IRON HEART PUBLISHING

UNDERSTANDING IBN 'ATA'ILLAH'S
BOOK
OF
WISDOM

TRANSLATION, ANNOTATION, AND COMMENTARY

BY

ABUBILAAL YAKUB

بِسْمِ اللهِ الرَّحْمٰنِ الرَّحِيمِ

الحمد لله وصلاة والسلام على رسول الله وعلى آله
وصحابته أجمعين
اللهم لا علم لنا إلا ما علمتنا إنك أنت العليم الحكيم
اللهم علمنا ما ينفعنا وانفعنا بما علمتنا وزدنا علما ورزقنا
فهما النبيين وحفظ المرسلين
اللهم افتح إلينا حكمتك وانشر علينا رحمتك يا ذا الجلال والإكرام

*In the name of God Almighty, the Most Merciful, the
Most Gracious, whose Divine Majesty perplexes the
Hearts and Minds of many a great people.
In the Hearts of our Beloved Prophets, His Light guides
them to guide us.
In the Hearts of the Enlightened Scholars of Islām,
esteemed as they are, His Light guides the Prophets to
guide them.
We are all but slaves and servants to His Greatness.
Like the thirsty in the desert, I yearn for every droplet
of Knowledge, from the Holy Prophet of Almighty Allāh
to the enlightened Scholars of Islām all to whom I
dedicate this book.*

*Lastly...
To my daughter, Naseem
and my sons, Bilaal and Maalik*

*May Almighty Allāh shower you with His Mercy and
Blessings, and guide you unto the path that will earn
you a special place in His Majestic Presence.*

آمين

Understand thyself, before probing the heavens;
For within it lay the truest questions.
Here poised, upon the isthmus of existence,
Honoured with wisdom yet raw in greatness.

The thinking fool on the edge of paradox,
Wise, yet skeptic and rudely unorthodox.
Too eager to embrace the manifest real,
Too frail to embody the prudent ideal.

Darkly suspended between action and inertia,
To wrestle with the riddle of one's own nature.
Are we angels aspiring, or beasts enchained?
Do we exalt the mind, or remain entertained?

Born only to die, we pride only to stumble,
Alike in ignorance and knowledge as such.
Lost in the void of thinking too little,
Or drowning in the fathoms of thinking too much.

CONTENTS

THE HIKAM OF IBN 'ATA'ILLAH

﴿ ٱدْعُ إِلَىٰ سَبِيلِ رَبِّكَ بِٱلْحِكْمَةِ وَٱلْمَوْعِظَةِ ٱلْحَسَنَةِ . . . ﴾

Invite to the path of Allāh with wisdom and profound speech...
~Sūrah an-Nahl 16:125~

﴿ يُؤْتِى ٱلْحِكْمَةَ مَن يَشَآءُ وَمَن يُؤْتَ ٱلْحِكْمَةَ فَقَدْ أُوتِىَ خَيْرًا كَثِيرًا

وَمَا يَذَّكَّرُ إِلَّا أُوْلُوا ٱلْأَلْبَٰبِ ﴾

*He gives wisdom to whom He wills, and whosover is given wisdom, has indeed
been given much good. Yet none will be mindful save the people of understanding.*
~Sūrah al-Baqarah 2:269~

PREFACE

My encounter with the Hikam of Ibn ʿAṭāʾillāh came abruptly during a study of Sūrah al-Kahf through the lens of Ibn ʿAjībah's Tafsīr entitled *al-Baḥr al-Madīd*. In his commentary, Ibn ʿAjībah observed that true reality is often veiled from those who cling to the chains of causality. Using this profound insight, he pointed to an aphorism by Ibn ʿAṭāʾillāh, that creation is outwardly form and inwardly discernment, and that the soul is ever transfixed by the outward allure of the form, while the heart is ever yearning for the inward discernment of meaning.

It is my habit, as a discipline of scholarship, to seek the source of any citation or quotation, even one from the most trustworthy authorities, before granting it my assent. Thus began a deeper engagement with the Hikam, a text I had already studied under two of my distinguished teachers in both Arabic and English. Yet at that time, my study was confined to the curriculum, tethered to the letter; much less its spirit. When, however, I approached the Hikam through an eschatological, philosophical, and psychological lens, and this shift in perspective illuminated dimensions I had not previously discerned. What I learned in this refreshed exploration became the fire that has kindled the work you now hold in your hands.

I am convinced, now more than ever, that the Hikam must become foundational in the study and teaching of philosophy, psychology, and spirituality. Indeed, I contend it holds unparalleled value for therapy, counseling, and the treatment of the human psyche. Yet I harbour no illusions about its reception within the frameworks of modern academics, for these structures often lack the conceptual space to accommodate the depth of such wisdom. Consequently, I expect little resonance from the so-called Muslim psychologists of our time. No matter—I have no desire to persuade by force. The sweetness of the Hikam can only be tasted by those whose hearts are prepared to savour its truths.

As always, I find myself in a necessary position to explain myself with a disclaimer of sorts. This is both an unfortunate and rather ridiculous thing for a scholar to do, but we are living in a society that is so incredibly opinionated and biased, much to our own dismay, that one wonders what has truly become of scholarship and what is now fated.

Let it suffice, then, to say that I am neither 'Salafī' nor 'Sūfī,' neither 'Māturīdī' nor 'Ash'arī.' I belong to no particular creed, order, or sect, nor am I pledged to any 'Shaykh,' 'Qutb,' or 'Pīr.' I do not disdain nor deride those who do ascribe to a particular identity, or who hold regard for such positions, nor do I belittle the tradition as it were. I only hold that these should not become impediments to knowledge and truth, and thus far I have not found failure in this principle. My teachers hail from all the above diverse paths of understanding, and my aim has always been to maintain a scholarship that is objective and open-hearted, within the necessary boundaries of the Sharī'ah. Where the Sharī'ah is breached, I keep my distance, and where sectarian and doctrinal prejudice is placed above the purity of knowledge, I condemn, but I do so without prejudice.

As one of my teachers often reminded me, there are no different creeds; there is only one creed. There are no different paths; there is only one Path. There are what we call 'schools of thought' that are but varying attempts to illuminate the same truth and draw nearer to the same Divine Presence. In this spirit, I have approached the Hikam, just as I approach every other scholarly work.

This book is neither a representation nor a promotion of any particular Sūfī order or related theological framework. As our beloved Prophet ﷺ declared: 'Wisdom is the lost property of the believer; he claims it wherever he finds it!' I have thus simply endeavoured to present the insights of the true Sūfiyyah as articulated by Ibn 'Atā'illāh, a master whose wisdom I distinguish from the broader populace of the *Mutasawwifah*.[1]

May this work serve as a bridge for seekers of truth and a guide for those yearning to deepen their understanding of the self and the Sacred.

Jumādā al-Awwal 1446/2024
Trabzon, Türkiye.

---

1   One who aspires to be a Sūfī, but is not actually, or is not yet, a Sūfī. The term is also used to denote those who pretend to be Sūfī or on a spiritual path.

INTRODUCTION

Western civilization and the idea of 'science' as developed and presented by the modern west, being constructed over materialistic and positivistic values, either ignores, underestimates, or altogether negates the spiritual dimension of reality because, as it were, feelings and states do not fit in a test tube and cannot be measured. Consequently, the psychological dimension, if at all acknowledged, is done so as being inseparable from the biology of the human being, severed from any spiritual affiliations, producing the apparent capitalistic behaviors, thoughts, emotions, and states influenced by the materialist paradigms.

Thousands of years of spiritual accumulation, which is necessarily a part of the human condition, has been driven out by modern civilization through the rules of these paradigms, thus producing perhaps the greatest contradiction of our age. The modern despairing and miserable society seeks solutions from psychologists who do not themselves believe in their own values, who do not believe in truth from a higher order, who do not believe in the power of belief, who themselves do not know who they are outside the titles that embellish their names and government issued identities. And yet these are the people to be trusted in their evaluation of what the human being's normal-to-abnormal scale needs to be and what constitutes happiness and contentment for the human being.

Those thousands of years of spiritual worldviews expressed by cultures physically disconnected have been dismissed as myth and fantasy, and the valuation of what or *who* the human being is has been reduced to chemical and biological causal functions that are spontaneous and meaningless.

17

The fault does not lie in the lack of evidence, for indeed there is no material evidence of these higher dimensions of the human being. After all, in what reality might one find material evidence for a spiritual actuality when the two are fundamentally divergent? A physical body cannot be dissected to reveal a soul and spirit. Even thoughts and emotions evade the most sophisticated of instrumentations. The fault lies in the epistemic process that attempts to force a material confession, built on the stubborn argument that if it exists it must be readily available to the senses. Yet, one might ask, if the instrument is material and the senses are material, how might they perceive the immaterial?

The solution is simple. Either the spiritual must itself become material, or its perception must necessarily become spiritual. One is possible, the other is not, and hence all evidence would indicate that the soul and spirit cannot be discerned through conventional scientific processes. Empirical knowledge alone will not suffice an understanding, as the scientific processes are themselves inherently limited to the quantifiable and measurable dimension. Beyond that, scientific inquiry must necessarily give way to a higher kind of inquiry. Wisdom, not knowledge, avails the truth of these inner realities.

The pursuit of knowledge in this age, pronounced in its faulty epistemologies, produces and applies knowledge not for revealing the truth but for dominating the truth. For he who can control knowledge can control the truth, and he who can control the truth possesses the power to alter perception of reality. Under this regime, it is impossible to justify progress in light of preceding morals and ethics. These must be altered to appear abnormal, and what is in light of them abnormal must then be normalized. The process of normalization sits at the same agenda-driven table that forwards the notion that in this 'modern age' supposedly advanced and civilized, morality is no longer dictated by the so-termed figments of imagination that spawned religion as the underlying governing body of the human being. No, this is 'backward thinking.' Morality must be reinvented to accommodate the modern notion of happiness, which is itself capitalistic and materialistic driven.

The key to achieving this lies in severing the human condition from any and all acknowledgment of a spiritually psychological dimension, while replacing it with a materialistic psychological framework void of wisdom. Knowledge can still be pursued under the guise of liberty and privilege, but only as far as the processing and transmission of information. Beyond that, it is fantasy and imagination. The very use of the word 'God' is limited to a customary expression in conventional speech. Its mention, if at all, is void of belief and conviction in what it means.

As a result, the very institutes of learning have become factories installed with conveyor belts that take the raw, creative, and imaginative minds of the young, producing biological computers by the masses. Each one is equipped with a certificate of inspection called a 'degree' or 'diploma' and each one is sent out into the workforce to trade precious time in exchange of a material benefit, which can then be redeemed in a point-based system for fleeting manufactured material joys in the form of leisure and entertainment. This is the modern pursuit of knowledge, mechanized, industrialized,[2] and packaged as 'progress.' The same is true of religious institutes, where one might tread on eggshells, cautious of spewing secular theories, where the turbaned and robed professionals spew their biased theologies and doctrines. The title of 'Shaykh' is either bestowed through conventional popularity, or affixed to the title of 'PhD'. The true honour of a 'Shaykh' as a 'Wise and Knowledgeable' individual is now entirely contingent upon the approval of his sect and doctrine, far removed from the worth and virtue of knowledge and wisdom itself.

A world void of wisdom is wild and uninhabitable. Societies are riled with crime and immorality, which, though manifested causally, owe their evil roots to ignorance. Darkness is to ignorance what Light is to knowledge, but what good is knowledge if it lacks in wisdom? Knowledge may facilitate the sowing of seeds, but it is wisdom that nurtures the tree and sweetens the fruit. The healing comes not from the treatment, but the one who administers it. How might one find spiritual and psychological healing, when the very psychology of the human being is left to the hands of a materialistic and pragmatic control paradigm. How can the human conscious possibly develop to produce useful solutions? When every textbook has its opening chapters discussing the 'biological origins of behavior,' and hardly two words might remotely hint the spiritual essence of the human being. The same books will doubly emphasize that the root of all psychological disorder, per their 'expert' studies and analyses, is the presence of religion, as if the complete removal of religion and all religious thought might solve, overnight, all the problems of the modern age. Yet we might ask, for thousands of years humanity has existed on the foundations of religious wisdom, how now are humanity's problems so prevalent as to blame religion itself?

Religion and spirituality are not mere concepts that enter life at specific times or conditions. They are not products of imaginative minds necessarily invented to fill the void of modern scientific discovery. These are fundamental ways of life that have been rigorously explored, experienced, their empowerment attested, and their truths affirmed. The veracity of religion as both a healing and sustaining axiom of mental wellness has been experimented upon and its results reproduced time and again, which necessarily negates the propagation that 'religion is unscientific.' The human need to believe and hold conviction in a higher truth has persisted in every society for as long as mankind has existed until the advent of the materialistic sentiments of the European-centered Enlightenment, which gave rise to the substitution of heavenly ordained virtues with worldly arbitrary values. Such has been the impact of western influence over the past few centuries that acknowledging spirituality as a rational foundation of psychological wellbeing has become an alien and novel concept explored only as 'mystical beliefs,'

---

2   There quite literally exists something called 'The Education Industry.'

We propose the following. If the pursuit of truth is genuine, the human being cannot ignore the spiritual dimension. Modern psychology has indeed made notable semantic advances, but draws a limit, succeeding only so far as to distance and provide temporary relief through brief momentary reflections. Spirituality, on the other hand, aims for a state of constant peace, healing the psychological impairment and laying the roots for healthy mental states. This is the conviction of the wise, and this is the essence of their wisdom presented in these pages.

As to the subject of this book, the wisdoms presented are not compiled in any chronological or structured theme. However, there is a certain deliberate order to them where the themes are placed in such a way as to take the seeker in gradual steps, from the basics of understanding to the more sophisticated of concepts. As such, we have grouped some of the aphorisms where the concept is thematic, and highlighted where there is an interconnectivity to those concepts with other aphorisms. There are no chapters in the book, but the table of contents provides a reference for which pages to follow. Each aphorism has been presented with the original Arabic, followed by a translation and brief commentary. The language used in both translation and commentary is balanced so as not to be too sophisticated nor too simple. This is to ensure that the reader's intelligence is respected, and the language of the Hikam is equally protected from being reduced. Unlike most other translations floating the Internet, ours is straightforward and as precise as possible to the meanings, subtleties, and nuances in the original Arabic. In some places the translation may seem too literal, and possibly unintelligible, which is owed to the metaphoric style of Ibn 'Aṭā'illāh that cannot truly be replicated in other than the source language. Rather than tamper with the intended meanings, our interpretations have been inserted, instead, in the commentaries and explanations.

Finally, to truly benefit from this work, we urge an approach that is active and conscious, rather than a passive read. Immerse yourself, dear reader, in an actual study of the text by writing the Arabic yourself along with notes and explanations. This is the method of the scholars, and I myself have always studied this way and can attest to the immense benefits of this discipline. This will imprint the meanings and understandings of the scholar's knowledge and wisdom deeper into your mind and heart, and will further be, from you to him, an act of honouring his efforts of bringing us these precious pearls and gems.

THE LEGACY OF
THE ALEXANDRIAN SAGE

The 'Golden Age' of Islāmic Scholarship was marked by the phenomenal advent and exponent rise of both material and religious scientia, intertwined in a harmonious manner that no civilization prior or after has ever been able to replicate. The pursuit of both streams were unitedly aimed not only at the betterment of mankind in this world, but for man's afterlife as well. Scholars were qualified with the highest honours in both the material and spiritual sciences becoming the only civilization in the world that produced literate bedouins, educated peasants, and esteemed polymaths by the numbers. Because the pursuit of knowledge was less for titles and riches and progress and industry and development, and was more for mental and spiritual wellbeing.

The pursuit of knowledge, in principle, can be seen from three perspectives. Knowledge for progress' sake, and this the modern industrialistic and technocratic agenda, whose progress, or lack thereof, can only be measured by material value, if any. Or, knowledge for knowledge's sake, and this is the worldview of the medieval gnostic and esoteric, whose ambitions lay in creating spiritual dimensions other than what really is. And knowledge for virtue's sake, and this is the worldview of Islām, which defines the material limits of science, respects the Divinely Decreed parameters, and as a fruitful consequence produced knowledge and knowledgeable individuals in quality over quantity, whose wisdom and understanding, unlike what has been produced and pursued by the West, still endure and prove to be both cure and saviour from the trials, tribulations, and complexities of modern societies.

Among these countless polymaths, few figures have been known to have left behind a legacy as luminous as Tāj ud-Dīn Abū'l-Fadl Ahmad bin Muhammad bin 'Abd al-Karīm Ibn 'Atā'illāh al-Iskandarī,[3] renowned as the third 'spiritual pillar'[4] of the Shādhilī order, though also deserving recognition in the fields of Fiqh, Usūl, language, philosophy, logic, psychology, Tafsīr, Qirā'ah, Hadīth, and most certainly, Belles-lettres.[5]

He was born in the middle of the 13th century in Alexandria during the peak of the Mamluk reign. His family were renowned Mālikī scholars from the Banū Judhām. His grandfather, 'Abd al-Karīm was distinguished as an expert in Fiqh, Usūl, and Language, having studied under the Mālikī jurist, Abū'l-Hassan al-Abyārī. Incidentally, 'Abd al-Karīm was known to be incredibly hostile to Sūfī orders and doctrines, himself preferring the juristic path, upon which he also set his son, Muhammad, and grandson, Ahmad. Muhammad, however, though a Faqīh himself, was less inclined to follow in his father's footsteps, and became a disciple of Abū'l-Hassan ash-Shādhilī, the founder of the Shādhilī order.

As a youth, Ahmad, being influenced by both his father and grandfather, received his education in the above-mentioned disciplines from some of the best and most illustrious teachers of Alexandria, including his father and grandfather. However, in spite of his father's attachment to Abū'l-Hassan ash-Shādhilī, he was, like his grandfather, heavily opposed to the Sūfiyyah, which he subtly admits in his book *Latā'if al-Minan*.[6]

Then, following an argument with one of Abū'l-Abbās al-Mursī's[7] disciples, who proclaimed the Shaykh as 'a man of truth and signs that cannot be hidden,' Ahmad decided to see for himself who this man truly was. He said that upon meeting Al-Mursī, something touched his heart and mind, that in that moment Allāh removed all objections he previously held, and was thus driven home to seek solitude. He subsequently returned to visit Al-Mursī, who received him with such warmth as to humble him greatly. This marked his initiation as a disciple of Al-Mursī, and remained so for twelve years until Al-Mursī's passing ﷺ.

3   His name is Ahmad, his father's name is Muhammad, and his grandfather's name is 'Abd al-Karīm. The moniker *Tāj ud-Dīn* (crown of the religion) is an honourary title. There is no widely known historical record about his children and it is assumed that the *kunya* of *Abū'l-Fadl* (lit. Father of Virtue) might also have been an honourary title.

4   A *Qutb* قطب, or *Murshid* مرشد, in Sūfī hierarchies, a pillar of spiritual guidance for disciples of the order.

5   *Belles-lettres* (French phrase) meaning 'beautiful' or 'fine' writing, valued for aesthetic qualities and originality of style and tone in literature.

6   *Latā'if al-Minan fī Manāqib al-Shaykh Abī'l-Abbās al-Mursī wa Shaykhihi ash-Shādhilī Abī'l-Hassan* — The Subtleties of Grace in the Virtues of Shaykh Abū'l-Abbās and his Shaykh Abū'l-Hassan.

7   Successor of Abū'l-Hassan ash-Shādhilī, and the second pillar of the Shādhilī order. Both Abū'l-Hassan and Abu'l-Abbas are the subjects of Ibn 'Ata'illah's *Latā'if al-Minan*.

Ibn 'Atā'illāh grew up under the rigor of jurisprudence and the rational sciences with both religious devotion and intellectual vigor. His journey, however, was not merely one of scholarship or piety; it was a journey from resistance to surrender, from the mind to the heart, and ultimately, from human strife to Divine realization. He is testament that the soul's journey is guided by providence, and it was in the companionship of Al-Mursī that Ibn 'Atā'illāh's heart began to soften, his mind expanded, and his spirit released its guarded rationality, awakened to the subtleties of the soul and the heart. This became pronounced in his career as a teacher at Al-Azhar, and as a guide and counsellor to his students and disciples.

His most notable works include:

- كتاب الحكم
  Kitāb al-Hikam
  The Book of Wisdom

- كتاب اللطائف المنن في مناقب الشيخ أبي العباس المرسي وشيخه أبي الحسن
  Kitāb Latā'if al-Minan fī Manāqib al-Shaykh Abī'l-Abbās al-Mursī wa Shaykhihi ash-Shādhilī Abī'l-Hassan
  The Subtleties of Grace in the Virtues of Shaykh Abū'l-Abbās and his Shaykh Abū'l-Hassan.

- مفتاح الفلاح ومصباح الأرواح
  Miftāh al-Falāh wa Misbāh al-Arwāh
  The Key of Success and the Lamp of Spirits

- كتاب التنوير في إسقاط التدبير
  Kitāb al-Tanwir fī Isqāt al-Tadbīr
  The Enlightenment in Abandoning Self-Direction

- القصد المجرد في معرفة الاسم المفرد
  Al-Qasd al-Mujarrad fī Ma'rifat al-Ism al-Mufrad
  The Pure Goal Concerning Knowledge of the Unique Name

- تاج العروس الحاوي للتهذيب النفوس
  Tāj al-'Arūs al-Hāwī li-Tahdhīb an-Nufūs
  The Bride's Crown Containing the Discipline of Souls

- عنوان التوفيق في آداب الطريق
  'Unwān at-Tawfīq fī ādāb at-Tarīq
  The Sign of Success Concerning the Discipline of the Path

His writings affirm that true understanding lies not in intellectual conquest but in spiritual surrender, not in the rigid structures of legalism but in the gentle flow of divine trust and reliance. And at the heart of his teachings is the Hikam, a work revered for its depth, its insight, and its unyielding call to sincerity.

The wisdoms compiled are more than words. They are gateways into an inner realm where the ego is humbled, where the worldly is shed, and where the self is called to divine servitude. They pierce right through the veils of human desire and invite the seeker into a state of realization, in which one finds a safe harbor from the storms of life. For the human heart is the locus of divine presence, the inner sanctum where he might converse with his Creator. This simple yet profound truth is the cornerstone of Ibn 'Aṭā'illāh's work and a timeless message of spiritual clarity.

In light of human psychology, the Hikam might well be the cure to the mental and spiritual turmoils of our age. These words are not a form of escapism from the hardships of existence, but rather a way to confront them with equanimity. True liberation from suffering, in search of happiness, arises not from bending the world to one's will, but from a peaceful surrender to the Divine Unfolding. In relinquishing control and abandoning one's illusions of independence, the heart finds not despair but profound relief. This, perhaps, is one of Ibn 'Aṭā'illāh's most striking insights. That freedom lies in recognizing one's own poverty before the Divine, in embracing vulnerability as a path to inner strength. He further pairs this with an emphasis on *ikhlās* اخلاص, which urges a stripping away of pretense, a removal of the masks that society, ambition, and fear impose. True happiness, he contends, is not achieved through worldly successes or social accolades but through a purified heart that stands unadorned before its Creator, to be adorned by His honour and grace.

In this way, Ibn 'Aṭā'illāh's legacy endures because his teachings transcend the specificities of time and place. Where modernity's epistemic processes suggest a continual reinvention of morals and ethics, works such as the Hikam remain rooted in the universality of Divinely Ordained morality and virtue as the sole source of sound thought and harmonious existence when rightly understood and implemented. His is an invitation not to caress the soul's whims and desires with mystical sayings, but to confront the self's illusions and to strive toward a higher, truer way of being. He maintains a constant assertion that the path to enlightenment is not traversed in leaps of intellectual achievement or grand ambition, but in gentle steps of humility, trust, and surrender. For those struggling with the anxieties, discontent, and disillusionments of the modern age, such wisdom comes with both solace and a transformative strategy for engaging with the vicissitudes of life.

In this translation and commentary, we have aimed to present the Hikam not as a distant, historical text, but as a living tradition. It is meant to speak to the heart's timeless yearning for peace, for understanding, and for God. Ibn 'Aṭā'illāh's words are as much a psychological journey as they are a spiritual one, leading one from self-absorption to self-transcendence, from restless striving to inner contentment. In a world that often equates success with material gain and identity with external arbitrary roles, the Hikam hopes to invite us back to a truer understanding of selfhood and realization of humanity, anchored in the Divine, and open to the fullness of being and existence.

As for the wisdom itself, Ibn 'Atā'illāh delivers, with remarkable restraint and concision, that wisdom cannot be contained in volumes of discursive prose, for it concerns matters that transcend worldly articulation. These aphorisms are written, as it were, upon the wind, enriched with subtle and nuanced metaphors, for their meanings touch upon the ineffable and address the root of the heart's yearnings, through words that, like well-wrought stones, provide solid footing for the wayfarer. Yet, they are not the mere construction of lofty statements on the mystical and metaphysical. Ibn 'Atā'illāh was a scholar rooted in practice. Much of his work is also influenced by the likes of Imām al-Junayd al-Baghdādī and Imam al-Ghazzālī, among other predecessors whose wisdom is encompassed the art of bringing such spiritual concepts into the practicality of everyday life. He both instructs and reveals the tender humanity of spiritual masters, highlighting the pitfalls and dangers of journeying though life blind and heedless, emphasizing on the human need for Divine Guidance, to attain, if granted, a glimpse of true reality and what awaits one's inevitable return to the Divine.

Ibn 'Atā'illāh was widely known for his influential oratorical style in sermons and conversations, which deeply impacted the masses during his time. This is reflected in the quality of all his works, especially the Hikam. It is a bold thing to do, for one to claim wisdom, let alone compose a collection of one's thoughts and ideas central to the human being's spiritual growth, as even the most wise know well enough not to boast wisdom. Rather the wise know wisdom as a closely guarded secret, imparted in sparse and prescribed measures, and above all they know that the very act of claiming to be wise is, in truth, a sign that one is indeed bereft of all wisdom. Yet the wise also know that knowledge alone does not suffice the human being, for without wisdom, knowledge, even if acted upon, is often lifeless. Wisdom is the spirit that guides the path of morality, and to share it is the impetus of the wise. In that regard, we would not perceive Ibn 'Atā'illāh as audacious, but as being wise enough to recognize that his thoughts and experiences are better served in the hands of the people than to be kept guarded by his silence.

It is evident from his writings that he understands more than most the void in the human condition that must be filled, a bridge built to carry the mind and heart across the pathways of discernment to the enlightenment of Revelation and Guidance. In this way, the expressions of the Hikam serve to address the core qualities of human nature, to nurture those qualities from hindrances and obstacles to becoming the very vessels that might bring the human being closer to his destiny.

Contrary to what is conventionally perceived, the expressions in this magnificent work are not compiled with the intent of expressing the mystical discoveries of this Sūfi Master,[8] nor are they intended to facilitate mystical thinking. As is common in academics, any work produced by a scholar marked as a Sūfi is unfortunately also perceived with a sense of

---

8   And he is, undeniably, a *true* Sūfi Master.

mystery and enlightenment, paired with the oftly false presumption that what is contained within that work is a grand revelation of the discoveries of those mysteries and an outpouring of enlightenment. Yet, as any true Sūfī Master will attest, attested also within these pages, such mysteries and discoveries are the treasures of the heart and innermost dimensions, and any attempt to express them squanders their wealth and worth. Rather, in truth, such mysteries and discoveries are so profound, there are no words in all the tongues of man that can express them. They are called mysteries and secrets because they *are* mysteries and secrets. As soon as they are expressed, they are no longer such. So, no, this is not a book of mystical concepts and their expressions, and any who approach this work as such have neither grasped its essence nor given it its due right.

What this is, is an expansive and most valuable resource to address the human condition in its spiritual and psychological dimensions. The aim, the ultimate aim of these expressions, is to remind us of the essence of our humanity, the grand purpose of our creation, the journey of life, its destination, and how to realize both.

We begin, then, in the Name of Allāh, Most Merciful, Most Benevolent. We send salutations and prayers upon His beloved Messenger, Muhammad ﷺ, and upon all the noble Messengers and Prophets, and upon all their blessed families and their righteous companions. We beseech Allāh's Divine aid in enabling and empowering us to reach the fruition of our quests and objectives, such as in the completion of this book. We seek His Mercy and Blessing in all our efforts, and we ask of Him that should there be good in our deeds, and should that good be of benefit to others, that He bring it to light, and should there be fault in it, that He forgives and draws over it a cover, and should it, or any part of it, be to His disliking, that He, in His power and Majesty, cause it to wither and wane in the annals of time.

شرح كتاب الحكم العطائية

للإمام تاج الدين أبو الفضل أحمد بن محمد
ابن عطاء الله الإسكندري

مُعَقّب : سيدي أبو بلال شاه نواز بن محمد شاكر بن أحمد ابن يعقوب الميموني

①

مِنْ عَلَامَاتِ الإِعْتِمَادِ عَلَى العَمَلِ، نُقْصَانُ الرَّجَاءِ عِنْدَ وُجُودِ الزَّلَلِ.

From among the signs of dependency on deed, is the loss of hope upon the occurrence of error.

Dependency upon a thing means placing one's trust in that thing, and things are, by their nature, subject to the vicissitudes of a causal reality. Dependency on deeds and actions, therefore, means one has placed faith in that which is itself dependent, and has not placed faith in their intentions, for actions and deeds are themselves contingent and dependent on the intentions.[9] The latter emerge from a realm untouched by causation, while the former are subject to the alterities and vicissitudes, such that though the action is performed to perfection, the outcome, either undesirable or ever vulnerable to error, may manifest into other than what one intended, and this results in a loss of hope.

Actions are parted into four general categories. Actions performed in accordance with, and submission to, the law; Actions performed in accordance with faith; and Actions performed in accordance with virtue, piety, and purification. These three correspond with Islām, Imān, and Ihsān. The fourth, oft overlooked, regards actions performed in accordance with one's *being* and true reality, which itself transcends the outward materiality and serves as the root of all their manifestations. These are the *inner* actions, or actions of the Heart, wherein the intention to do takes form. For instance, the Law dictates that you worship Him, your faith dictates that you aim for Him, and to draw nearer to His presence entails virtue and purification, while to realize one's being and reality is to perfect all three. Dependency, hence, is hierarchical. To depend on the actions solely is to depend on one's lower self, and to trust that what one does purely from a reaction to the outward reality will bear fruit. To depend on the actions performed in collaboration with one's lower self and their rationality, or higher self, is to have faith that the manifestation of their deeds would be favourable, and one risks losing hope should the outcomes on both dependencies be unfavourable, meaning, should there be error in their manifestation.

Dependency, therefore, should not be upon the actions, outward or inward, but upon the intentions and their surrender to the Will of the Almighty, for the outcome of all that manifests rests solely in His Hands. One does what is in their means, and trusts the outcomes to His Will, thereby accepting whatever the results. Should there be error on one's part, it serves to rectify their journey, rather than harm their psychological state.

---

9   Sahīh Hadīth, إِنَّمَا الْأَعْمَالُ بِالنِّيَّاتِ *"Indeed, actions are only contingent upon Intentions."*

(٢)

إِرَادَتُكَ التَّجْرِيدَ مَعَ إِقَامَةِ اللهِ إِيَّاكَ فِي الْأَسْبَابِ ... مِنَ الشَّهْوَةِ الْخَفِيَّةِ،

وَإِرَادَتُكَ الْأَسْبَابَ مَعَ إِقَامَةِ اللهِ إِيَّاكَ فِي التَّجْرِيدِ ... انْحِطَاطٌ عَنِ الْهِمَّةِ الْعَلِيَّةِ.

Your want for withdrawal when Allāh has established you in causality... is
from a concealed desire,
And your want for causality when Allāh has established you in withdrawal...
is from a lofty aspiration.

Withdrawal entails isolation or alienation from causation. The heart, not designed for a realm of causality, often finds itself unwanting of the occurrences and happenings of the world, and desires to be removed from it. Such a desire arises from its innocence, but is counterintuitive to Divine Decree. Allāh Decrees placement among the vicissitudes to aid the servant in his objective of purification. To desire removal when one has been placed in hardship, though innocent, remains a hidden desire, demonstrating a lack of fortitude and perseverance. It is akin to the desire to leave, without being granted permission to leave. If he should exercise patience, then when Allāh Decrees removal from the vicissitudes, it is to grant the servant respite from them. It is thus a fall from a lofty aspiration to want the vicissitudes at a time of reprieve, for it demonstrates the servant's lack of appreciation.

Almighty Allāh plunges the being into worldly means, not to indulge and satisfy themselves, the satisfaction of which is itself temporary and ultimately unsatisfactory. Rather he is subjected to the world that he may seek from it the provision to endure the journey, and ultimately return to a seclusion from the world. To desire a seclusion is from the being's innocence, and is praiseworthy indeed. Such a desire, when fulfilled, is a blessing from the Creator, as it now serves as respite from the worldly.

If the being should find themselves in seclusion from the world, where it may appear as though one is deprived of its niceties, such a state is indeed a blessing. For we may say that only in seclusion, far removed from the worldly, can one find the Divine Presence. Why then should the being seek out the worldly? Is that not a fall from a lofty aspiration?

The word التَّجْرِيد means to 'strip away,' such as the stripping away of a garment. One may 'strip away' only the outward, or only the inward, or in essence, both. The outward stripping is the removal of worldly causes and physical habits. The inward is the stripping of psychological and illusory chains. When one strips the physical but not the psychological, they risk being a liar and hypocrite. They may beautify the outward, but the inward is ugly. To strip away both, is to free oneself from both the outward causality and the psychological delusions, so that both the outward and inward exhibit beauty and purity.

(٣)

سَوَابِقُ الهِمَمِ لَا تَخْرِقُ أَسْوَارَ الأَقْدَارِ.

Antecedent aspirations cannot tear down the walls of destiny.

Aspirations هِمَمّ stem from هَمّ, a purpose or intention that is strong, or holding, powerful enough to propel one ahead. It is akin to the potential and kinetic energy stored in an arrow before it is released. The arrow does not aim itself, hence its yield does not depend on its potential energy, which determines how powerfully it will travel, nor its kinetic energy, which determines how far and swift it will travel. These, as mere energies, will be released upon the archer's directive. What determines the yield is whether or not the arrow will strike true. Ultimately, the archer is only concerned with striking the right target. Hence, preceding the aspiration هَمّ is the whim وهمّ or the trigger that releases the aspiration.

The archer is also subject to a 'Will', and that will can be his own, or be one that is directed to him. The directed 'Will' can either be Divine or worldly. As such, aspirations can either be praiseworthy, when targeted toward the praiseworthy, being those that are guided by Divine Will, so that the archer strikes the target that is desired, not by himself or the world, but by Almighty Allāh. Alternatively, aspirations can also be blameworthy, when targeted toward the worldly, being those that are guided by the whims of the individual or the whims of others. Nevertheless, aspirations remain as potential powers, which whence released, take the path upon which they are aimed.

These are strong and powerful desires emanating from the heart, and can often rush ahead, or be prematurely released. This is what we refer to as سبق or a 'forward position', a preemptive strike, if you will. And here we find something remarkable, that regardless of how strong the potential, or power, and regardless of how quick, swift, or ahead of the mark the aspiration is released, ultimately, it must submit to the Will that precedes the whims of the archer and world. This is the Will of the Divine, the Will that determines the fate, or destiny of one's aspirations, what they hope to achieve, how far they are willing to go to achieve them.

One must understand that nothing comes into being save by what Divine Destiny and Decree contains. So when the being's aspirations are directed towards a praiseworthy target, they rush forth in accordance with, but do not surpass Divine Decree. If the aspirations find the walls of destiny erected before them, they can never break through, regardless of how strong and powerful they, or the whims that precede them, may be. And if they are righteous, meaning, targeted towards that which is praiseworthy, they submit and revert to their attributes. They are not aggrieved or saddened, rather they rejoice in reverting to their proper place and attribute.

(٤)

أَرِحْ نَفْسَكَ مِنْ هَمِّ التَّدْبِيرِ ... فَمَا قَامَ بِهِ غَيْرُكَ عَنْكَ ... لَا تَقُمْ بِهِ لِنَفْسِكَ.

Rest yourself from Self-contrivance, for what is being done for you by others, do it not by yourself.

Life is not about control, it is about correction. We oft find ourselves wanting, from a sense of self-confidence, to manage and contrive ourselves individually, admirable when the task is of a praiseworthy nature, but blameworthy when the task is mundane and worldly. It is blameworthy especially when accompanied by resolve and tenacity, as it contains within it a lack of discipline and hastens fatigue, resulting in its failure. The task in point underlies the very purpose of one's existence. And such is not a task achievable by oneself, especially not by attempting to control one's own life and its outcomes. That which one begins by themselves, unaided by the pious and righteous, is often followed by trouble and turbulence. One of the attributes of a sincere seeker is that he realizes his only need rests in that which his Lord has established for him in the moment. It is a mark of true humility and respect that when someone else comes to your aid, you allow them to aid you, and not attempt to seize control yourself. After all, we have no say in all the choices and measures of the Sharī'ah; they have been chosen for us by Allāh, and we simply heed and obey.

(٥)

اجْتِهَادُكَ فِيمَا ضَمِنَ لَكَ وَتَقْصِيرُكَ فِيمَا طُلِبَ مِنْكَ ... دَلِيلٌ عَلَى انْطِمَاسِ الْبَصِيرَةِ مِنْكَ.

Your struggle to hasten what has been assured for you, and your inadequacy in [delivering] what is sought from you... is evidence of the obliteration of true intelligence from you.

True intelligence entails knowing one's purpose and what is expected from them. It also entails realization of the One True and Absolute, and that He, in His wisdom, has assured the best for His servant. Hence true intelligence exercises patience in expectation, while striving to deliver what is expected. But if the being struggles to hasten the outcome, directing all their efforts in pursuit, thereby failing to deliver what is expected of them in obedience, such is a sure sign that one's inner intelligence has dulled. Should they then replace the striving with absorption and consumption, and replace the inadequacy, or laxness, with complete abandonment, the dullness or obscurity of intelligence becomes complete blindness, resulting in disbelief. Though they may have proclaimed 'Muslim' on their tongues, the spirit of Islām does not penetrate their hearts.

٦

لَا يَكُنْ تَأَخُّرُ أَمَدِ العَطَاءِ مَعَ الإِلْحَاحِ فِي الدُّعَاءِ... مُوجِبًا لِيَأْسِكَ،

فَهُوَ ضَمِنَ لَكَ الإِجَابَةَ فِيمَا يَخْتَارُ لَكَ، لَا فِيمَا تَخْتَارُ لِنَفْسِكَ،

وَفِي الوَقْتِ الَّذِي يُرِيدُ، لَا فِي الوَقْتِ الَّذِي تُرِيدُ.

No... the delay in the giving, though with intensity in supplication... should not cause you despair. As He guarantees for you a response in what He chooses for you, not in what you choose for yourself. And at a time that He intends for you, not at the time that you intend for yourself.

Be careful what you wish for... It may be that you desire a thing and it is harmful for you, or you despise a thing and it is beneficial for you. You do not know, but your Lord knows. Therefore, trust in His wisdom and judgment to favour you what is from His kindness. For though He has invited you openly to ask from Him, He may choose to give you instantly, or delay the giving, or withdraw it entirely should it not be of benefit to you, as His mercy far supersedes anything you may ask from Him. Thus, His giving to you has been guaranteed, as long as you fulfill your part in asking of Him and only Him. So do not despair, lest it lead you to withhold from asking, if what you asked for did not manifest, or what manifested was not what you asked for. He will give you what He deems worthy of you and at a time ripe for giving.

٧

لَا يُشَكِّكَنَّكَ فِي الوَعْدِ عَدَمُ وُقُوعِ المَوْعُودِ وَإِنْ تَعَيَّنَ زَمَنُهُ؛
لِئَلَّا يَكُونَ ذَلِكَ قَدْحًا فِي بَصِيرَتِكَ وإِخْمَادًا لِنُورِ سَرِيرَتِكَ.

Do not doubt in the Promise if it does not occur, though its time has been appointed. Lest that happen, it will cloud your intelligence and extinguish the light of your conscience.

So though you may feel that His promise is due, that the time is nigh for His intervention, let not doubt enter your heart should it appear to be delayed. Doubt is like a film of crude oil upon glass. The thicker the layer of oil, the greater the doubt. Whatever visibility it permits is distorted, and it cannot so easily be wiped clean. Your heart, likened to a glass orb,[10] must not be stained by this crude oil, for it will prevent insight and the light of intuition from entering it to illuminate your consciousness.

---

10 Sūrah an-Nūr 24:35

٨

إِذَا فَتَحَ لَكَ وِجْهَةً مِنَ التَّعَرُّفِ... فَلَا تُبَالِ مَعَهَا إِنْ قَلَّ عَمَلُكَ؛

فَإِنَّهُ مَا فَتَحَهَا لَكَ إِلَّا وَهُوَ يُرِيدُ أَنْ يَتَعَرَّفَ إِلَيْكَ؛

أَلَمْ تَعْلَمْ أَنَّ التَّعَرُّفَ هُوَ مُورِدُهُ عَلَيْكَ وَالْأَعْمَالَ أَنْتَ مُهْدِيهَا إِلَيْهِ؟

وَأَيْنَ مَا تُهْدِيهِ إِلَيْهِ مِمَّا هُوَ مُورِدُهُ عَلَيْكَ؟

If He opens for you a way to make Himself known to you, do not be concerned if your deeds do not measure to expectations. For indeed, He has not opened it for you save that He wants to make Himself known to you [not your deeds]. Do you not know that He is the One who has presented realization of Himself to you, while you are presenting to Him your deeds.
Where is what you present to Him, and what He presents to you?

When He opens up a facet by which you come to know Him, do not concern yourself with the measure of your deeds. Rather, embrace that moment wholeheartedly. For how can one compare what He is granting you, to what you are presenting to Him? You are like the farmer who goes to the king with an offering of a bale of hale, while He, the King, is presenting you with a chalice of gold. The wise one knows the worth of his offering to what is being presented to him, and knows that the King is well aware of that worth. So he accepts what is gifted to him with deepened gratitude, for to simply be in the presence of the King is worth more than all the deeds of all the creatures in all the realms combined.

٩

تَنَوَّعَتْ أَجْنَاسُ الْأَعْمَالِ لِتَنَوُّعِ وَارِدَاتِ الْأَحْوَالِ.

Deeds differ, because the inspirations of the states of being differ.

Actions differ in their outcomes because the spiritual states in which they are performed also differ. One might wonder, how it is that two people perform the same act of obedience, yet one is permeating an intense glow in their performance, and its manifestation spreads to great extent, while the other's seems to diminish and wither before it has even reached completion. Consider then, were you to perform your prayer beside AbūBakr as-Siddīq ﷺ, whose deed would bear greater luminance, and why? Certainly, *his* deed would supersede yours by magnitudes, simply due to his spiritual state. After all, he was not called '*As-Siddīq* ﷺ' for other than the purity and sincerity of his heart!

⟨١٠⟩

الأَعْمَالُ صُوَرٌ قَائِمَةٌ، وَأَرْوَاحُهَا وُجُودُ سِرِّ الإِخْلَاصِ فِيهَا.

Deeds are but erected forms, and their spirits are existent of the secrets of sincerity in them.

Then, on that note, deeds are lifeless forms. They are personified, but are not the personifiers. They are but physical enactments that enter the stream of causes and effects, the physical movements originated from the metaphysical intentions of the heart. What gives them 'life,' or the secret of what enlivens them is the spirit of sincerity. Was it not sincerity that granted AbūBakr 🙵 the title of As-Siddīq, and was it not his sincerity that enlivened his deeds?

Sincerity is when the heart is devoted to attributing its actions to Allāh. When the doer of the deed attributes it not to himself, but to the One in whom rests the power to manifest the deed and its outcome. It contains both the core of the intention and its secret. At its core, it negates self-regard, self-satisfaction, and showing off, while in its secret, it negates pride and arrogance. Through these two tenets, the actions manifest with sincerity, as self-regard detracts from the soundness of the deed, while pride detracts from its perfection and attribution to Allāh.

⟨١١⟩

ادْفِنْ وُجُودَكَ فِي أَرْضِ الخُمُولِ، فَمَا نَبَتَ مِمَّا لَمْ يُدْفَنْ ... لَا يَتِمُّ نِتَاجُهُ

Bury your existence in the earth of obscurity. As that which sprouts without being buried, does not sprout with completeness.

This is the obscurity of ingloriousness and namelessness. A flower does not blossom as a flower unless it sprouts from obscurity of the dirt and grime of its 'flowerness.' One cannot hope to receive honour and glory from the merit of name or legacy. For them to sprout with completeness, they must be buried in obscurity. They must be unknown and strive to remain unknown. Only then can they truly come to know themselves, untainted by what is projected of them by others.

Obscurity is defined as a state of being unknown, or rather a state of being without societal fame and renown for those aspects that are trivial and frivolous. It a blessing that the self rejects, and its rejection is a thing that the self desires. In an age defined by individuality and self-entitlement, one needs no proof to understand why a pursuit of fame and renown is a disease. Evident it is to see that those who delight in the glow of fame are a people who are hollow and empty.

34

(١٢)

مَا نَفَعَ القَلْبَ شَيْءٌ مِثْلُ عُزْلَةٍ... يَدْخُلُ بِهَا مَيْدَانَ فِكْرَةٍ.

Naught benefits the Heart a thing such as seclusion. It [the Heart] enters by it [seclusion] into the domain of thought.

The domain of thought is an enclosure of reflection that is sacred to the heart. The heart is an entity that has been originated with the sole purpose of receiving and embracing Divine Truth. To understand and realize that truth, to reach that degree of *true knowing* is only achieved when the heart has withdrawn from all else but Almighty Allāh. It is to be in a state where one is no longer seeking, but has arrived, and is open to receiving and reflecting upon that which is received rather than probe inquiry into other than that.

---

(١٣)

كَيْفَ يُشْرِقُ قَلْبٌ وَصُوَرُ الأَكْوَانِ مُنْطَبِعَةٌ فِي مِرْآتِهِ ؟

أَمْ كَيْفَ يَرْحَلُ إِلَى اللهِ وَهُوَ مُكَبَّلٌ بِشَهَوَاتِهِ ؟

أَمْ كَيْفَ يَطْمَعُ أَنْ يَدْخُلَ حَضْرَةَ اللهِ وَهُوَ لَمْ يَتَطَهَّرْ مِنْ جَنَابَاتِ غَفَلَاتِهِ ؟

أَمْ كَيْفَ يَرْجُو أَنْ يَفْهَمَ دَقَائِقَ الأَسْرَارِ وَهُوَ لَمْ يَتُبْ مِنْ هَفَوَاتِهِ ؟

How can the Heart shine while the forms of the world are impressed in its mirror?
Or how can it journey to Allāh while it is shackled by its lusts?
Or how can it yearn to enter the presence of Allāh while it is not cleansed from the impurities of its heedlessness?
Or how can it hope to understand the subtleties of secrets while it has not repented from its lapses?

The heart has been likened to a mirror upon which is reflected the Divine Ordinance emanating from the Preserved Tablet اللوح المحفوظ. The heart has four praiseworthy inclinations. To rise and shine with purity. To return to the Divine Presence from which it has been distanced. To enter the Divine Presence from whence it originates. And to realize the secrets of Divinity from which it has been deluded. To each of these, there are obstructions. The heart cannot shine if the forms of the created world are impressed upon its surface, as their lingering effects taint its reflective quality. It cannot journey if it is shackled by lust and greed. It cannot enter the Divine Presence if it is impure, for the impure cannot come upon the pure. And it cannot understand and realize truth if it is confounded with error.

Four essential qualities have been highlighted here against four essential impediments to these qualities.

The first are the forms of the world. In the hierarchy of man's internal governance, the heart must sit sovereign over the soul. If the heart is weakened, it is subject to the soul's inclinations. The soul, by its nature is transfixed on the outward forms of the realm, while the heart is seeking their internal essences and discernments,[11] since the heart's innate attribute is to know and understand, which it achieves through discernment. Thus if the heart is crippled in its governance of the soul, it has no choice but to obey the soul and its fixation on the forms of the world. And if its focus is on the forms, it cannot achieve discernment, and without discernment of creation it cannot reach the discernment of the Divine.

The second is the rising to a lofty position, the loftiest being the Divine Presence. Like a bird whose feet are chained to the ground, however much it may struggle to flap its wings, it is unable to take flight. Similarly, one's desires are grounded in the earthly realm, and when one is shackled to their desires and lusts, regardless of how much they may struggle in the rites and rituals, they find themselves unable to take flight to reach that lofty rank.

The third pertains that which is pure and that which is impure. The former is of a higher rank, the latter of a lower rank. As a principle, that which is pure cannot descend to a level of impurity, for if it should, it would be tainted and would lose its purity. Rather that which is impure must strive to purify itself, and by doing so, rise to the rank of purity.

The fourth pertains one's errors and mistakes, one's sins. These become blemishes upon the heart. Since the heart is likened to a glass sphere, for it to unravel and gain an understanding of divine mysteries and secrets, it must be readied to receive Divine Light, since light alone can reveal what is kept concealed. The blemishes and stains of sin upon the heart prevent light from penetrating its surface, and this impedes the heart from receiving the unveilings of divine secrets and mysteries.

١٤

الْكَوْنُ كُلُّهُ ظُلْمَةٌ، وَإِنَّمَا أَنَارَهُ ظُهُورُ الْحَقِّ فِيهِ، فَمَنْ رَأَى الْكَوْنَ وَلَمْ يَشْهَدْهُ فِيهِ أَوْ عِنْدَهُ أَوْ قَبْلَهُ أَوْ بَعْدَهُ... فَقَدْ أَعْوَزَهُ وُجُودُ الْأَنْوَارِ... وَحُجِبَتْ عَنْهُ شُمُوسُ الْمَعَارِفِ بِسُحُبِ الْآثَارِ.

The World in its entirety is darkness. And indeed it is only illuminated by the manifestation of Truth in it. So whosoever sees the realm but does not witness the manifestation of the Truth in it, or by it, or before it, or after it... Verily he is destitute of the existence of light... And is veiled from the Radiances of Knowing by the clouds of antiquities.

---

11 See Hikam 85

The realm, *al-Kawn* الكون, is a 'phenomenological entity' formed by a Higher Power, and manifested to being observable. We may call it the 'world' 'cosmos' or 'universe,' but it remains a created domain that is both finite and temporal. Hence, it is, and all that exists within it, is likewise, finite, temporal, and lifeless, unless given life and longevity by other than itself. It cannot bring itself into existence nor take itself out of existence into non-existence, as it cannot will itself into being, nor is it able to sustain itself, and as such it cannot illuminate itself, nor can it illuminate others, save by acting as a vessel of sustenance, and of light.

In that regard, it is, by its very nature, an entity of darkness, and it is so because it is a veil for the one who halts at its outward shell and does not see its inward essence. It is, by clear validation, that the world, and all that which is manifest in it, cannot elucidate itself. Cannot illustrate its own origin, nor define its longevity. A star cannot explain its luminance, a planet cannot explain its roundness, a tree cannot explain its greenness, and the oceans cannot explain their moistness. A created being cannot explain its creation or its being. For lack of their knowability, all that is created necessitates the Creator to explain what He has created, how, and why. If knowledge is regarded as an illuminating light, then lack of knowing is regarded as darkness, iterated thus as an 'absence of light.'

The 'Truth' is therefore not a construct of facts, figures, and expressions of reality, but *Al-Haqq* الْحَقّ, as *'The Truth'* being the Creator Himself. Thus, whosoever does not witness the Creator in creation, by it, before, or after it, has been deprived of the Light of the Truth, and thus veiled from the rays of knowing by the veils of externalities.

The true 'knower' is one, who, once he realizes Almighty Allāh and sees (witnesses) His Divine manifestation in all things, sees nothing else of import beside Him. The knower achieves this by sharpening the sight of faith in his heart such that he finds Allāh in everything, with everything, at everything, before everything, after everything, above everything, and encompassing everything. This is further elucidated in the next two Hikam. For it is not He, Allāh, who is veiled, but veiled are those who deliberately deprive themselves of witnessing Him despite being granted the ability to see. And they are not blinded in their eyes, but blinded in the hearts that are in their breasts.[12]

(١٥)

مِمَّا يَدُلُّكَ عَلَى وُجُودِ قَهْرِهِ سُبْحَانَهُ أَنْ حَجَبَكَ عَنْهُ بِمَا لَيْسَ بِمَوْجُودٍ مَعَهُ

From what indicates to you of the existence of His omnipotence, Glory be unto Him, is that He has veiled you from Himself with what does not have existence alongside Him.

12 Sūrah al-Hajj 22:46

كَيْفَ يُتَصَوَّرُ أَنْ يَحْجُبَهُ شَيْءٌ وَهُوَ الَّذِي أَظْهَرَ كُلَّ شَيْءٍ؟

كَيْفَ يُتَصَوَّرُ أَنْ يَحْجُبَهُ شَيْءٌ وَهُوَ الَّذِي ظَهَرَ بِكُلِّ شَيْءٍ؟

كَيْفَ يُتَصَوَّرُ أَنْ يَحْجُبَهُ شَيْءٌ وَهُوَ الَّذِي ظَهَرَ فِي كُلِّ شَيْءٍ؟

كَيْفَ يُتَصَوَّرُ أَنْ يَحْجُبَهُ شَيْءٌ وَهُوَ الَّذِي ظَهَرَ لِكُلِّ شَيْءٍ؟

كَيْفَ يُتَصَوَّرُ أَنْ يَحْجُبَهُ شَيْءٌ وَهُوَ الظَّاهِرُ قَبْلَ وُجُودِ كُلِّ شَيْءٍ؟

كَيْفَ يُتَصَوَّرُ أَنْ يَحْجُبَهُ شَيْءٌ وَهُوَ أَظْهَرُ مِنْ كُلِّ شَيْءٍ؟

كَيْفَ يُتَصَوَّرُ أَنْ يَحْجُبَهُ شَيْءٌ وَهُوَ الوَاحِدُ الَّذِي لَيْسَ مَعَهُ شَيْءٌ؟

كَيْفَ يُتَصَوَّرُ أَنْ يَحْجُبَهُ شَيْءٌ وَهُوَ أَقْرَبُ إِلَيْكَ مِنْ كُلِّ شَيْءٍ؟

وَكَيْفَ يُتَصَوَّرُ أَنْ يَحْجُبَهُ شَيْءٌ وَلَوْلَاهُ مَا كَانَ وُجُودُ كُلِّ شَيْءٍ؟

يَا عَجَبًا! كَيْفَ يَظْهَرُ الوُجُودُ فِي العَدَمِ !

أَمْ كَيْفَ يَثْبُتُ الحَادِثُ مَعَ مَنْ لَهُ وَصْفُ القِدَمِ !

How can it be conceived that He should be veiled by a thing... And He is the One who Manifests every thing?

How can it be conceived that He should be veiled by a thing... And He is the One who is Manifest through every thing?

How can it be conceived that He should be veiled by a thing... And He is the One who is Manifest in every thing?

How can it be conceived that He should be veiled by a thing... And He is the One who is Manifest to every thing?

How can it be conceived that He should be veiled by a thing... And He is the Manifest before the existence of every thing?

How can it be conceived that He should be veiled by a thing... And He is more Manifest than every thing?

How can it be conceived that He should be veiled by a thing...And He is the One whom alongside is no thing?

How can it be conceived that He should be veiled by a thing...And He is closer to you than every thing?

How can it be conceived that He should be veiled by a thing... And were it not for Him, no thing would exist?

O' what a marvel! How existence has manifested into non-being!

Or how the temporal has been established with the One to whom is the attribute of eternity!

He has veiled *you*, not Himself, with that which has no existence beside Him, and truly has no existence compared to His existence. His existence is the only true existence, while all else exists *because* He exists. In this way, what we regard as existence, being our existence or the existence of the rest of creation, is, in truth non-existence. For though we are manifest in reality, our manifestation is because of His manifestation. Were He to withdraw, even for the most minute measure of a moment, all would cease to exist. And in this way, that which is temporal, non-permanent, finite, and limited, is manifest with the One to whom is the attribute of eternity, a manifestation everlasting.

$$ ١٧ $$

مَا تَرَكَ مِنَ الجَهْلِ شَيْئًا مَنْ أَرَادَ أَنْ يَحْدُثَ فِي الوَقْتِ غَيْرُ مَا أَظْهَرَهُ اللهُ فِيهِ

Not has he parted from ignorance a thing, one who wants that there occur in a moment other than what Allāh manifests in it

For naught can manifest in a moment save that which Almighty Allāh decrees. Knowing and realizing this is truly from the purest and most praiseworthy of knowing. To then anticipate an occurrence in any given moment, other than what the Almighty decrees in it, is ignorance.

$$ ١٨ $$

إِحَالَتُكَ الأَعْمَالَ عَلَى وُجُودِ الفَرَاغِ مِنْ رُعُونَاتِ النَّفْسِ

Your remittance of deeds upon the convenience of leisure is from the frivolities of your self (ego)

The unfolding moment is therefore not in your control, and is beyond your knowing. You are alive in the present, not the past, nor future. You but have a remnant memory of what was, and but a glimpse of what may come to be. Even those who may profess the deepest wisdom and insight cannot perceive the entirety of what lay beyond the moment. The interconnected threads of fate and consequence extend beyond our horizon of understanding, the ultimate outcomes veiled in uncertainty and mystery. It is wiser, therefore, to 'seize the moment' and remit your deeds with every fiber of your being, than to assume the luxury and leisure to remit them later. For there is no greater ignorance than to prioritize convenience over excellence. To do so is to think not with your heart, but with the frivolities and mediocre logics of your self, for it is the self that anchors you with foolishness to comfort and leisure, manifesting lethargy and laziness in you.

(۱۹)

لَا تَطْلُبْ مِنْهُ أَنْ يُخْرِجَكَ مِنْ حَالَةٍ لِيَسْتَعْمِلَكَ فِيمَا سِوَاهَا...

فَلَوْ أَرَادَ... اسْتَعْمَلَكَ مِنْ غَيْرِ إِخْرَاجٍ.

Seek not from Him that He removes you from a state in order to make use of you in a different state... If He so desired, He could make use of you without removing you (altering your state).

Your present state is one in which *He* has established you, wherein your usefulness has already been established, and your servitude is expected regardless of your circumstances. To think that you could have been a better servant if only your conditions improved is indeed foolish. It is to assume that His establishment of you in that state was an error on His part, when the *Adab* of the believer is to be content and satisfied with one's placement, and be ever willing to serve, rather than vow one's servitude only when the conditions are improved. Who are we to place a condition on our Lord before serving Him? He is Doer of what He wills, and can alter our individual or collective states without the need to ask our consent.

(۲۰)

مَا أَرَادَتْ هِمَّةَ سَالِكٍ أَنْ تَقِفَ عِنْدَ مَا كُشِفَ لَهَا إِلَّا وَنَادَتْهُ هَوَاتِفُ الْحَقِيقَةِ...

الَّذِي تَطْلُبُ أَمَامَكَ،

وَلَا تَبَرَّجَتْ ظَوَاهِرُ الْمُكَوَّنَاتِ إِلَّا وَنَادَتْهُ حَقَائِقُهَا...

﴿ إِنَّمَا نَحْنُ فِتْنَةٌ فَلَا تَكْفُرْ ﴾

Not does the passion of the seeker intend to cease when it is unveiled to him, but that the voices of reality call out to him, "That which you seek is ahead of you". And not do they adorn, the externalities of formations (created things) but their realities call out, "Indeed we are but a trial, so disbelieve not..." [13]

The '*Himmah*' (passion) of the '*Sālik*' (seeker) is a force that compels his journey, such that he does not linger to awe upon marvels. As when he witnesses them, they call out to him, propelling him onward. That what he truly seeks lies further ahead. He is not distracted by the externalities of created things, for he hears their call to him, declaring themselves to be distractions, urging him to maintain his focus on the Divine.

---

13 Sūrah al-Baqarah 2:102

(٢١)

طَلَبُكَ مِنْهُ اتِّهَامٌ لَهُ...

وَطَلَبُكَ لَهُ غَيْبَةٌ عَنْهُ...

وَطَلَبُكَ لِغَيْرِهِ لِقِلَّةِ حَيَائِكَ مِنْهُ...

وَطَلَبُكَ مِنْ غَيْرِهِ لِوُجُودِ بُعْدِكَ عَنْهُ...

Your demanding from Him is impeachment of Him...
And your searching of Him is to your absence from Him...
And your expecting from other than Him is to your lack of shame from Him...
And your seeking from other than Him is to your distance from Him...

The word طلب, is a broad term that holds the meanings of 'search, find, seek, demand, pursue, inquire, expect, ask, appeal,' among others. When you demand from Allāh, you are challenging His supreme authority, and undermining the very essence of His sovereignty. A servant does not impose demands upon the Master. To do so would be an act of profound disrespect and arrogance. The Divine owes you nothing, despite any self-conceived notions of entitlement or deservedness you may hold.

And when you embark on a quest to find Him, it is not because *He* is absent or distant, but rather because *you* have become estranged from Him, lost in the illusions of your own existence. The Divine Presence is ever near, closer to you than your own breath, eternally sustaining your very being. Your search is a reflection of your inherent need for Him, not a consequence of His absence from you. He remains omnipresent, a constant in your life, while it is you who have wandered away.

When you place your expectations in other than Him, you commit an act of profound folly and shamelessness. Who among mortals possesses the power to fulfill promises with the certainty and perfection that the Divine does? By turning to others for what only He can provide, you betray a misunderstanding of His infinite capabilities and grace.

When you then seek Him, it is a manifestation of your spiritual estrangement, not an indication of His distance from you. You mistakenly perceive Him as missing from your life, yet it is only by His grace that you have life. If you choose to seek fulfillment or solace in anything other than Him, you reveal the depth of your separation from His essence. For if you truly realized the proximity and intimacy of His presence within you, how could you ever turn elsewhere? Your seeking from other sources is a testament to the chasm between you and the Divine, a gap born of your ignorance, heedlessness, and forgetfulness of His omnipresence.

So search not, but with sincerity. Ask not, but with humility. Demand not, but from yourself. And expect not, but from Him.

۲۲

مَا مِنْ نَفَسٍ تُبْدِيهِ إِلَّا وَلَهُ قَدَرٌ فِيكَ يُمْضِيهِ

*Not from a breath do you exhibit (manifest) but that to it is a decreed destiny
within you that proceeds it further.*

۲۳

لَا تَتَرَقَّبْ فَرَاغَ الْأَغْيَارِ فَإِنَّ ذَلِكَ يَقْطَعُكَ عَنْ وُجُودِ الْمُرَاقَبَةِ لَهُ فِيمَا هُوَ مُقِيمُكَ فِيهِ

*Do not anticipate dissolution from the vicissitudes (of life), as that severs you
from the presence of observation (vigilant attention) to Him in what He has
established for you.*

The 'breath' is the moment in time, the duration between inhaling
and exhaling, whereby each exhaled breath is a manifestation of a moment
of your life. Whatever manifests with that breath, meaning, whatever you
do, or is done to you, or around you, has been Decreed, and this you must
acknowledge, whether or not you understand it. The 'Decree' is Allāh's
fore-knowledge and complete measure, قَدَرٌ, of all aspects of His creation,
seen (physical) and unseen (spiritual). Within it is included all necessary
outcomes, all possible outcomes, and all impossible outcomes, the sum
of which are infinite and cannot be estimated, let alone measured, by
creation, even if all of creation was to gather and exert all their efforts into
its deliberation. Hence, the moment only manifests if it has been willed
by the Highest of Wills, and this is what precedes all manifestation.

In that regard, the believer's role does not become one of 'controlling'
the moment and its outcomes, but one of 'witnessing' what is becoming
of the moment. For it is only in Almighty Allāh's Decree, that He wills a
thing to 'BE' and thus it 'Becomes.'

Do not seek to be dissolved and removed from the moment, be it a
moment of tranquility or a moment of turbulence, for you will be severing
yourself from the vigilance of witnessing what He, in His wisdom,
has established for you. The vicissitudes of time, being the unfolding
moment, subjects the being into a state of constant change. Time itself is
never static, as that which occurs in time is also never static. Reality is in
a constant state of change, and these changes have a direct effect on the
being. They influence the manner in which intentions are enacted, the
outcomes of the enactments, and even affect the intentions themselves.
Most will find themselves often changing their decisions and intentions
in relation to the unfolding circumstances, and this is proof of one's inner
state being affected by the externalities. It is evidence of weakened Will
and discipline, and a dependency on externalities, evidence of vicissitudes
having dominance over their will and their being.

لَا تَسْتَغْرِبْ وُقُوعَ الْأَكْدَارِ، مَا دُمْتَ مُقِيمًا فِي هَذِهِ الدَّارِ، فَإِنَّهَا مَا أَبْرَزَتْ لَكَ إِلَّا مَا هُوَ
مُسْتَحَقٌّ وَصْفِهَا وَوَاجِبُ نَعْتِهَا

Do not find strange the occurrence of sorrows so long as you reside in this world. For indeed it (the world) demonstrates not but its rightful characteristic and necessary attribute.

To perceive a thing as 'strange' is to perceive its occurrence as being other than the norm, or to perceive it as being 'out of place' or 'extraordinary,' meaning other than ordinary. It is to assume, at a time of peace that the occurrence of turbulence is odd, wherein the turbulence has disrupted the norm of peace.

However, for one to find it strange is also counterintuitive and in opposition to one's intelligence, since the nature of the world is not, as previously iterated, static. No moment remains a moment but that it transforms into another moment, either distinct from the previous or something in similitude but not the same. Such is the nature of the realm we presently inhibit, and it is but demonstrating its rightful characteristics and what is innate of its attributes.

A prime stipulation of Belief, is never to assume that any occurrence is 'out of place' or extraordinary, in that, if one understands that each unfolding moment is a moment decreed, then that which occurs, though appearing distinct from the norm, is itself part of the norm. Indeed, this realm is a realm of turbulence, not stability. It is a domain of sorrow, not joy. The one who understands this, does not rejoice in its ease, neither is he saddened by its grief. For he understands that Almighty Allāh fashioned this realm as a realm of affliction, of trials and tribulations, and established the HereAfter as a realm of permanence. He fashioned this realm as a repository for the reward of the HereAfter, and that reward as a recompense for the afflictions endured in this realm. So in His taking, He gives, and in His testing, He recompenses.

This realm, and everything within it, was designed to fade and vanish. So beware of the sweetness of its suckling for the bitterness of its weaning. Be wary of its immediate pleasure for its hateful end. Strive not to cultivate here, nor to obtain it now, for this realm is but a bridge. Seek not to establish a sense of permanence upon it, rather cross over it to the ultimate destination. It is an abode of worry, sorrow, affliction, and trial. This is its true nature. Expect with certainty that part of its gift will never be to your liking. What little joy you receive is meant only to alleviate the difficulty, and this a mercy from your Lord, that you may be thankful for His care and nurture. He knows of your pain, and will never withdraw His providence so long as you remain grateful towards Him.

۲٥

مَا تَوَقَّفَ مَطْلَبٌ أَنْتَ طَالِبُهُ بِرَبِّكَ وَلَا تَيَسَّرَ مَطْلَبٌ أَنْتَ طَالِبُهُ بِنَفْسِكَ

*Not is halted a quest you seek with your Lord. And not is facilitated a quest
you seek by yourself.*

۲٦

مِنْ عَلَامَاتِ النُّجَاحِ فِي النِّهَايَاتِ، الرُّجُوعُ إِلَى اللهِ فِي البِدَايَاتِ

From among the signs of success in the end, is the turning to Allāh in the beginning.

۲۷

مَنْ أَشْرَقَتْ بِدَايَتُهُ أَشْرَقَتْ نِهَايَتُهُ

He who rises to shine in the beginning, rises to shine in the end.

Every quest has a beginning, an initial step when one considers
whether they will embark it by themselves, or with aid. To embark it
with aid is to beseech the aid of Allāh, wherein one places the trust of a
favourable outcome in His hands, and is thus distracted from the possible
negative results. Should it bear fruition, it is only by His permission,
where as seeking it by oneself, though with complete confidence in one's
abilities, though with diligent planning and strategy, the quest inherently
becomes difficult and constricted.

If you should beseech His aid in the task, its outcome is fulfilled with
meaning, intrinsically, even if it is not satisfied extrinsically. However, if
you should embark it yourself, you may find your efforts disappointed
and your time wasted, even if your desire and need is satisfied. Thus a sign
of success at the end of the quest is the beseeching of Allāh's aid in the
beginning, such success having an intrinsic meaning and contentment,
even if the outcome was not physically favourable.

This traces back to the first Hikam regarding the dependency on deeds,
as opposed to dependency on Allāh, such that even though the outcome
was physically favourable, one does not find an intrinsic satisfaction in it.
To put it bluntly, 'there was no Barakah in it.'

Upon this, Ibn Ata'Illah says, that turning to Allāh for aid in the
beginning is a sign of one's luminance. A sign of one's rising to shine,
such that he shall, by the Grace of Allāh, and due to this alone, rise to
shine in the end. One who diligently seeks Allāh's aid in the beginning, by
turning away from any intimacy with creation, will have his end radiant,
his outcome praiseworthy, and his goal obtained. He will find himself
content, regardless of what causality may manifest.

(۲۸)

مَا اسْتُودِعَ فِي غَيْبِ السَّرَائِرِ ظَهَرَ فِي شَهَادَةِ الظَّوَاهِرِ

What is entrusted in the unseen of the consciousness is manifested in the seen of phenomena.

The Arabs say, اللسان ترجمان القلب, *'The tongue is a translator of the Heart.'* What appears on the tongue is not of its own origin. It is merely relaying what already lay in the innermost of the heart and expressing it in the realm of physicality. It does not interpret, nor add, nor subtract from what is expressed. Thus it demonstrates precisely what the inner state is. What one does or says, how they conduct themselves, the subtleties and nuances of their actions and behaviours, is all manifested in the realm of physical phenomena from the unseen of their consciousness. If it utters uncontrolled, it demonstrates a lack of inner control. If it utters with intelligence, with knowledge and wisdom, it demonstrates the being's intelligence, knowledge, and wisdom. The same is true for all that manifests in the outward; it is but an extension of what is inward.

(۲۹)

شَتَّانَ بَيْنَ مَنْ يَسْتَدِلُّ بِهِ وَ بَيْنَ يَسْتَدِلُّ عَلَيْهِ، فَالْمُسْتَدِلُّ بِهِ... عَرَفَ الْحَقَّ لِأَهْلِهِ، فَأَثْبَتَ الْأَمْرَ مِنْ وُجُودِ أَصْلِهِ، وَالِاسْتِدْلَالُ عَلَيْهِ مِنْ عَدَمِ الْوُصُولِ إِلَيْهِ وَإِلَّا مَتَى غَابَ حَتَّى يُسْتَدَلَّ عَلَيْهِ؟ وَمَتَى بَعُدَ حَتَّى تَكُونَ الْآثَارُ هِيَ الَّتِي تُوْصِلُ إِلَيْهِ؟

What a difference between one who confers (creation) by Allāh and the one who confers upon Allāh through creation. For one who confers by Allāh understands the truth of its qualification and ascertains the command from the existence of its origin. And the inference upon Him through creation is a void of attainment (of understanding Him). Elseways, when was He absent that inference had to be made upon Him? And when was He distant that the traces of created things must lead to Him?

There are two primary approaches to discerning the origin of reality. Either one examines the origin through the lens of manifestation, or one examines manifestation through the lens of the originator. The word *Shattāna* شتّان, here is used to distinguish the perspectives and approaches. One can, for instance, either examine physical phenomena and then attempt to validate what is found in revelation, or one can examine revelation and discern the reality of physical phenomena. The former is discerning reality through a language constructed purely of his own whims, through variant theories, hypothesis, equations, and such.

45

His understanding may be quantitative of the world, but not qualitative of the Originator. As we would ask, when was He absent such that He must be substantiated through created things? And when was He distant such that created things must be used to lead to Him? Is He to be known through the comprehension of this or that theory, constructed from a perceptive that only acknowledges the quantitative outward and overlooks the qualitative essence? Why then would He reveal to you, in His own words, a description of what He has created and why? Was it for you to marvel at His creation? Or was it that *you* come to understand *Him?*

---

(٣٠)

﴿ لِيُنفِقْ ذُو سَعَةٍ مِّن سَعَتِهِ ﴾ ... الْوَاصِلُونَ إِلَيْهِ

﴿ وَمَن قُدِرَ عَلَيْهِ رِزْقُهُ ﴾ ... السَّائِرُونَ إِلَيْهِ

"Let him spend, the one of means, from his means" ... these have attained closeness with Him.
"And one whose provision is withheld upon him" ... these are journeying towards Him. [14]

(٣١)

اهْتَدَى الرَّاحِلُونَ إِلَيْهِ بِأَنْوَارِ التَّوَجُّهِ ، وَالْوَاصِلُونَ لَهُمْ أَنْوَارُ الْمُوَاجَهَةِ ، فَالْأَوَّلُونَ لِلْأَنْوَارِ ،

وَهَؤُلَاءِ الْأَنْوَارُ لَهُمْ ؛ لِأَنَّهُمْ لِلَّهِ لَا لِشَيْءٍ دُونَهُ

﴿ قُلِ اللَّهُ ثُمَّ ذَرْهُمْ فِي خَوْضِهِمْ يَلْعَبُونَ ﴾

Guided are the migrants (those journeying) to Him by the Lights of orientation. And those who have arrived, to them are the Lights of Confrontation. As for the first, they belong to the Lights. And these (others) the Lights are to them, for indeed to them there is no thing other than Him. "...Say Allāh; then leave them [those who are defiant] to their debates, amusing themselves." [15]

There are two kinds of seekers. Those who have attained closeness to the Divine, and those who are yet journeying toward Him. The first are the elite few خاص, saints and prophets among them. They are those whose essences have risen out of the constriction of phenomenal states to an expanse of knowledge and understanding, and they spend freely from these treasures. The second are the common many عام, who are constricted by the phenomenal world, whose knowledge and understanding is constricted, to whom the openings and unveilings have not yet come.

14 Sūrah at-Talāq 65:7

15 Sūrah al-An'ām 6:91

The *'Lights'* أَنْوَارُ, are the lights of guidance and understanding. Light is, by its very nature and quality, that which reveals what is concealed. For in order to see, light must fall upon that which is sought, unveiling it for the eye, and by its unveiling does it come to be known. Hence light is that which unveils for the seeker what he was ignorant of, so that by its revelation to him, he comes to know and understand it. Revelation وحي, is therefore regarded as 'Light' نور, and Almighty Allāh guides His Light unto whomsoever He Wills.[16]

These lights take on multiple forms and attributes. There are lights awarded to the senses that unveil the physical material realm, by which one's physical eyes can perceive and understand the outward forms of things. There are lights awarded to the intellects that unveil the symbolic realm, by which the symbolic forms can be perceived and interpreted to understand the realm of essences. Then, there are lights awarded to the hearts and the innermost dimensions that unveil the spiritual aspects of reality and their secrets, by which one can understand the meanings of the innermost dimensions. And among them all are several other lights, some lesser, other greater.

Those defined as الواصلون, are seekers to whom the lights are of confrontation, meaning they are encountering the higher and greater lights without any veils between them, hence earning both the title and its meaning of 'the Enlightened.'

۳۲

تَشَوُّفُكَ إِلَى مَا بَطَنَ فِيكَ مِنَ الْعُيُوبِ خَيْرٌ مِنْ تَشَوُّفِكَ إِلَى مَا حُجِبَ عَنْكَ مِنَ الْغُيُوبِ

Your aspiration to (discern) what is within you from shame (vices and shortcomings) is better than your aspiration to seek what is hidden from you from the Unseen [mysteries and wonders].

Existence is an unending odyssey of discovery for the existing entity, an inexhaustible, ceaseless quest for meaning and enlightenment. The essence of existence itself remains unassuming as its very nature is not inherently significant on its own; rather it is the purpose and meaning we ascribe to it that imbues it with significance to us. This intrinsic drive toward exploration and enlightenment is a universal trait among sentient beings. However, it is the direction in which we channel this drive that determines whether our endeavors lead to fulfillment or to futility. As beautifully and eloquently articulated in the Holy Qur'ān;

True success lies in the refinement and purification of the self, while failure manifests in obstructing it from its intended purpose.[17]

---

16   Sūrah an-Nūr 24:35

17   Sūrah ash-Shams 91:9-10

All men, by their very nature, desire to know.[18] Undoubtedly, the vast expanse of existence offers boundless opportunities to satiate the human thirst for knowledge. Beyond the confines of our limited perceptions lie realms unimagined, where the mysteries of the heavens and the earth await revelation. Indeed, as it has been said, there are more things in the Heavens and the Earth than are dreamt of in our philosophies.[19] Yet, the human capacity for focus and attention is finite, and there is only so much to which one's gaze can be directed. It therefore becomes imperative to discern that which holds paramount importance, and what greater pursuit to quenching man's desire to know than knowing not what is created but the *One* who created and creates all.

As iterated before,[20] however, He who is of that loftiest degree of absolute purity cannot be expected to lower Himself and cater to the whims and conveniences of we who have inherently determined ourselves to be steeped in states of impurities. The flaws and vices that mar and taint our inner essence are undeniable, and it behooves us to acknowledge that part of the preparation for true discernment of the Absolute necessitates purification of the self to be readied for that loftier discernment. The foremost task, therefore, lies not in the mere investigation of the unseen and unknown mysteries and wonders of reality, however alluring their call, but in the introspective journey towards recognizing and rectifying our own imperfections.

Within this realization lies the crux of our quest for knowledge and enlightenment. For how can we, the imperfect, hope to realize Him, the Perfect, without first striving to achieve some measure of perfection? Is not the pursuit of greater mysteries and secrets of existence, while neglecting the deeper quest for self-purification, a misguided endeavor? Indeed, only by cleansing oneself of those imperfections can the Absolute be perceived in His pristine clarity, and therein lies the key to unlocking the profound mysteries of existence.

Your time is precious. Limited. Spend it not in the pursuit of marvels and wonders. The time for marvel and wonder will come, promised to those who are successful, not in conquest of the world, but in conquest of themselves. So waste not precious moments in the wonder of mysteries and secrets, rather direct your thoughts and manifest righteous actions with the aspiration of removing from your essence the very blemishes that would cloud your inner sight from witnessing those wonders and marvels. What a loser is he who shall be prevented, by his own volitions, from seeing eternal beauty simply because he squandered the temporal opportunity to earn the right to witness and bask in Divine Glory!

---

18 Aristotle, *Metaphysics.*

19 Shakespeare. *Hamlet.*

20 Hikam 13

(٣٣)

الْحَقُّ لَيْسَ بِمَحْجُوبٍ، وَإِنَّمَا الْمَحْجُوبُ أَنْتَ عَنِ النَّظَرِ إِلَيْهِ،

إِذْ لَوْ حَجَبَهُ شَيْءٌ لَسَتَرَهُ مَا حَجَبَهُ، وَلَوْ كَانَ لَهُ سَاتِرٌ ... لَكَانَ لِوُجُودِهِ حَاصِرٌ،

وَكُلُّ حَاصِرٍ لِشَيْءٍ ... فَهُوَ لَهُ قَاهِرٌ

﴿وَهُوَ الْقَاهِرُ فَوْقَ عِبَادِهِ﴾

The REAL (Al-Haqq) is not veiled. Indeed the only one veiled is you from
seeing Him. For if there were to veil Him a thing, it would indeed cover Him,
and were there to Him a covering it would indeed be to His existence a siege,
and that which besieges a thing, upon it has power. And yet...
"He is Al-Qāhir [the Overpowering, the Omnipotent] over His subjects." [21]

All of existence is parted into that which exists boundless, independent,
and absolute, and that which exists bound, dependent, and temporal. The
latter is contingent upon the former, hence the former cannot be
overpowered by the latter. The latter is creation while the former is the
Creator. Being omnipresent and transcendent means that Almighty
Allāh remains unobscured by any element. He is manifest in all things,
preceding and succeeding all existence. If He is all-Seeing, then no veil
can obstruct Him, as that which obstructs a thing has power over it,
and any entity that is overpowered by a thing cannot be superior to that
thing. Hence the veils are not upon Him, but upon all else that must
derive existence from Him. You are not 'all'-seeing. Your sight can only
fall upon one thing at a time. Your gaze can either be seeking Him, or
remain affixed on other than Him. In that regard, He remains concealed
from you so long as you are distracted by otherness. Were your heart truly
devoted to seeking the Divine, turning away completely from all else, you
would perceive the light of the Absolute shining forth in every aspect of
creation, dispelling the illusions that veil your sight.

Though all bear witness to the omnipresent evidence of His Divinity,
few truly realize and comprehend. Most swim in the ocean of existence
yet remain oblivious to the depths and pearls within. In truth, none are
veiled from Him; it is only the illusion of separation that blinds you. The
illusion of separation, rather than any actual concealment, is identified
as the root cause of spiritual blindness. This illusion, empty of substance,
holds no sway in the realm of actuality, where nothing exists alongside
Almighty Allāh in absolute essence. If He is the Absolute while all else is
temporal, how can it be said that the temporal has veiled the Absolute?
Such is the illusion of multiplicity, and it is owed to the failure of realizing
His unity that obscures your vision.

---

21 Sūrah al-Anʿām 6:18 and 6:61

It is emphasized that even the mere suggestion of a physical entity being capable of veiling the Divine would imply a limitation upon His omnipotence, which contradicts His boundless and uncontainable essence. For He transcends all limitations; His essence boundless, incapable of containment. Indeed, any entity contained by another is subservient to it. How then could this be true of the Almighty, who reigns supreme over all creation, by virtue of His sovereign will and power?

His elevation above His subjects signifies not spatial superiority, but rather eminence in rank and authority, as one might say, "The sultan surpasses the vizier," or "the master is superior to the slave." This concept denotes sovereignty and superiority, negating the notion of proximity. Such matters are beyond the limitations of time and space, known only to Allāh, the Most Wise.

Thus, the barrier between the soul and enlightenment is but an illusion. It is a malady of the human condition, a sickness of the heart that hinders recognition of the Divine. Were it to free itself from ailment, it would perceive the Truth and Real with unhindered clarity.

---

(٣٤)

اخْرُجْ مِنْ أَوْصَافِ بَشَرِيَّتِكَ عَنْ كُلِّ وَصْفٍ مُنَاقِضٍ لِعُبُودِيَّتِكَ،

لِتَكُونَ لِنِدَاءِ الْحَقِّ مُجِيبًا وَمِنْ حَضْرَتِهِ قَرِيبًا

Depart from the characteristics of your humanness, from every trait that is contradictory to your veneration. So you can be, to the call of Truth, responsive, and from His presence, closer.

(٣٥)

أَصْلُ كُلِّ مَعْصِيَةٍ وَغَفْلَةٍ وَشَهْوَةٍ ... الرِّضَا عَنِ النَّفْسِ،

وَأَصْلُ كُلِّ طَاعَةٍ وَيَقَظَةٍ وَعِفَّةٍ ... عَدَمُ الرِّضَا مِنْكَ عَنْهَا،

وَلَأَنْ تَصْحَبَ جَاهِلاً لَا يَرْضَى عَنْ نَفْسِهِ خَيْرٌ لَكَ مِنْ أَنْ تَصْحَبَ عَالِمًا يَرْضَى عَنْ نَفْسِهِ،

فَأَيُّ عِلْمٍ لِعَالِمٍ يَرْضَى عَنْ نَفْسِهِ؟ وَأَيُّ جَهْلٍ لِجَاهِلٍ لَا يَرْضَى عَنْ نَفْسِهِ؟

The root source of every sin, heedlessness, and lust, is self-satisfaction. And the root source of every obedience, virtue, and vigilance is lack of self-satisfaction. And that you keep the company of an ignoramus not pleased with himself is better for you than to accompany an academic satisfied with himself. For what knowledge is there to an academic satisfied with himself? And what ignorance is there to the ignoramus not satisfied with himself?

50

Sever yourself from your humanness, from those traits and behaviours that hinder your devotion and servitude to Him. Indeed, though you possess a human form, your essence is of the Angelic Genus. You were created to seek the light, to pursue knowledge and virtue, not to succumb to carnal desire and fester in brutish darkness. Only when you realize this quality do you find yourself open and responsive to the call of the Truth that would draw you closer to His presence.

Indeed, the source of all evil originates not from the world outside and around you, but from the depths of your human flaws, from the core of your vices, the poison within you, birthed by negligence, desire, and a misguided sense of self-satisfaction. From the delusion that you are, yourself, perfect and blameless. That you know all there is to know, that you are right and correct in every aspect of your valuation and inquiry.

Conversely, the source of your obedience, your virtue and vigilance, is embracing a state devoid of self-satisfaction. This is the medicinal elixir to your poison, that counters and heals your spiritual illnesses, and enlivens your being to a higher state. Such a state keeps you alive and cognizant, it keeps you humble and ever eager to persevere.

Hence it is more prudent to keep the company of an ignoramus unsatisfied with himself, than a learned who is satisfied with himself. The former has everything to gain, including enlightenment. The latter has deluded himself into thinking he has acquired all there is to acquire.

(٣٦)

شُعَاعُ الْبَصِيرَةِ يُشْهِدُكَ قُرْبَهُ مِنْكَ،

وَعَيْنُ الْبَصِيرَةِ يُشْهِدُكَ عَدَمَكَ لِوُجُودِهِ،

وَحَقُّ الْبَصِيرَةِ يُشْهِدُكَ وُجُودَهُ ،

لَا عَدَمَكَ وَلَا وُجُودَكَ.

The Rays of Intelligence let you witness His closeness to you...
The Eye of Intelligence lets you witness your non-being to His Being...
The Truth of Intelligence lets you witness His Being...
Not your non-being, nor your being...

(٣٧)

كَانَ اللّٰهُ وَلَا شَيْءَ مَعَهُ، وَهُوَ الْآنَ عَلَى مَا عَلَيْهِ كَانَ

He was Allāh, and no thing was with Him. And He is now as He always was.[22]

---

22 This is derived from the Hadīth in Sahīh al-Bukhāri 3191 and 7418

(٣٨)

لَا تَتَعَدَّيَنَّ هِمَّتُكَ إِلَى غَيْرِهِ، فَالْكَرِيمُ لَا تَتَخَطَّاهُ الْآمَالُ

Let not your ambitions extend to other than Him; Hopes and aspirations cannot exceed the Most Generous One.

The Rays of Intelligence are those that are cast by the intellect upon creation, by which their essence is abstracted, and through which the truth of their nature is realized. It is the intelligence that recognizes the worlds and all that they contain as created entities, and that if they are created there must be a Creator. Such is a necessary inference, and anything contrary becomes a fallacy. Through this the being realizes his closeness to the One who created him, as he sifts through the multiplicities and particularities to arrive at the Divine Unity.

The Eye of Intelligence is that which see the true nature of things and of itself. The being understands himself as a created entity that cannot sustain his own existence. This is also a necessary inference, and anything contrary is a fallacy. As such, He who brought the being into existence can only be He who has always *been* existent. In light of His existence, all else becomes non-existent. It is not because of your thought that you are,[23] but because of His being that you came to be. Your being, to His being, is in effect a non-being.

The Truth of Intelligence is that which transcends the mere abstraction and discernment of creation and the understanding of one's existence, to witnessing the Divine and naught else. For once you realize your non-being to His being, all that matters is His being. Not your existence, nor your non-existence. Such a truth, when dawned upon the heart, reveals that nothing but He Almighty truly is.

Hence, He *was*, *is*, and always *will be*, and there was no thing beside Him, nor will there ever be. All that exists in the realms shall perish, and forever will remain the existence of your Lord full of majesty and nobility. This is the testimony you affirmed in your faith as لَا إِلٰه إِلَّا الله, when you swore featly and submission to His will.

Now, realize what that testimony truly means.

And thereby, realize who *you* are before Him. What worth do you hold in His gaze, and are you truly worthy of His gaze? These hopes and aspirations you bear, that heedlessly carry you to higher states of delusion; do you think they can surpass He who is Most High?

---

23 René Descartes's *"Cogito, ergo sum;* I think therefore I am,"* which is an ideology that posits reason as the primary source of truth and knowledge. Islām opposes this ideology with emphasis on Revelation as the primary source of truth and knowledge. While the human being can be aware of himself as an existent being, his existence and its truth and knowledge cannot originate from himself. He must rely on his Creator to unveil that truth to him.

（٣٩）

لَا تَرْفَعَنَّ إِلَى غَيْرِهِ حَاجَةً هُوَ مُوْرِدُهَا عَلَيْكَ... فَكَيْفَ يَرْفَعُ غَيْرُهُ مَا كَانَ هُوَ لَهُ وَاضِعًا؟

مَنْ لَا يَسْتَطِيعُ أَنْ يَرْفَعَ حَاجَةً عَنْ نَفْسِهِ... فَكَيْفَ يَسْتَطِيعُ أَنْ يَكُونَ لَهَا عَنْ غَيْرِهِ رَافِعًا؟

*Do not seek to alleviate to other than Him, a need that He has brought upon
you... For how can someone else alleviate what He has authored?
One who is not able to alleviate his own need from himself... How can he be
able to alleviate the needs of someone else?*

Each individual is apportioned their share of burden, their share of
trial and tribulation, and upon each is the test of faith and trust upon He
who burdens them. Regardless, all are burdened, and it is affirmed that
no soul is burdened beyond its capacity.

Hence, we inquire, if Allāh has decreed a specific circumstance for
an individual, can any other entity alter that ordained condition? This
is the essence of Divine Providence and Omnipotence. He possesses,
over all things, complete knowledge and exact measure. His decrees
are irrefutable, for any attempt to contravene them would negate His
supreme authority. Hence, if He imposed the trial upon you, He alone
can truly alleviate it.

And to that we ask, if one cannot even relieve the burdens upon
their own shoulders, how can they possibly alleviate the burdens borne
by others? The believer understands, that none can truly alleviate his
burden save the One who burdened him. It is, therefore, unwise to seek
alleviation from others who are themselves subject to their own trials.

It is paramount to understand that no burden is imposed with the
intention of inflicting suffering, but rather to fortify, to challenge one's
limits, to test endurance and perseverance, and ultimately to lead one to
realize their deepest potential and capabilities. Allāh did not create you
in the essential likeness of the beasts whose limitations lie in their basic
instincts of ruminance and predation. He knows that if you only do what
you can do, you will never be more than you are. That you are a being
capable of great knowledge and virtue, that through you, the world can
be tamed, cultivated, and nurtured with piety and righteousness. Each
burden placed upon you, therefore, serves to strengthen you, as that
which does not destroy ultimately fortifies.

Indeed, He fashioned you with His own hands, with profound care
and attention. His providence is never removed from your side. And as
the Creator, He loves His creation, a love that is boundless. Should not
that love be reciprocated, if but a measure?

We posit that all the trials, all the predicaments and burdens, are but
intended to draw your attention to Him. He *wants* that you turn *only* to
Him, that you would ask only *Him* for ease!

۴۰

إِنْ لَمْ تُحَسِّنْ ظَنَّكَ بِهِ لِأَجْلِ وَصْفِهِ، فَحَسِّنْ ظَنَّكَ بِهِ لِأَجْلِ مُعَامَلَتِهِ مَعَكَ، فَهَلْ عَوَّدَكَ إِلَّا حَسَنًا؟ وَهَلْ أَسْدَى إِلَيْكَ إِلَّا مِنَنًا؟

If you have not improved your thinking of Him to the perfection of His attributes, then improve your thinking of Him on account of His treatment with you. For has He accustomed you anything but good? And has He conferred upon you anything but favour?

It is faulty to think the predicament upon you was bestowed for other than good. Though you may not see it in its immediate, the predicament tests your trust in Him to bring fruition from the trial. Indeed, you may desire a thing though it is harmful for you, or despise a thing though it is beneficial for you. Truly, your Lord knows while you do not. As not even the wisest can see all outcomes, one may either trust that their Lord, in His mercy and wisdom, will bear them good, or despair that they have been forsaken. Should you then despair, it is only to your loss. For when has He, the Merciful, granted anything but good? And when has He, the Benevolent, bestowed anything but favour? He, Almighty, has said, أَنَا عِنْدَ ظَنِّ عَبْدِي بِي *"I am as My servant thinks of Me."*[24] Should one think *nothing* of God, then God will be *nothing* to him. But if he should think *everything* of God, then God will be *everything* to him!

۴۱

الْعَجَبُ كُلُّ الْعَجَبِ مِمَّنْ يَهْرُبُ مِمَّا لَا انْفِكَاكَ لَهُ عَنْهُ، وَيَطْلُبُ مَا لَا بَقَاءَ لَهُ مَعَهُ ﴿ فَإِنَّهَا لَا تَعْمَى الْأَبْصَارُ وَلَكِن تَعْمَى الْقُلُوبُ الَّتِي فِي الصُّدُورِ ﴾

The marvel of all marvels is one who flees from what is inescapable and seeks what does not remain with him.
"For indeed they are not blinded in their eyes, but blinded are the hearts that are in their breasts."[25]

This is the profound paradox of the human condition. It marvels at the irony of those who often attempt to escape that which is certain and unavoidable, while aimlessly chasing after that which is transient and impermanent. This juxtaposition between the inescapable and the ephemeral illustrates the futility in resisting the inevitable and the vanity of pursuing what cannot endure.

---

24 Al-Bukhāri 7505

25 Sūrah al-Hajj 22:46

The wisdom lies in recognizing and accepting reality as it stands, by acknowledging that certain aspects of life are beyond our control. It is to focus on internal growth, spiritual fulfillment, and lasting virtues over superficial and temporary gains, to direct one's efforts towards what endures rather than what merely passes.

The folly of clinging to impermanent things and the wisdom of embracing what is inevitable is rooted in human wisdom. It echoes across all dispensations and is not merely a religious propagation. It teaches the nature of attachment and impermanence, reflects on fate and control, and emphasizes the weakness in the transient nature of worldly life. By bringing attention to the absurdity of our common pursuits and fears, it encourages a more enlightened outlook on life, rather than being driven by fear or a relentless quest for fleeting satisfaction.

(٤٢)

لَا تَرْحَلْ مِنْ كَوْنٍ إِلَى كَوْنٍ فَتَكُونَ كَحِمَارِ الرَّحَى؛

يَسِيرُ... وَالْمَكَانُ الَّذِي ارْتَحَلَ إِلَيْهِ هُوَ الَّذِي ارْتَحَلَ مِنْهُ!

وَلَكِنِ ارْتَحَلْ مِنَ الْأَكْوَانِ إِلَى الْمُكَوِّنِ...

﴿ وَأَنَّ إِلَى رَبِّكَ الْمُنْتَهَى ﴾

فَانْظُرْ إِلَى قَوْلِهِ صلى الله عليه وسلم،

...فَمَنْ كَانَتْ هِجْرَتُهُ إِلَى اللهِ وَرَسُولِهِ فَهِجْرَتُهُ إِلَى اللهِ وَرَسُولِهِ، وَمَنْ كَانَتْ هِجْرَتُهُ لِدُنْيَا يُصِيبُهَا

أَوِ امْرَأَةٍ يَنْكِحُهَا فَهِجْرَتُهُ إِلَى مَا هَاجَرَ إِلَيْهِ...

وَتَأَمَّلْ هَذَا الْأَمْرَ إِنْ كُنْتَ ذَا فَهْمٍ... وَالسَّلَامُ.

Move not from created thing to created thing that you become like a donkey at the mill that moves, and to where it travels becomes from where he departed. Rather move from created thing (the world) to the Originator.
"And that to your Lord, is the final destination..." [26]
Look then to the Prophet's saying, peace and blessings be upon him, "For whoever migrated to Allāh and His messenger, migrated to Allāh and His messenger. And whoever migrated for the worldly, to acquire it, or to wed (and establish a progeny/legacy) then he migrated to whatever he migrated." [27]
So ponder this behest that you may be of understanding.
And peace upon you.

---

26 Sūrah an-Najm 53:42

27 *Muttafaqun ʿAlayh* متفق عليه

Change is inevitable. Each thing is perpetually in motion, if not physically, then certainly metaphysically, and spiritual change is of greater importance than any material transformation. For if one does not spiritually move from one state to a better state, it does not matter where they physically establish themselves.

Yet this motion should be directed towards higher degrees. To journey from one created entity to another created entity is akin to the donkey at the mill, whose motion returns it from whence it began. It achieves nothing other than to repeat the same journey over and over again, yet never reaching greater heights, never escaping from its confines.

Rather, the motion should be from created entities to the Creator Himself. The objective of the journey, the ultimate destination should be other than the point of origin. Hence, he who migrates to Allāh and His messenger, has migrated from a lower state to a higher state. While he who migrates for worldly acquisition, for progeny and legacy, has merely shifted in a planar direction and has gained nothing of intrinsic or everlasting value.

---

(٤٣)

لَا تَصْحَبْ مَنْ لَا يُنْهِضُكَ حَالُهُ وَلَا يَدُلُّكَ عَلَى اللهِ مَقَالُهُ

Accompany not the one who, by his state, does not raise you, and by his speech, does not lead you to Allāh.

Language bears the remarkable power to take the soul from one state to another. Depending on the speaker and what they say, what words are articulated, what meanings they signify, one can take a soul from a sound state to an agitated state, or from an agitated state to a sound state. If we say that the soundest state is a state of being in the Divine Presence, which is attained through His mention and remembrance, then he whose speech brings you no closer to that state is not worth your company.

---

(٤٤)

رُبَّمَا كُنْتَ مُسِيئًا فَأَرَاكَ الْإِحْسَانَ مِنْكَ صُحْبَتُكَ إِلَى مَنْ هُوَ أَسْوَأُ حَالًا مِنْكَ

It may be you are in a bad state, so you see good in you when you are in the company of one who is in a worse state than you.

You may well be in a bad state, but allowing yourself the company of someone in worse state than yourself, might enable you to see the good in you. As the poet said, *I lamented for want of shoes until I met a man who had no feet.* And thus his lament turned to gratitude.

---

(٤٥)

مَا قَلَّ عَمَلٌ بَرَزَ مِنْ قَلْبٍ زَاهِدٍ ، وَلَا كَثُرَ عَمَلٌ بَرَزَ مِنْ قَلْبٍ رَاغِبٍ

*Not does it diminish, a deed arising from a heart that is ascetic, and not does
it grow, a deed arising from heart that is desirous.*

A deed that rises from the heart untouched and untethered by any
worldly affiliation, any material expectation, is a deed pure in its origin. It
is a deed performed with sincerity, free from any restrictions or hesitations,
and is thus a deed that does not diminish. It manifests perpetually, ever
growing, ever yielding rewards that transcend the worldly to manifest in
the Hereafter.

Then again, should the deed rise from a heart that is desirous, a heart
that expects recompense and immediate reward, a heart that does the
deed not for the deed itself nor for the pleasure of its Creator, but for its
own motives, then such a deed does not surpass its quantitative bounds.
Sure, the reward might be dealt, proportionate in measure to the deed,
but other than that, the being will receive no higher satisfaction.

(٤٦)

حُسْنُ الْأَعْمَالِ نَتَائِجُ حُسْنِ الْأَحْوَالِ، وَحُسْنُ الْأَحْوَالِ مِنَ التَّحَقُّقِ فِي مَقَامَاتِ الْإِنْزَالِ

*Good deeds are the result of good states, and good states are from the realization
of the waystations of Revelation (guidance).*

Good states are realized by those who have attained and risen
the spiritual degrees by embracing the guidance of Revelation. Each
waystation مقام is a rank and a minor destination along the journey, a
place of alightment مَنزِل. Each station is earned through a process of
spiritual or internal realization of Divine Guidance during the various
stages of one's spiritual development.

This is about the relationship between one's actions, their mental
and spiritual state or condition, and the fulfillment of certain rites that
enable ascent and establishment in higher spiritual stations or degrees.
The quality of one's actions is influenced by the state of being in good
conditions, and achieving these good conditions requires reaching certain
spiritual levels or stages. There is hence a deep connection between one's
inner states and their outward actions, in that the goodness of one's
actions is a direct result of the goodness of their internal conditions.

Each waystation represents a different stage of spiritual awareness and
purification, and each one determines the degree of the action and its
intrinsic value. The higher the station, the more profound the deeds.

(٤٧)

لَا تَتْرُكِ الذِّكْرَ لِعَدَمِ حُضُورِكَ مَعَ اللهِ فِيهِ،

لِأَنَّ غَفْلَتَكَ عَنْ وُجُودِ ذِكْرِهِ أَشَدُّ مِنْ غَفْلَتِكَ فِي وُجُودِ ذِكْرِهِ؛

فَعَسَى أَنْ يَرْفَعَكَ مِنْ ذِكْرٍ مَعَ وُجُودِ غَفْلَةٍ إِلَى ذِكْرٍ مَعَ وُجُودِ يَقَظَةٍ،

وَمِنْ ذِكْرٍ مَعَ وُجُودِ يَقَظَةٍ إِلَى ذِكْرٍ مَعَ وُجُودِ حُضُورٍ،

وَمِنْ ذِكْرٍ مَعَ وُجُودِ حُضُورٍ إِلَى ذِكْرٍ مَعَ وُجُودِ غَيْبَةٍ عَمَّا سِوَى الْمَذْكُورِ...

﴿ وَمَا ذَلِكَ عَلَى ٱللَّهِ بِعَزِيزٍ ﴾

Do not forsake remembrance on account of not realizing your presence with
Allāh in it. Because your heedlessness of His remembrance is more severe than
your heedlessness in remembrance.

As it may be that He raises you from remembrance with heedlessness to
remembrance with awareness, and from remembrance with awareness
to remembrance with presence, and from remembrance with presence to
remembrance with absence of all but the One Remembered.

"And not is that upon Allāh difficult..." [28]

Dhikr ذِكْر is not merely the sifting of beads and repetitive recitation
of the Divine Names. Rather it is the very remembrance of the Divine in
all forms, a remembrance that is sincere and devotional. One should not
give up the practice of remembering their Lord in every wakeful moment,
even if one feels that their heart is not fully present or attentive during
the act of remembrance. It is not for certain that every act of devotion
necessarily manifests into a spiritual experience. The act is your offering
to Him. Its spiritual experience is His to manifest for you. It is not your
acts He desires, but your sincerity and perseverance in them. Though
you may not experience the Divine Presence, it should not deter you
from persevering. Lack of a spiritual experience is worse than a lack of
devotion, as the true servant worships not for the experience of it, rather
for the sole purpose of pleasing his Lord.

The sincerity of your devotion may be the very thing that grants
you rise to a higher station, from simple devotion to awareness of Him,
and from awareness of Him to being present with Him, and from being
present with Him to being absent of all else but Him. Maintaining
the continuous effort in remembering your Lord, despite moments of
forgetfulness or inattentiveness, can, by His Will, gradually lead to a
deeper spiritual connection and awareness.

---

28   Sūrah Ibrāhīm 14:20

مِنْ عَلَامَاتِ مَوْتِ الْقَلْبِ...

عَدَمُ الْحُزْنِ عَلَى مَا فَاتَكَ مِنَ الْمُوَافَقَاتِ،

وَتَرْكُ النَّدَم عَلَى مَا فَعَلْتَهُ مِنَ الْمُخَالَفَاتِ

From among the signs of the death of the heart... is the absence of grief over what you have let expire from the acts of obedience, and the forsaking of regret over what you have done from the violations.

The concept of a 'living' or 'dead' heart, in spiritual terms, is denoted by its sensitivity or lack thereof. The heart is not sustained by food or drink. Its sustenance comes from its proximity to goodness and distance from evil. It softens and becomes more subtle and ethereal when in proximity to righteousness and piety. It hardens and becomes more rigid and opaque when distanced from goodness. Hence a heart that is not troubled by wrongdoing and equally not troubled by the absence of doing good, as a heart distanced from goodness and proximate to evil, is a heart either dead or dying.

A living heart is sensitive, responsive, and attuned to moral and spiritual dimensions. It is troubled and sorrowed by the missed opportunities for good deeds, and regretful of sinful actions. The sorrow keeps it aware of not wanting to miss more opportunities, and the regret keeps it conscious of its errors. Both of these keep it alive and agile from falling into a state of stagnation followed by its death. This sensitivity is a sign of spiritual vitality and a consciousness that is aware of its duties and the importance of moral integrity. A heart that is troubled by wrongdoing and equally troubled by the absence of doing good is a healthy and full of life.

Likewise, a spiritually dead heart is one that is indifferent to good undone, and is untroubled by past wrongdoings. This indifference is a grave spiritual ailment. The absence of sorrow for missed opportunities is a symptom for a lack of appreciation for virtuous actions and a disconnection from the moral compass that guides one towards goodness. The lack of regret for wrong actions is likewise a symptom of a hardened or desensitized state where the individual is no longer moved, through shame or guilt of the consequences of their actions, losing the motivation to repent or seek rectification.

This emphasizes the importance of keeping one's heart and conscience alive and responsive. It reflects a key aspect of spiritual practice, which is to remain vigilant and conscious of one's actions and their moral implications. It also embodies the concept of '*taqwa* تقوى' (God-consciousness), where the individual must always be mindful of their relationship with Allāh and their ethical responsibilities towards fulfilling His rights.

⟨٤٩⟩

لَا يَعْظُمُ الذَّنْبُ عِنْدَكَ عَظَمَةً تَصُدُّكَ عَنْ حُسْنِ الظَّنِّ بِاللَّهِ تَعَالَى ،

فَإِنَّ مَنْ عَرَفَ رَبَّهُ... اسْتَصْغَرَ فِي جَنْبِ كَرَمِهِ ذَنْبَهُ

Let not your sin reach such proportions that it deters your good opinion of Allāh, Exalted be He. For indeed one who knows his Lord... his sin is insignificant in Light of Allāh's Generosity.

⟨٥٠⟩

لَا صَغِيرَةً إِذَا قَابَلَكَ عَدْلُهُ ، وَلَا كَبِيرَةً إِذَا وَاجَهَكَ فَضْلُهُ

There is no sin too small when His Justice confronts you, and there is no sin too great when His Grace faces you.

Truly, he who knows himself, knows his Lord. And he who knows his Lord, knows his non-being to his Lord's Majestic Being. Hence, his sins, in light of Allāh's boundless mercy, benevolence, and generosity, are insignificant. For Him to erase those sins is not difficult. And for Him to forgive you is more preferable to Him than to punish you. His mercy far exceeds His wrath, and He would much rather do the former than the latter, if but you realize your error and seek His mercy.

The way to achieving that is to strive and ensure that your sins do not reach such great a proportion that you fall into despair and hopelessness. That you opine yourself as being beyond His forgiveness. Not only will you have undermined His Divinity, you will also have condemned yourself from returning to His presence.

⟨٥١⟩

لَا عَمَلَ أَرْجَى لِلْقُلُوبِ مِنْ عَمَلٍ يَغِيبُ عَنْكَ شُهُودُهُ وَيُحْتَقَرُ عِنْدَكَ وُجُودُهُ

No deed is more hopeful to the heart than the deed absent from you witnessing it and its presence being despised by you.

The incredible value of humble actions, done without seeking recognition or without being conscious of their significance. These hold special merit for the heart. They emphasize humility and sincerity, where the worth of an action is not in its external recognition but in the purity of its intention. Actions performed without a desire for praise or acknowledgment are more genuine and reflective of a sincere heart.

۵۲

إِنَّمَا أَوْرَدَ عَلَيْكَ الْوَارِدَ لِتَكُونَ بِهِ عَلَيْهِ وَارِدًا

Indeed, He only brought upon you the Inspiration that you may, by it, go to Him.

۵۳

أَوْرَدَ عَلَيْكَ الْوَارِدَ لِيَتَسَلَّمَكَ مِنْ يَدِ الْأَغْيَارِ ، وَلِيُحَرِّرَكَ مِنْ رِقِّ الآثَارِ

He brought upon you the Inspiration that you may be delivered from the grasp of otherness and that you may be freed from the bondage of created things.

۵٤

أَوْرَدَ عَلَيْكَ الْوَارِدَ لِيُخْرِجَكَ مِنْ سِجْنِ وُجُودِكَ إِلَى فَضَاءِ شُهُودِكَ

He brought upon you the Inspiration that you may exit from the prison of your existence to the vastness of your witnessing.

The inspiration[29] has been granted for three primary reasons.

Firstly, that by it, one can go to Him. It enables the individual to attain a profound recognition of the Divine, thus reminding them of their existential purpose and elucidating the means by which to fulfill that purpose. This awareness and clarity safeguards the individual from descending into despair and despondency. Consequently, their heart is enlivened, imbued with renewed lofty and praiseworthy aspirations, and settled in contentment.

Secondly, that one can be liberated by it from the bondage of worldly distraction. By illuminating the transient nature of temporal existence, it unveils an understanding of the Real and Absolute. Through this, the individual realizes the trivialities of the created world, thereby aligning their heart with the Creator.

And thirdly, that one may be emancipated from their greatest adversary; themselves. It frees them from the illusion of self-deification and cultivates a recognition of the Divine as the sole True God. That it inspires within the being a sense of selflessness and magnanimity, releasing them from the entanglements of the material realm and the deceptive whisperings of their own desires.

---

29 The word الوارد carries the meanings of *thinkable; conceivable; imaginable; possible; expected; foreseen; anticipated; arrival; coming; incoming; forthcoming,* among others. We have chosen to translate it in context as 'Inspiration,' being that which comes from the Divine. In this regard, the *wārid* وارد, as the *inspiration*, is that which results from the *wird* ورد, often translated as 'prayer.' We may say that if the purpose of the prayer is to beseech aid from the Almighty, the response comes in the form of an inspiration.

٥٥

الأَنْوَارُ مَطَايَا الْقُلُوبِ وَالأَسْرَارِ

Lights are the expedients (mediums) of the Hearts, and their innermost secrets.

٥٦

النُّورُ جُنْدُ الْقَلْبِ كَمَا أَنَّ الظُّلْمَةَ جُنْدُ النَّفْسِ،

فَإِذَا أَرَادَ اللهُ أَنْ يَنْصُرَ عَبْدَهُ... أَمَدَّهُ بِجُنُودِ الأَنْوَارِ وَقَطَعَ عَنْهُ مَدَدَ الظُّلَمِ وَالأَغْيَارِ

Light is the army of the heart, as darkness is the army of the self.
So when Allāh intends to aid His servant, He reinforces him with the Army of Lights, and severs from him the enforcements of darkness and otherness.

٥٧

النُّورُ لَهُ الْكَشْفُ، وَالْبَصِيرَةُ لَهَا الْحُكْمُ، وَالْقَلْبُ لَهُ الإِقْبَالُ وَالإِدْبَارُ

To light belongs the unveiling; to intelligence belongs the discernment; to the heart belongs the approach and the retreat.

Light serves as the medium upon which the heart قلب and its concealed dimensions traverse towards a profound comprehension of Divine Realities. It embodies divine knowledge, guidance, and spiritual illumination, facilitating the journey of the heart towards deeper understanding and the unveiling of its most profound mysteries. The innermost secrets, *asrār* أسرار, are the subtle and often hidden aspects of knowledge and absolute truths. These truths do not belong to the rational world. They are *supra-rational*, and cannot be apprehended through intellect and reason alone. Rather they are accessible through realization by the heart, and hence attained only from divine illumination.

Each level of ascendancy is accompanied by its corresponding degrees of lights and unveilings. The lights of each stage reveal their specific realities to the heart, and as it ascends through the veils, it draws ever nearer to the purest manifestation of Light, where it is confronted with *Light upon Light* نور على نور. To the heart, then, light is the army that combats the darkness of ignorance, guiding it from a state of dire need for illumination to a state of becoming a source of luminance.

Darkness is conversely the absence of light. It lacks substance, form, and inherent meaning, serving only to contrast and thus highlight the substance, form, and meaning of Light. Darkness is to the self نفس what light is to the heart. The realm of created things is darkness, devoid of intrinsic illumination, and the self, by its very nature, is allured by this realm. Thus darkness is its allied army.

When the Almighty intends to bestow goodness upon His servant, He draws them nearer to the light and distances them from darkness. He bestows upon them deep understanding and illumination, guiding them away from ignorance and towards spiritual enlightenment. This Divine intervention elevates the servant's spiritual state and transforms them into a source of light for others, reflecting the Divine Illumination they have received, as has been said by the Prophet ﷺ;

$$ * مَنْ يُرِدِ اللهُ بِهِ خَيْرًا يُفَقِّهْهُ فِي الدِّينِ * $$

For whomsoever Allāh intends goodness, He grants him a [deep] understanding of the Religion. [30]

The word دين is often translated as 'religion,' but it encompasses a far more profound meaning than this translation suggests. It signifies guidance for mankind, from the lowest of the low to the highest of the high, as a ladder that elevates one from the depths of their humanness, of darkness, to the angelic heights of light. *Dīn* includes the lights that unveil higher realities drawing the seeker closer to the Divine Presence.

Hence, to light belongs the attribute of unveiling, as it is, by its very nature, a revealer of that which is concealed in darkness, making known what is unknown. It is what the being experiences of perceiving divine realities beyond ordinary sensory experience.

Only when this light penetrates the heart and illuminates the lamp of intelligence can discernment truly take place. Intelligence itself does not unveil. It can only receive the unveiling and ratify its absolute veracity. This is the ability to distinguish and ratify ﴿ truth from falsehood, moral from immoral, virtue from vice. Following this illumination, the heart is endowed with the ability to choose... To approach إقبال the Divine, driven by love and longing, and retreat إدبار from the distractions and temptations of the worldly life. The heart itself does not unveil nor illuminate nor discern the illumination. It can only receive the unveiling and its discernment. By this, it may enter the light, and be safeguarded by its illumination.

This dual movement, towards the Divine and away from the worldly, reflects the dynamic nature of the being's spiritual progress. The seeker is continually navigating between the Divine Presence and the mundane world, striving to remain anchored in the light while engaging with the challenges and responsibilities of earthly existence.

In this ceaseless journey, this interplay between light and darkness, between the heart and self, the ultimate aim is not merely the accumulation of knowledge or adherence to ritual but the attainment of a direct and intimate experience of the Divine, without which all pursuits are hollow and lifeless. The being's very existence is impossible without the Divine, and is likewise meaningless without Him, as He alone is the source of all Light and illumination.

---

30 متفق عليه

This true illumination, when it penetrates the heart, transforms the individual's entire being, aligning their actions, thoughts, and desires with the transcendent reality of Divine Will. This alignment leads to a state of spiritual maturity, where the servant becomes not only a vessel of Divine Knowledge but also a radiant exemplar of Divine Love and Mercy. In this state, the servant's existence itself becomes a testament to the Divine Light, guiding others towards the path of enlightenment and serving as a living witness to the boundless grace and wisdom of the Creator. The journey from darkness to light is not a physical motion through space and matter, but a spiritual elevation of the soul through time, to its highest potential in every facet of its life.

٥٨

لَا تُفْرِحْكَ الطَّاعَةُ؛ لِأَنَّهَا بَرَزَتْ مِنْكَ، وَافْرَحْ بِهَا لِأَنَّهَا بَرَزَتْ مِنَ اللهِ إِلَيْكَ

﴿ قُلْ بِفَضْلِ اللَّهِ وَبِرَحْمَتِهِ فَبِذَٰلِكَ فَلْيَفْرَحُوا هُوَ خَيْرٌ مِّمَّا يَجْمَعُونَ ﴾

Let not obedience make you feel good about yourself on the merit that it came from you. But be joyous by it because it came from Allāh to you.
"Say, 'By the bounty of Allāh, and by His mercy.' And by that let them rejoice. It is better than what they accumulate." [31]

Those who rejoice in their goodly actions are of three kinds; [32]

The first are those who hope that their actions will bring them the bliss of paradise and avert from them the punishment of the abyss. These see the origin (of the deed) as being from themselves and to themselves, and they do not renounce their own power and strength in it. They are those who represent the words of Allāh, إِيَّاكَ نَعْبُد *'You alone do we serve.'*

They attribute their actions and achievements solely to their own efforts, without recognizing any divine assistance or influence. They believe these actions and their outcomes originate entirely from within themselves and are for their own benefit. They do not disavow or distance themselves from reliance on their own power and strength. Albeit performing good deeds, this manifests a lack of humility and acknowledgment of a higher power's role in their successes.

Their association with the people of إِيَّاكَ نَعْبُد expresses a complete and exclusive devotion to God, acknowledging that worship and servitude are directed solely towards Him. The contrast here highlights a paradox; these individuals claim to be among those who worship God alone, yet they fail to fully internalize the essence of this worship by not relinquishing their attachment to their own perceived agency, autonomy, and strength.

---

31 Sūrah Yūnus 10:58

32 From Ibn ʿAjībah's commentary, *Īyqādh al-Himam fī Sharh al-Hikam*

The second are those who rejoice as the deeds are intrinsically signs of pleasure and acceptance, and a reason for nearness and arrival to the Divine Presence. They are gifts from the Divine, and vessels that carry them to the bliss of paradise. These individuals do not assume to possess action or inaction, nor power nor strength as being from themselves, rather they believe it all to be conveyed by the Higher Power and turned by primal will. They are those who represent the words of Allāh, إِيَّاكَ نَسْتَعِين 'You alone do we beseech for aid.'

In contrast to the first group, whose worship is for Allāh, the worship of the second group is both for Allāh and by the power of Allāh, and with that subtle addition lies this incredible distinction between them.

The third are those who rejoice not in their deeds nor their outcomes, but rejoice only in Allāh and nothing else, and are annihilated to themselves. Should they manifest obedience, they perceive it as a debt owed to Allāh, and if they manifest disobedience, they turn to Him with humility, beseeching forgiveness. Disobedience does not diminish their joy, nor does obedience increase it, as they are by Allāh and for Allāh. They are among those who represent the words of Allāh, لَا حَوْلَ وَلَا قُوَّةَ إِلَّا بِاللهِ 'There is no strength nor power save by Allāh.'

۵۹

قَطَعَ السَّائِرِينَ لَهُ وَالْوَاصِلِينَ إِلَيْهِ عَنْ رُؤْيَةِ أَعْمَالِهِمْ وَشُهُودِ أَحْوَالِهِمْ،

أَمَّا السَّائِرُونَ فَلِأَنَّهُمْ لَمْ يَتَحَقَّقُوا الصِّدْقَ مَعَ اللهِ فِيهَا،

وَأَمَّا الْوَاصِلُونَ فَلِأَنَّهُ غَيَّبَهُمْ بِشُهُودِهِ عَنْهَا

He severs, those who are journeying to Him and those who have arrived, from visualizing their deeds and witnessing their states.
As for those who are journeying, it is because they have not yet realized their sincerity with Allāh, Exalted be He, in their deeds.
And as for those who have arrived, it is because He has concealed them from witnessing their states by witnessing only Him.

Should obedience and goodness manifest from you, do not rejoice it as your achievement, for in truth, it did not issue from you. If you do so, you will bear the guilt of *shirk* شِرْك when you praise yourself rather than He who enabled you to manifest goodness. Rather, proclaim it all to be from the bounty of your Lord, and rejoice instead in that. Know that humility rests at the bottom step, while pride awaits at the topmost. The higher one ascends, the more trying the effort to maintain humility and sincerity, and even the slightest hint of pride may result in downfall.

For this reason, He, Almighty, prevents His sincere servants, both those who are journeying to Him and those who have arrived, from witnessing their deeds and the manifestations of their states.

As those who are journeying, they have not fully realized their sincerity, as they are still in the process of spiritual striving, *sulūk* سلوك. Part of them seeks to attribute their being to Allāh, while a part of them yet clings to self-praise. They are hence veiled from perceiving their own actions and spiritual states. This veiling is a form of mercy, preventing them from falling into self-admiration or complacency, which can arise from recognizing one's own spiritual achievements. The absence of true sincerity, where actions are performed solely for the sake of Allāh without any self-interest, necessitates this veiling, as they have not fully aligned their intentions and actions with Divine Will.

As for those who have arrived and are in proximity to the Divine, His presence becomes so overwhelming and consuming that they become absorbed in it. Their focus and consciousness are entirely directed towards Allāh, leaving no room for self-awareness or contemplation of their spiritual progress. However, though their sincerity may be fully realized, their humanness is still a part of them. Hence, they are veiled from realizing that state as there exists the possibility of faltering due to self-praise of having arrived.

---

(٦٠)

مَا بَسَقَتْ أَغْصَانُ ذُلٍّ إِلَّا عَلَى بَذْرِ طَمَعٍ

Not do the branches of dishonour extend save by the sowing of seeds of greed.

(٦١)

مَا قَادَكَ شَيْءٌ مِثْلُ الْوَهْمِ

Nothing leads you on like whims and speculations.

(٦٢)

أَنْتَ حُرٌّ مِمَّا أَنْتَ عَنْهُ آيِسٌ، وَعَبْدٌ لِمَا أَنْتَ لَهُ طَامِعٌ

You are free in what you despair (your state of hopelessness), and a slave in that which you are covetous.

From the seeds of greed sprout the branches of dishonour and humiliation. Greed itself becomes the root of abasement, as he who is greedy parts himself from the Mighty to attach himself to the lowly, like vines of a weed that cling to bare rock for its survival, and unlike the sturdy oak that reaches for the sky, breathing the clean air.

True freedom is when the individual is a slave only to Allāh, in that he becomes freed from all else, and true imprisonment is when the individual frees himself from Allāh to become enslaved by his greed and desires. This is cultured by love, for he who loves a thing becomes its slave.

66

If greed was asked, 'Who is your father?' it would reply, 'Doubt in the Decree.' And if it was asked, 'What is your craft?' it would reply, 'the earning of humiliation.' And if it was asked, 'What is your objective?' it would reply, 'Deprivation.'[33]

One who feels in himself love for the world has destroyed himself with the sword of greed, and whoever has greed of a thing becomes humiliated, and through his humiliation, he perishes![34]

This greed is fed by naught else but one's whims and speculations. As it is spawned from doubt in the Divine Decree, that urges one to seek and pursue that which they covet to be in their possession. The whim is the first pull, and it is weaker than doubt. It pulls the self toward greed for what is in the possession of others, yet uncertain if it ever will be in the possession of the self, and hence becomes illusory. It is the illusion that what others possesses, that the self is covetous of, has benefit or harm, is giving or withholding, and the self becomes desirous of it, becomes humble towards it, relies on it, and equally fears it. Ultimately, it becomes subservient both to what it desires and to desire itself.

And thus, one is free in what they despair of the worldly, their state of hopelessness in not achieving what they desire, for this despair keeps them distanced and detached from that which seeks to enslave them.

———————

(٦٣)

مَنْ لَمْ يُقْبِلْ عَلَى اللهِ بِمُلَاطَفَاتِ الإِحْسَانِ قِيدَ إِلَيْهِ بِسَلَاسِلِ الامْتِحَانِ

He who does not draw closer to Allāh by the gentleness of Iḥsān, is chained to Him by the shackles of trials

'Iḥsān' is goodness and righteousness. It is gentleness and kindness in servitude to the Almighty, as iterated by the Prophet ﷺ;

* أَنْ تَعْبُدَ اللهَ كَأَنَّكَ تَرَاهُ، فَإِنْ لَمْ تَكُنْ تَرَاهُ فَإِنَّهُ يَرَاكَ *

'It is to serve Allāh as though you see Him, and if you cannot see Him, then [know that] indeed He sees you.'[35]

He ﷺ further said;

* مِنْ حُسْنِ إِسْلَامِ الْمَرْءِ تَرْكُهُ مَا لَا يَعْنِيهِ *

'From the goodness (beauty) of one's submission, is to leave that which does not concern him.'[36]

———————

33 From AbūBakr al-Warrāq, cited in Ibn 'Ajībah's commentary.

34 From AbulHassan al-Nīsabūrī, also cited in Ibn 'Ajībah's commentary.

35 متفق عليه

36 متفق عليه

Mankind is ever in a state of servitude. Whether willingly or unwillingly, we are all slaves of Allāh, and He has divided His slaves into three kinds;[37]

The first are those on the left, أصحاب المشئمة. These are a people who do not turn to Allāh, even by a measure. Their servitude is utterly unwilling and imperceptible to them. And when they have served their time in this world, with nothing to present of goodness in the Hereafter, their destination lies in the abysmal flame. Theirs is the path of condemnation. So long as they are alive, however, the doors to redemption lay open for them, should they choose to walk through. At this stage they are in utter heedlessness أولئك هم الغافلون,[38] and as a result commit حنث and كفر.

If and when they rise, they join the ones on the right, أصحاب الميمنة, who turn to Allāh by small measures, but have no elite status with Him, as they are content with the outward of His Decree and do not seek the pathways of inner reality. They abide by the letter of the law and perform the bare minimum, but scarcely grasp the spirit of the law. They halt at the limits of empirical proof and evidence, but do not rise to the stations of Divine Witnessing. Theirs is the path of salvation, and they are the people of إياك نعبد 'You alone do we serve.' Their transition from condemnation to salvation places them in a state of ظالم لنفسه, 'unjust to themselves.'

Then come the forerunners, السابقون. These seek out the paths of inner reality and turn to Allāh always and in all things, ever longing to bask in His presence. They rise through two degrees:

They first emerge from the people of the right as they strive to be among the forerunners. As they rise, they turn to Allāh through the bonds of trials and afflictions. These are the people of steadfastness. Through constant strife, they are reminded of the Divine, and turn to Him for aid. They are now the people of إياك نستعين 'You alone do we beseech for aid.' Their transition from salvation to sanctification elevates them to a state of مقتصد, 'the moderate.'

They then turn to Allāh through the tenderness and gentleness of His goodness, ever in gratitude for His blessing and grace. They become the people of gratitude, the people of لا حول ولا قوة إلا بالله 'There is no strength nor power save by Allāh.' They become ranked among the sanctified as those of سابق بالخيرات, 'forerunners with goodness.'

All three are mention in the āyah:

$$\text{﴿ ... فَمِنْهُمْ ظَالِمٌ لِّنَفْسِهِ وَمِنْهُم مُّقْتَصِدٌ وَمِنْهُمْ سَابِقٌ بِالْخَيْرَاتِ ... ﴾}$$

... and among them is the one unjust to himself, and among them is the one moderate (on the middle path), and among them is the forerunner with goodness... [39]

---

37 Sūrah al-Wāqi'ah 56:7-56

38 Sūrah an-Nahl 16:108 and Sūrah al-A'rāf 7:179

39 Sūrah Fātir 35:32

٦٤

مَنْ لَمْ يَشْكُرِ النِّعَمِ فَقَدْ تَعَرَّضَ لِزَوَالِهَا، وَمَنْ شَكَرَهَا فَقَدْ قَيَّدَهَا بِعِقَالِهَا

Whoever is not grateful for their blessings indeed risks their cessation, and whoever is grateful of them, tethers them with their chords.

Gratitude obligates the blessing to be tethered and rooted, which grants it growth and increase, as He Almighty has said;

﴿...لَئِن شَكَرْتُمْ لَأَزِيدَنَّكُمْ وَلَئِن كَفَرْتُمْ إِنَّ عَذَابِى لَشَدِيدٌ﴾

...If you are grateful, I will increase you, but if you are ungrateful, indeed My punishment is severe![39]

Gratitude nourishes the seeds of felicity, and distinguishes the forerunners السابقون, from the moderate مقتصد, and the unjust ظالم لنفسه. Repentance distinguishes the latter two from each other, while ingratitude distinguishes the unjust from the former two. There is no state of indifference. Being both grateful and ungrateful, or neither, is an impossibility, as Allāh says;

﴿إِنَّا هَدَيْنَهُ السَّبِيلَ إِمَّا شَاكِرًا وَإِمَّا كَفُورًا﴾

Indeed We have guided Him to the path. He is either grateful or ungrateful.[40]

One cannot be both, as they contradict each other. One can also not be either, as lack of gratitude breeds ingratitude, while lack of ingratitude, without gratitude to replace it, results in lifelessness. Gratitude itself serves as the root for sincerity and love in one's actions. Hence one can either be grateful or ungrateful, and failure to show gratitude necessarily makes one an ingrate, even if their actions are righteous or sinless.

As for the unjust, their deeds counterbalance their sins, and their compensation for good is upon the remaining aggregate of the two. They have no sense of measure of either, and are often heedless of their state. As for the moderate, their deeds are compensated to their measure, while their sins are forgiven by their beseeching and repentance. The repentance is what distinguishes them from the unjust, as they are not heedless of their actions. As for the forerunners, their deeds outlast their sins on two accounts. They are ever in a state of repentance for their sins and ever in a state of gratitude for their deeds, and are never heedless of either. Repentance cleanses them of their sins, so that their deeds are not wasted in counterbalancing the sins, and gratitude increases the quality of their deeds, so that they are not measured only by their quantity.

---

39 Sūrah Ibrāhīm 14:7

40 Sūrah al-Insān 76:3

۶۵

خَفْ مِنْ وُجُودِ إِحْسَانِهِ إِلَيْكَ وَدَوَامِ إِسَاءَتِكَ مَعَهُ... أَنْ يَكُونَ ذَلِكَ اسْتِدْرَاجًا لَكَ

﴿... سَنَسْتَدْرِجُهُم مِّنْ حَيْثُ لَا يَعْلَمُونَ ﴾

Fear! From the presence of His goodness to you, and your continued wrongdoing with Him… that it may become a lure to ruin.

…'We shall lure them gradually from whence they know not (in ways they cannot comprehend)' [41]

۶۶

مِنْ جَهْلِ الْمُرِيدِ أَنْ يُسِيءَ الْأَدَبَ فَتُؤَخَّرُ الْعُقُوبَةُ عَنْهُ، فَيَقُولُ: لَوْ كَانَ هَذَا سُوءَ أَدَبٍ لَقَطَعَ الْإِمْدَادَ، وَأَوْجَبَ الْبِعَادَ؛ فَقَدْ يُقْطَعُ الْمَدَدُ عَنْهُ مِنْ حَيْثُ لَا يَشْعُرُ، وَلَوْ لَمْ يَكُنْ إِلَّا مَنْعُ الْمَزِيدِ، وَقَدْ يَقُومُ مَقَامَ الْبُعْدِ مِنْ حَيْثُ لَا يَدْرِي، وَلَوْ لَمْ يَكُنْ إِلَّا أَنْ يُخَلِّيَكَ وَمَا تُرِيدُ

From the ignorance of the disciple is that he behaves poorly, and as the consequences are delayed, he says, "if this was bad behavior, Allāh would have severed His aid (provision) and necessitated banishment (from His presence)." It may be that He severs aid from him and he (the disciple) is not even aware, even if it is only by preventing its increment. And He (Allāh) places (you, the disciple) in a station of distance without him knowing, even if it is by Him (Allāh) leaving you to do what you want.

Fear is a psychological motivator. It keeps the being within certain boundaries that safeguard it from harm. Such harm includes the consequences of transgressing those boundaries. There also exists the interim region between safe sanctuary and transgression, and herein lay the subtle dangers of experiencing continuous kindness from Allāh while persisting in wrongdoing. It is to mistaken the assumed absence of immediate retribution for one's misdeeds by the veil of Allāh's favour, and to take for granted that favour, such that it becomes not a sign of divine mercy, but rather a form of *istidrāj* استدراج, a gradual lure and entrapment, where one is slowly led to their downfall without them realizing it.

This happens when one's righteous actions bear swift recompense and reward, while one's wrongdoing appears inconsequential. Through the first, they assume themselves on the right path and think themselves among the pious, bolstered by the withholding of punishment for their misdeeds. They move gradually from a state of clarity into a state of delusion. When in this state, they are unable to realize that the rewards for their deeds hardly accumulate or increase, and the guidance so direly needed to save one from their misdeeds has been withdrawn.

41 Sūrah al-A'rāf 7:182

It is not without forewarning, in that they are constantly reminded, but when they continuously sin and are met with blessings instead of punishment, it may be a sign that they are being ensnared by their own actions, with consequences looming unbeknownst to them.

Thus does He, Almighty, say;

$$ \text{﴿ فَلَمَّا نَسُوا مَا ذُكِّرُوا بِهِ فَتَحْنَا عَلَيْهِمْ أَبْوَابَ كُلِّ شَيْءٍ حَتَّىٰ إِذَا فَرِحُوا بِمَا أُوتُوا أَخَذْنَاهُم بَغْتَةً فَإِذَا هُم مُّبْلِسُونَ ﴾} $$

So when they forgot of what We reminded them, We opened for them the doors to everything, until when they rejoiced with what they were given, We seized them suddenly and they fell to despair [42]

The sophisticated essence of this teaching lies, strangely so, in its paradoxical nature, as what one assumes to be divine benevolence upon them might actually be a test or a prelude to divine justice. One must consciously and mindfully reflect on their actions, to be vigilant of their wrongdoing, and not be lulled into complacency by the absence of immediate retribution. It is hence a critical fault in one's inner discipline that he remains oblivious to his wrongdoing or undermines it altogether, ignorant that the lack of consequences is in reality a concealed opportunity to seek forgiveness which in turn is a greater progression towards intimacy with his Lord than his righteous actions. Divine favour rests more profoundly in the admission of fault and wrong, and the plea for guidance. The disciple must not forget that it was not the victim's innocence that granted Ādam and Ḥawā their Lord's favour. It was their sincere admission of ربنا ظلمنا أنفسنا, *'Our Lord, we wronged ourselves,'* and their realization that وإن لم تغفر لنا وترحمنا لنكونن من الخاسرين, *'if You do not forgive us and have mercy on us, we shall surely be among the greatest losers.'*

The greatest 'aid' from Allāh, Exalted be He, is guidance, and so it is also, in its withholding from you, the greatest deprivation. If you should be one to estimate your worth with Him, look to the abundance of guidance or the lack thereof. Its abundance far supersedes any material reward, for it is the vehicle to the greatest of all reward, the everlasting abode of the Hereafter. Its withdrawal far outlasts any physical retribution or punishment, for it is the void of condemnation that chains one to the abyssal pit. Thus does He Almighty say;

$$ \text{﴿ ... لَئِن شَكَرْتُمْ لَأَزِيدَنَّكُمْ وَلَئِن كَفَرْتُمْ إِنَّ عَذَابِي لَشَدِيدٌ ﴾} $$

...If you are grateful, I will increase you, but if you are ungrateful, indeed My punishment is severe! [43]

---

42 Sūrah al-Anʿām 6:44

43 Sūrah Ibrāhīm 14:7

(٦٧)

إِذَا رَأَيْتَ عَبْدًا أَقَامَهُ اللهُ تَعَالَى بِوُجُودِ الأَوْرَادِ، وَأَدَامَهُ عَلَيْهَا مَعَ طُولِ الإِمْدَادِ...

فَلَا تَسْتَحْقِرَنَّ مَا مَنَحَهُ مَوْلَاهُ، لِأَنَّكَ لَمْ تَرَ عَلَيْهِ سِيمَا الْعَارِفِينَ، وَلَا بَهْجَةَ الْمُحِبِّينَ؛

فَلَوْلَا وَارِدٌ... مَا كَانَ وِرْدٌ

When you see a servant whom Allāh, Exalted be He, has established in the invocation of Awrād, and has preserved him upon them with longevity in His assistance, do not despise what his Lord has bestowed upon him, on the premise that you do not see upon him the mark of those who know or the splendour of those who love Him.
If there was no Wārid, there would be no Wird.[44]

Seeing a believer engaged in prayer, fasting, continual recitation and invocation, and yet unqualified among scholars or saints should not be the premise of judgment upon them. For such is a servant whom Allāh Himself has established in those apparent acts and continuous verbal remembrances, and has further fortified him in that capacity. So do not find insignificant his state because you do not see upon him the mark of the gnostics nor the splendor of the spiritual. Were it not for Allāh's guidance upon them, they would not be able to continue to worship Him in their capacity. They are, like yourself, like the saints and the learned, also included within Allāh's special concern and protection. It is not upon you to judge and find small what He has given them nor the rewards they would gain from such. Passing judgment is from your own ignorance and deficiency in spiritual intelligence, and none looks down upon worship, however small, save those who are ignorant.

---

44 *Awrād* أوراد being the plural of *wird* ورد, and *wārid* وارد being the one engaged in *wird* (see footnote 25). Sūfi orders generically define 'wird' as a form of 'spiritual medication' prescribed by the disciple's 'Shaykh' or 'Sūfi Master' to be performed at specific times and often under the supervision of the Shaykh. These maybe collections of special invocations, Āyāt from the Qur'ān, and voluntary prayers. It is important to note that while they serve certain spiritual benefits, they are not a core constitution of the religion and cannot be imposed by law. Rather, they are, fundamentally, innovations (albeit from within the religion and not necessarily extraneous) whose ritualistic practices are often debated for validity in religion.
However, in context of the Hikam, the *wird* can be performed by any devout Muslim, Sūfi or otherwise, and is not restricted to any order or sect. It simply is, an invocation, a supplication, and an intimate calling upon the One Almighty. It is performed with utter sincerity and from deep within the heart far detached from worldly affairs and influences. The *wird* and its performing can have certain powerful effects on one's spiritual states, and is recommended that one only perform those *Awrād* that are outlined by scholars and spiritual masters, and only within the measures prescribed, as *Awrād*, when overdone, can possibly lead to delusion, confusion, and psychological disorder.

٦٨

قَوْمٌ أَقَامَهُمُ الْحَقُّ لِخِدْمَتِهِ، وَقَوْمٌ اخْتَصَّهُمْ بِمَحَبَّتِهِ وَمَعْرِفَتِهِ،

﴿ كُلًّا نُمِدُّ هَٰؤُلَاءِ وَهَٰؤُلَاءِ مِنْ عَطَاءِ رَبِّكَ وَمَا كَانَ عَطَاءُ رَبِّكَ مَحْظُورًا ﴾

Some people, He establishes them rightly to serve Him, and some people He
distinguishes them to love Him and realize Him.
'To each We extend, to these and these, from the gift of your Lord. And not is
the gift of your Lord restricted.'[45]

Some He has established in servitude until they are, through their
servitude, readied for paradise. These are of apparent abstinence and
worship. They are ever engaged in worshipful acts demanded of physical
strife and are among those learned in the letter of His law.

Others He has established on the path of spiritual seeking for His love
until they are, through their love for Him and His love for them, fit to
enter into His presence. They are the knowers of Allāh and those learned
in the spirit of His law.

To each of these He extends His gifts, in various forms, in the ability to
worship Him, the capacity to fulfill His given rights, and the opportunities
to serve Him. He gifts them with guidance, with understanding, with
enlightenment. And to neither of these, so long as they maintain their
honesty, humility, and sincerity, are His gifts ever restricted.

٦٩

قَلَّمَا تَكُونُ الْوَارِدَاتُ الْإِلَهِيَّةُ إِلَّا بَغْتَةً، صِيَانَةً لَهَا أَنْ يَدَّعِيَهَا الْعِبَادُ بِوُجُودِ الِاسْتِعْدَادِ

Rarely do Divine Inspirations come, but suddenly, in order to preserve them
from the claims of the servant's readiness to receive.

A *Wārid* realizes praiseworthy thoughts which come to his heart
upon which he has no bearing. The *Wāridāt* can be of joy or sorrow,
contraction or expansion. These Divine Inspirations do not come upon
demand or claim, and are not affected by any cause. They do not come
in any natural form nor at an expected time. This is the protection upon
them that they differ from the demonic whisperings or the suppositions
of the self. They are like ethereal breezes that blow upon the hearts and
spirits, that makes them withdraw into the Divine Presence. They come
in sudden flashes because they are not sought nor earned. Rather, they
are openings granted by the Generous Giver, and if they had been earned
through effort and strife, the recipients would lay claim upon them by the
obligation of predisposition and preparation.

45 Sūrah al-Isrā 17:20

They would then become mere acquisitions, and would lose all spiritual value, and hence there are three aspects behind the wisdom of their unanticipated and unexpected arrival.

First is that they bear the mark of being gifted exclusively from Allāh. They are of His choosing and His mercy, by His saying;

$$ \text{﴿ ... وَٱللَّهُ يَخْتَصُّ بِرَحْمَتِهِ مَن يَشَآءُ وَٱللَّهُ ذُو ٱلْفَضْلِ ٱلْعَظِيمِ ﴾} $$

...and Allāh selects for His Mercy whomsoever He wills, and Allāh is the possessor of great bounty [46]

$$ \text{﴿ ... يَهْدِى ٱللَّهُ لِنُورِهِ مَن يَشَآءُ ... ﴾} $$

...Allāh guides His Light unto whomever He wills...[47]

Second is that they are given their due right and their due value, so that from them result incredible joy unmeasured by any physical attribute. And third is that from them come great passion and zeal and esteem for them as they are from the Most Noble, and anything from the Most Noble is precious.[48]

This makes them precious gifts and divine secrets from the Most Generous, Most Benevolent, All-Forgiving, granted only upon the people of trust and protection, not to those of treachery and betrayal.

٧٠

$$ \text{... مَنْ رَأَيْتَهُ مُجِيبًا عَنْ كُلِّ مَا يُسْأَلُ، وَمُعَبِّرًا عَنْ كُلِّ مَا شَهِدَ، وَذَاكِرًا كُلَّ مَا عَلِمَ} $$

$$ \text{فَٱسْتَدِلَّ بِذَلِكَ عَلَى وُجُودِ جَهْلِهِ} $$

Whoever you see has answers to everything he is asked, and expresses all what he witnesses, and mentions all what he learns... conclude by that the presence of ignorance.

This requires little explanation. He who responds to every question, often without a moment of thought or even hesitation, who declares openly all that comes to him, in knowledge and experience, who presents himself thus as he who knows everything about everything...

Such an individual is far removed from knowledge and understanding. This person demonstrates all the signs of ignorance, and we live in an age of prevalent ignorance, overwhelmingly ruled by the ignorant.

It is as the Arabs say, كل من هب ودب يتكلم , *'Every creeping and crawling thing wants to speak!'*

---

46   Sūrah al-Baqarah 2:105

47   Sūrah an-Nūr 24:35

48   Ahmad Zarrūq, in the commentary of Ibn 'Ajībah

(٧١)

إِنَّمَا جَعَلَ الدَّارَ الآخِرَةَ مَحَلًّا لِجَزَاءِ عِبَادِهِ الْمُؤْمِنِينَ؛ لِأَنَّ هَذِهِ الدَّارَ لَا تَسَعُ مَا يُرِيدُ أَنْ يُعْطِيَهُمْ،

وَلِأَنَّهُ أَجَلَّ أَقْدَارَهُمْ عَنْ أَنْ يُجَازِيَهُمْ فِي دَارٍ لَا بَقَاءَ لَهَا

Indeed, He has only placed the Realm of the HereAfter as a place of rewarding
His believing servants. Because this worldly realm cannot encompass what
He wants to give them, and because He deems their worth too high to reward
them in a world that has not permanence in it.

The reward of this realm, from the human perspective, is vast and abundant. It has an outward beauty that appeals to the human eye, and an arbitrary value that allures the soul.[49] It is, however, a quantifiable shell. Each material thing has a unit of measure that in itself is material and measured by another thing, and when seen with a holistic lens, all things balance themselves. Nothing truly supersedes another in extrinsic value, and all things present themselves as non-permanent entities, perishable within their designated terms of existence.

How then can this abode be used to reward those efforts that are themselves not measurable extrinsically? When much of this abode is also given to those who themselves do not, deliberately so, serve the Giver? If the contents of this realm, in varied quantity and length of existence, are granted to all, believer and disbeliever, should not the worthy one be granted more, or perhaps, other than this — something that does not bear the same measure?

If the wealth of this world, finite and temporal, satisfies the disbeliever despite his disbelief, then the natural reward for the believer must be infinite and eternal. Because the worth of the believer over the disbeliever is far greater to be given that which is limited and perishing. Because the believer, in his servitude to the Giver, sacrifices the worldly for the Giver's pleasure. His reward is therefore the otherworldly, the HereAfter, infinite and eternal.

Thus does the Prophet ﷺ say;

* قَالَ اللهُ أَعْدَدْتُ لِعِبَادِيَ الصَّالِحِينَ مَا لَا عَيْنٌ رَأَتْ، وَلَا أُذُنٌ سَمِعَتْ،

وَلَا خَطَرَ عَلَى قَلْبِ بَشَرٍ *

Allāh has said, "I have prepared for My righteous servants what no eye has
seen, and no ear has heard, and no heart can conceive."[50]

---

49 See Hikam 85

50 Sahīh al-Bukhārī 7498

(٧٢)

مَنْ وَجَدَ ثَمْرَةَ عَمَلِهِ عَاجِلًا ... فَهُوَ دَلِيلٌ عَلَى وُجُودِ الْقَبُولِ آجِلًا

*Whoever finds the fruits of his deed coming sooner [in this domain], then that
is proof of their acceptance being deferred [to the HereAfter].*

No good deed exists but with hardship with which one must endure
patiently. Whoever perseveres through its difficulty will ultimately find
ease. This brings with an arduous strife against the self, against one's
appetites and desires. Then bearing the distress of detaching from the
material world, which, with hope, leads to eternal delights and pleasures,
and such are the true fruits of one's deeds. They manifest in the bliss
of obedience, the sweetness of intimate communion, the heart's affinity
for vigilance, the soul's ecstasy in direct witnessing, and the secret joy in
direct speech with the Divine. As He Almighty affirms;

﴿ ... قَدْ عَلِمَ كُلُّ أُنَاسٍ مَّشْرَبَهُمْ ... ﴾

...Verily, every group of people knew their drink... [51]

Meaning, each soul has its rightful share of this spiritual fruit. The
evidence for its manifestation is found in the vitality that arises from
within, the pleasure derived from it, the persistence in performing those
deeds, and the increasing Divine Support it attracts. This is among the
signs that guidance has descended into the heart, by His declaration;

﴿ وَيَزِيدُ اللّٰهُ الَّذِينَ اهْتَدَوْا هُدًى وَالْبَاقِيَاتُ الصَّالِحَاتُ خَيْرٌ عِندَ رَبِّكَ ثَوَابًا وَخَيْرٌ مَّرَدًّا ﴾

*He increases those who are guided with more guidance, and the enduring
righteous deeds are better with your Lord for reward and better for recourse* [52]

And as the poet so eloquently expressed:

وإذا حلّت الهداية قلبا ... نشطت للعبادة الأعضام

'When guidance settles in a heart ... the limbs become engaged in worship.' [53]

When we witness someone's actions flourishing and their spiritual
state rising, we take by it that they have tasted the fruit of their deeds, an
auspicious sign that their efforts have been accepted. We experience the
soul's estrangement from worldly distractions and from the company of
other people, longing instead for intimacy with the Sovereign Truth. We
find the soul's contentment with Allāh's knowledge, sufficiency in His
presence, and independence from all else.

51 Sūrah al-Baqarah 2:60

52 Sūrah Maryam 19:76

53 Al-Būsayrī from his 'Hamziyya'

There manifests a life of ease, words of power, and the dispelling of sorrow by joy in Divine favour.[54] A life of ease is contentment, and its pleasure is through submission. Words of power are those that manifest in this divine stewardship. And the dispelling of sorrow is experienced by the sweetness of sincere action.

Yet one must be vigilant, for there is a hidden danger in becoming attached to the sweetness of obedience itself. This attachment is a subtle poison. Just as we distinguish between actions accepted and rejected, we must also distinguish between the beloved servant and the one turned away. Likewise, when one's actions diminish or their states decline, we fear the rejection of their deeds.

---

(٧٣)

إِذَا أَرَدْتَ أَنْ تَعْرِفَ قَدْرَكَ عِنْدَهُ... فَانْظُرْ فِي مَاذَا يُقِيمُكَ

If you want to discern your worth with Him... look to what He has established you in.

There exist, fundamentally, two kinds of people. The wretched and the righteous. The first kind are ever in despair, drenched in criticism, objection, and grievance. When given, they are boastful and arrogant. When deprived, they bewail and deplore. The second kind are ever in gratitude, regardless of the state they find themselves in. When given, they are humble and charitable. When deprived, they are patient and faithful.

Either group finds themselves precisely where Allāh has placed them, and to each is a test of faith. When those of the first realize this and express gratitude rather than despair, they rise to be among the righteous. And when those of the second express grievance rather than contentment, they fall to be among the wretched.

To both of these groups, it is not their external environs, the materiality of their reality, nor abundance or scarcity that determines their rank with Allāh. Rather, it is the states of their hearts and innermost, regardless of their external states. If one desires to know what worth they hold before Him Almighty, they must look to the states of their hearts and what worth their hearts hold for Him.

He has Himself declared, أنا عند ظن عبدي بي *'I am what My servant thinks of me.'*[55] If you hold Him in high regard, He will hold you in High regard. If you think nothing of Him, He will think nothing of you. This is fair and just. After all, how can you expect *Him*, Most High, to make *you* a priority, when in your life He is just an option?

---

54 Aḥmad Zarrūq, in the commentary of Ibn ʿAjībah

55 Ḥadīth al-Qudsī; متفق عليه

(٧٤)

مَتَى رَزَقَكَ الطَّاعَةَ وَالْغِنَى بِهِ عَنْهَا، فَاعْلَمْ أَنَّهُ قَدْ أَسْبَغَ عَلَيْكَ نِعَمَهُ ظَاهِرًا وبَاطِنًا

When He bestows upon you obedience and abundance of it, then know that indeed He has liberally imparted upon you His blessings manifest and intrinsic.

(٧٥)

خَيْرُ مَا تَطْلُبُهُ مِنْهُ مَا هُوَ طَالِبُهُ مِنْكَ

The best of what you seek from Him, is what He seeks from you.

(٧٦)

الْحُزْنُ عَلَى فُقْدَانِ الطَّاعَةِ مَعَ عَدَمِ النُّهُوضِ إِلَيْهَا... مِنْ عَلَامَاتِ الاغْتِرَارِ

Grievance over the loss of obedience along with the absence of proactively reviving it, is from the signs of delusion.

The ultimate mark of true happiness is freedom, and freedom itself is defined by that to which one is bound against that to which one is freed from. Freedom does not have a shape or form, nor any measurable parameters. When one is bound to that which is finite and temporal, they are freed from that which is infinite and eternal.

True freedom, which leads to true happiness, is when one is bound to He who can give in abundance, to whom everything belongs, even the finite and temporal. It is defined by being in servitude to Him, thereby freeing oneself from all else. Thus, when He Almighty bestows upon you the ability to obey and serve Him without restriction and hesitation, He has indeed showered you with the blessings of freedom and felicity. There can be no greater gifting, nor greater liberty than that.

If happiness and contentment is what you seek, then ask for how you can serve Him, not how He can serve you. Ask for the ability and capacity to obey Him, as that is what He asks of you. Ask for the ability and capacity to manifest righteousness and piety, as that is what He expects from you. One who does not feel sorrow for the inability to obey, nor does he seek to revive himself to a state of obedience, rather he who believes that contentment and felicity is to be gained from other than the Divine, has indeed deluded himself, for that is not what reality avails. The fleeting moments of joy felt upon acquiring from the materiality of this world is temporal. Its betrayal upon you is intrinsically its quality. Who then, but the deluded, would think to find eternal happiness in the temporal?

۷۷

لَيْسَ الْعَارِفُ... مَنْ إِذَا أَشَارَ وَجَدَ الْحَقَّ أَقْرَبَ إِلَيْهِ مِنْ إِشَارَتِهِ،

بَلِ الْعَارِفُ... مَنْ لَا إِشَارَةَ لَهُ لِفَنَائِهِ فِي وُجُودِهِ وَانْطِوَائِهِ فِي شُهُودِهِ

He is not an 'ārif [56] (gnostic) the one who when he alludes a symbol, the presence of truth draws near to him through his allusion. Rather the ārif is one who has no symbolic allusion because of his own self-annihilation in Allāh's presence and self-withdrawal in His witnessing.

Knowledge begins with the allusion of symbols and what they signify, but that is not its destiny. Its destiny is in manifesting an understanding deep in one's innermost, a dimension not of symbols. True understanding is not arrived at through the allusion of symbols. Symbols and words are but carriers of meaning, not meaning itself. One to whom reality is unveiled knows to establish meaning as the root and symbols and words as followers. This is the true *'ārif*, the one who knows, the one who understands. Not the one who seeks to find meanings in symbols and words, but one who sees the meaning in the form and realizes the symbol as a mere carrier, as the poet said;

إنما الكون معان ... قائمات بالصور

كل من يدرك هذا ... كان من أهل العبر

'The world is but meaning, erected as form...
He who realizes this is from the people of discernment.' [57]

The *'ārif* is one who holds no symbolic allusion, having mentally transcended the domain of the soul[58] and settled in the domain of the heart. This is what is meant by 'self-annihilation' in the presence of Allāh, where one does not gain understanding by their own mental processes, but receive knowledge directly from Allāh in the form of guidance and inspiration. In doing so, they see not themselves as the enlightened ones, but they witness the Glory and Majesty of Allāh who grants them enlightenment.

---

56 Most texts translate the word عارف *'ārif* as 'gnostic.' In English, the word 'gnostic' is defined as 'possessing esoteric knowledge,' which can become problematic because 'esoteric knowledge' in the language of Islām does not have the same meaning as is rendered in western languages, theological or otherwise. Hence we have opted not to translate it so as to preserve the meaning simply as 'one who knows; has deep knowledge, or understanding.'

57 From the Dīwān of Muhammad ibn al-Habīb (d.1972)

58 Which is also the domain of metaphors, allegories, symbols, and symbolic allusion, عالم المثال, *'ālam al-mithāl.*

79

الرَّجَاءُ مَا قَارَنَهُ عَمَلٌ، وَإِلَّا فَهُوَ أُمْنِيَّةٌ

Hope is what accompanies deed, elseways it is just wishful thinking.

Hope is nourishment for the soul. It is a station among the stations of certainty as it encourages one to strive in righteous action. One who hopes for something proceeds towards it, and with the loss of hope flees from it. False hope is vain desire, wishful thinking, and is among the signs of delusion. The fruition of a deed is always accompanied by hope, and hope itself is always accompanied by action. Lack of either is mere fancy, like he who sins and hopes to be forgiven but does nothing to rectify himself or his wrong. Or he who desires paradise but does not strive in righteousness, hoping for intercession without just right.

مَطْلَبُ العَارِفِينَ مِنَ اللهِ تَعَالَى... الصِّدْقُ فِي العُبُودِيَّةِ، والقِيَامُ بِحَقِّ الرُّبُوبِيَّةِ

The search of the ʿārif from Allāh, Exalted be He, is sincerity in servitude, and rightful establishment of Lordship.

The ʿārif understands that his want is contingent upon Allāh's giving and not his own volition. Though he may pursue the means available to him, the fruition of his quest rests in Allāh's Divine Authority. He also understands that the greatest gift is not from the world of non-permanence. What he seeks, what will bring him true contentment, lies ahead, in the HereAfter, in the eternal and infinite abode. To that gain, his true search in this world rests in that which will avail him the HereAfter. This, he understands, is to be found only in obedience and servitude. He also understands that the fruition of his acts of obedience and servitude is incumbent upon his inner state. His honesty, humility, and sincerity. He thus understands that to gain what he wants he must ask for what he needs to achieve it. He must ask for sincerity in his servitude, for the ultimate source of truth and guidance is Allāh.

One must therefore strive to cultivate his heart with *Ikhlās* and fulfill the rights of his Lord in not merely a ritualistic manner but a heartfelt commitment to align one's will with the Divine, free of pretense or ulterior motives. Such an understanding transcends mere intellectual reasoning; it is a transformative insight into the nature of reality and the Divine. The pursuit of sincerity and fulfillment of Divine Rights *is* one's existential journey towards self-realization. Only he who understands this can be called an ʿārif.

（٨٠）

بَسَطَكَ كَيْ لَا يُبْقِيَكَ مَعَ الْقَبْضِ... وَقَبَضَكَ كَيْ لَا يَتْرُكَكَ مَعَ الْبَسْطِ...
وَأَخْرَجَكَ عَنْهُمَا كَيْ لَا تَكُونَ لِشَيْءٍ دُونَهُ...

He expanded you so as not to keep you in contraction, and He contracted you
so as not to keep you in expansion. And He took you out of both, so you belong
to no thing other than Him.

（٨١）

الْعَارِفُونَ إِذَا بُسِطُوا... أَخْوَفُ مِنْهُمْ إِذَا قُبِضُوا، وَلَا يَقِفُ عَلَى حُدُودِ الْأَدَبِ فِي الْبَسْطِ إِلَّا قَلِيلٌ

Those who know, when expanded, are more fearful than when contracted, as
none can stand within the limits of discipline when expanded, save but a few.

（٨٢）

الْبَسْطُ تَأْخُذُ النَّفْسُ مِنْهُ حَظَّهَا بِوُجُودِ الْفَرَحِ، وَالْقَبْضُ لَا حَظَّ لِلنَّفْسِ فِيهِ

The soul takes its share of joy from expansion, but contraction has no share in
it for the soul.

Expansion and contraction are the fundamental states of reality. The only true constant of this reality is change, and change is transformative between states of expansion and states of contraction. In the spiritual and psychological sense, expansion is a state of joy and euphoria, while contraction is a state of sorrow and depression. As a being in this reality, one must experience both, and likewise be tested in both. There is no 'status quo' in life, no permanent state of being. The world is in a state of change, and so too must the human being change. This is inevitable, but not without wisdom.

He Almighty, from His mercy, grants us moments of joy so as not to burden our souls with continued sorrow. He then, also from His mercy, bestows sorrow, so as not to delude our souls with joy and deprive us of vigilance. He is *Al-Bāsit* الباسط, the Expander, and *Al-Qābid* القابض, the Constrictor, and He continually changes the states of His servants, between expansions and contractions, so as to free us from the clutches of both, for they are of this world, and we belong to Him, not to this world.

The '*ārif* understands that the soul delights in expansive states, and holds no preference for constriction. He is thus fearful for expansion, fearful of losing his state of vigilance and becoming too comfortable in the temporal joy at the risk of losing eternal felicity.

(٨٣)

رُبَّمَا أَعْطَاكَ فَمَنَعَكَ، وَ رُبَّمَا مَنَعَكَ فَأَعْطَاكَ

It may be He gives you by depriving you, and it may be He deprives you by giving you.

(٨٤)

مَتَى فَتَحَ لَكَ بَابَ الْفَهْمِ فِي الْمَنْعِ، عَادَ الْمَنْعُ عَيْنَ الْعَطَاءِ

When He opens for you the doors of understanding in the deprivation, the deprivation returns to the source of the giving.

Sometimes He gives by withholding, and sometimes He withholds by giving. In the giving, He gives that which is beneficial, and in the withholding, He withholds that which is harmful, and this is all from His wisdom as He declares;

﴿ ... وَعَسَىٰ أَن تَكْرَهُوا شَيْئًا وَهُوَ خَيْرٌ لَّكُمْ وَعَسَىٰ أَن تُحِبُّوا شَيْئًا وَهُوَ شَرٌّ لَّكُمْ وَٱللَّهُ يَعْلَمُ وَأَنتُمْ لَا تَعْلَمُونَ ﴾

...and perhaps you despise a thing and it is good for you, or perhaps you desire a thing and it is bad for you, and Allāh knows but you do not know.[59]

The human power of evaluation is limited, narrow, and estimative as opposed to accurate. One might evaluate a thing in its entirety and assume it beneficial to them, yet there exists within it harm that is beyond the human capacity to grasp. This is because all things are existent subject to Time, the sole entity beyond the human capacity to measure. Time unveils the realities of all things as their temporal states are ever subject to change. That which appears good in the present moment may avail harm, and that which appears detrimental in the present may avail benefit. Such knowledge exists only with the Divine.

The wisdom here is to trust Divine Judgment and Decree. What may appear to you as cumbersome, tiresome, deprivation, is in reality a gift, either preventative of what would destroy you in this world, and if at all it benefits in this world it may be at the expense of your HereAfter.

The 'ārif understands this in its inner dimensions, and his understanding makes him realize that ultimately, both the deprivation and the giving, emerge from the same source. With this understanding, they become the same thing. Within the tragedy lies the tranquility, within the problem lies its solution. Solving the problem entails understanding the problem, and upon understanding, the doors to its solution are unveiled. One's felicity rests in the folds of tragedy, if not availed in this life, then certainly availed in the HereAfter.

---

59   Sūrah al-Baqarah 2:216

(٨٥)

الأَكْوَانُ ظَاهِرُهَا غِرَّةٌ وَبَاطِنُهَا عِبْرَةٌ،

فَالنَّفْسُ تَنْظُرُ إِلَى ظَاهِرِ غِرَّتِهَا،

وَالقَلْبُ يَنْظُرُ إِلَى بَاطِنِ عِبْرَتِهَا،

The realms of created things are outwardly allures and inwardly discernments.
And the soul is transfixed on the outward allure of it, while the heart is seeking
the inward discernment of it.

That which is immediately visible to the senses captivates, but is not the entire truth of it, and it hence distracts from the truth. This is why the outward is an allure. Its very nature is to captivate and retain one's intellective attention and prevent it from progressing deeper. It entices one into superficial understandings, leading away from deeper truths. Within human nature lies a zeal to uncover the logical understandings of reality, and yet reality is always several steps ahead of logic. Though rationality carries one forward into the domain of understanding, it is restricted to the surface. One who is enticed by the outward beauty of things and does not penetrate further has indeed fallen prey to the allure. This is the nature of the self. It receives from the sensorial and is delighted by what it receives. The world is indeed beautiful, for its Creator loves beauty and creates in beauty. But within that beauty lies a greater beauty, more intrinsic than the outward. This is what the heart desires, for its unveiling to the heart leads it closer to the presence of the Creator. For within this inner beauty He has placed meaning and purpose, the Divine Wisdom of why He has created and what it all avails.

This is why the inner essence is called *'ibrah* عبرة, 'discernment,' an act of perceiving first, then conceptualizing its meaning, and finally arriving at its true judgment. It comes from the root *'abara* عبر, meaning to 'cross over' from the apparent outwardness of things to their innermost secrets. The final judgment gives the heart a conviction of truth, firm and unyielding, a protection from doubt and uncertainty. This invites the heart to reflect on how the sensorial and experiential, while often tempting the self with superficial allurements, are filled with deeper lessons if we are willing to look beyond mere appearances.

The self is ever concerned with material desires, immediate satisfaction, and sensory experience. It is easily swayed by pleasure, wealth, status, and appearance. The heart is the seat of deeper understanding, wisdom, and spiritual realization. It is tasked with reaching beyond the illusions of the surface world and realizing the inner truths. The tension between these two, between the superficial and the profound, the material and the spiritual, is the truest struggle of the human being.

(٨٦)

إِذَا أَرَدْتَ أَنْ يَكُونَ لَكَ عِزٌّ لَا يَفْنَى ، فَلَا تَسْتَعِزَّنَّ بِعِزٍّ يَفْنَى

If you want honour (fame, might, glory) that does not perish (everlasting), then do not console yourself in an honour that perishes.

There is no honour in this world but an honour that perishes with the decay of time. If there is joy, it is not without grief. If there is longevity, it is not without annihilation, if there is power, it is not without incapacity, and if there is knowledge it is not without ignorance. Likewise, if there is honour it is not without disgrace. However, by the Wisdom of Allāh, there is an honour existent that does not fade. It is an honour that is itself anchored in that which does not perish. This is called *al-bāqiyāt as-sālihāt* الباقيات الصالحات, 'enduring righteousness,' found in those acts that earn the pleasure of Allāh, as He has Himself declared;

﴿ ٱلْمَالُ وَٱلْبَنُونَ زِينَةُ ٱلْحَيَوٰةِ ٱلدُّنْيَا وَٱلْبَٰقِيَٰتُ ٱلصَّٰلِحَٰتُ خَيْرٌ عِندَ رَبِّكَ ثَوَابًا وَخَيْرٌ أَمَلًا ﴾

Wealth and legacy are but allures of the life of this world. While enduring righteousness is better with your Lord in reward and better in aspiration! [60]

Such an honour,[61] with one's Lord, is lasting, eternal, and rooted in something higher and more permanent. It is a genuine honour that arises from integrity, moral strength, and faith, which are not subject to external changes or worldly influences.

---

(٨٧)

الطَّيُّ الْحَقِيقِيُّ ... أَنْ تَطْوِيَ مَسَافَةَ الدُّنْيَا عَنْكَ حَتَّى تَرَى الْآخِرَةَ أَقْرَبَ إِلَيْكَ مِنْكَ

The true fold (cover/kept concealed) is the folding of the far reaches of the world from you, such that you see the HereAfter closer to you than yourself.

The true concealment is the concealment of the worldly, removed from one's periphery, such that the heart sees only the HereAfter, closer than one's self. It is the folding of the world's allure and distraction, and the opening of the innermost, the availing of the otherworldly, that leads to a profound appreciation of the Divine. This is the ultimate gift granted in this life, to realize that there is more to living than mere living, that there awaits an existence no eye has seen, no ear has heard, no thought has ever entered the heart.

---

60   Sūrah al-Kahf 18:46

61   See Hikam 257

(٨٨)

العَطَاءُ مِنَ الْخَلْقِ حِرْمَانٌ، وَالْمَنْعُ مِنَ اللهِ إِحْسَانٌ

*The gift from creation (man) is a prohibition (deprivation), and a prevention
from Allāh (prohibition) is a goodness (benefaction).*

That which creation gifts to creation is limited and restricted. Within
it lies both the joy of the gift and the sorrow it brings. Both are inevitably
embedded in the created. But that which comes from Allāh, be it a
restriction, constriction, be it a prohibition, is invariably benefaction. For
He does not prohibit save that within the prohibition is a wisdom that
leads to goodness or protects from harm.

(٨٩)

جَلَّ رَبُّنَا أَنْ يُعَامِلَهُ الْعَبْدُ نَقْدًا فَيُجَازِيَهُ نَسِيئَةً

*Too Exalted is our Lord, that He would deal with His servant in coin, and
reward him in deference (credit).*

(٩٠)

كَفَى مِنْ جَزَائِهِ إِيَّاكَ عَلَى الطَّاعَةِ أَنْ رَضِيَكَ لَهَا أَهْلًا

*It is reward enough for your obedience that he accepts you and deems you
worthy of it.*

(٩١)

كَفَى الْعَامِلِينَ جَزَاءً مَا هُوَ فَاتِحُهُ عَلَى قُلُوبِهِمْ فِي طَاعَتِهِ،

وَمَا هُوَ مُورِدُهُ عَلَيْهِمْ مِنْ وُجُودِ مُؤَانَسَتِهِ

*It is reward enough for the doers (of good) what He has opened to their hears
in obedience to Him, and what He has bestowed upon them from the presence
of His cordiality (kindness/courtesy to them).*

(٩٢)

مَنْ عَبَدَهُ لِشَيْءٍ يَرْجُوهُ مِنْهُ ، أَوْ لِيَدْفَعَ بِطَاعَتِهِ وُرُودَ الْعُقُوبَةِ عَنْهُ... فَمَا قَامَ بِحَقِّ أَوْصَافِهِ

*Whoever worships Him for a thing he hopes to gain from Him, or to prevent,
by obedience to Him, His punishment, then not has (such a person) given His
Attributes their due right.*

A relationship with Allāh is not 'quid pro quo.' One does not serve and worship expecting a direct or immediate return as one might expect wages for labor. Divine reward is beyond the immediate and the material, from a higher, more spiritual dimension, and is not a 'thing' to be disposed in the temporal world.

So how foolish is the servant who seeks recompense from his Lord in the form of material wealth and benefaction? Or he who seeks recompense for a deed he has yet to perform? Does he think to reduce his Lord to the customs of man that he would be rewarded in coin or be granted blessing without righteous action?

Rather one should consider it reward enough that he has been granted the ability to obey, and that his deeds would be accepted by Him Almighty, and that He would indeed deem this servant worthy of worship and servitude. One should consider it reward enough that there has come to him guidance that leads him to servitude, and that this guidance has come in the highest form of cordiality and courtesy. Such is the true believer and servant. He is grateful for simply having the realization of himself and who his Lord is. It is not without Allāh's mercy that every deed will be recompensed, in this life or the other, in material benefaction as well as spiritual, but the true servant does not serve in lieu of reward. He serves simply out of love and to seek the pleasure of his Lord. The very fact that one is able to worship and obey Allāh is, in itself, a divine gift and a reward. Being chosen or given the capacity to obey is an honour, a sign of divine grace. One must shift their focus from external rewards to the internal, intrinsic value of obedience. Worship, in this view, is not about gaining something material but about being spiritually elevated and connected to Allāh through the act of obedience.

The inner spiritual rewards that come from worship and obedience are 'openings' in the heart, of spiritual insight, tranquility, and divine closeness. Rather than focus on material or external compensation, which are inclinations of the self, the true reward is the internal transformation and the sense of divine companionship that the heart experiences.

He who serves with aspiration of gaining from Him, yet lacks sincerity in his servitude, has not fully served him, nor will his servitude be with conviction. For when the reward is withheld, and when the self becomes dominant, he shall withdraw his servitude and find himself in greater loss. The same is true for he who serves simply to avoid retribution. For when the punishment is delayed, he will lapse and falter to a state of disobedience, thereby losing both rank and reward. Worship that is motivated by self-interest, either in seeking worldly or heavenly rewards or in attempting to avoid divine punishment, is blameworthy. True worship is not driven by personal gain or fear. Such a person has not realized the true rights of the Divine Attributes. Allāh is beyond being an object of transactional worship, and true devotion arises from love, awe, and recognition of His majesty and grace, independent of what one might receive in return.

⟨٩٣⟩

مَتَى أَعْطَاكَ... أَشْهَدَكَ بِرَّهُ، وَمَتَى مَنَعَكَ... أَشْهَدَكَ قَهْرَهُ،
فَهُوَ فِي كُلِّ ذَلِكَ مُتَعَرِّفٌ إِلَيْكَ وَمُقْبِلٌ بِوُجُودِ لُطْفِهِ عَلَيْكَ

When He gives you, He is making you witness His nobility, and when He denies you, He is making you witness His irresistible power. So He is, in each of these, making Himself known to you, and drawing you closer by the presence of His gentleness to you.

⟨٩٤⟩

إِنَّمَا يُؤْلِمُكَ الْمَنْعُ لِعَدَمِ فَهْمِكَ عَنِ اللهِ فِيهِ

Indeed, the deprivation only hurts because of your lack of understanding of Allāh (His reasons) in it.

When He grants a blessing, whether material or spiritual, He is revealing His kindness and mercy. The giving itself becomes a means of witnessing His generosity. Through it, one is reminded of Allāh's benevolence, love, and care, and this realization should be reciprocated with gratitude, for the giving is not simply a transfer of material or spiritual bounty, but an invitation to reflect on and recognize the divine quality of mercy and grace.

Then, when He withholds, He reveals His Power and Majesty. Withholding is not necessarily a punishment or a sign of neglect; rather, it is one among the ways in which He manifests Himself to His servants. By not granting a request or a desire, He reminds the believer of His absolute control and authority. This invites reflection on our dependency and that human will is ultimately subject to Divine Wisdom and Decree.

Whether He gives or withholds, He is continuously revealing Himself to his servants, making Himself known in different ways. Both generosity and power are aspects of His Divinity. Even when He withholds, it is an expression of His gentleness and subtle kindness. This, whether perceived as favourable or unfavourable, is an act of divine engagement. He is constantly drawing His servants closer, teaching them through both abundance and deprivation, guiding them to a deeper understanding of who He is.

The pain or discomfort one feels when something is withheld arises not from the act itself, but from a lack of understanding of its divine purpose. If one could truly grasp Allāh's wisdom and recognize that even withholding is a form of care and guidance, the suffering would lessen, disappear even. This is encouraging enough a thought for believers to trust that even in deprivation there is wisdom and mercy.

(٩٥)

رُبَّمَا فَتَحَ لَكَ بَابَ الطَّاعَةِ وَمَا فَتَحَ لَكَ بَابَ الْقَبُولِ، وَرُبَّمَا قَضَى عَلَيْكَ بِالذَّنْبِ فَكَانَ سَبَبًا فِي الْوُصُولِ

It may be that He opened for you the door to obedience, and did not open the door to acceptance, and He sentenced you to sin that it becomes a means of reconciliation.

(٩٦)

مَعْصِيَةٌ أَوْرَثَتْ ذُلًّا وَافْتِقَارًا خَيْرٌ مِنْ طَاعَةٍ أَوْرَثَتْ عِزًّا وَاسْتِكْبَارًا

Disobedience that bequeaths humiliation and desperation is better than obedience that bequeaths renown and pride.

Outward acts of obedience are not always accompanied by divine acceptance. One might be given the opportunity to perform righteous acts, such as prayer, charity, or fasting, but these acts alone do not guarantee spiritual success. The deeper dimension of obedience lies not in the mere performance of duties, but in whether those acts are accepted by Allāh. Hence, one should not be complacent or prideful merely because they engage in outward acts of piety. The real goal is to achieve divine acceptance, which requires sincerity, humility, and inner transformation. It is a warning against self-righteousness or assuming that outward compliance with religious duties naturally means spiritual success.

Here, sin itself can paradoxically become a means of spiritual awakening. When one sins, especially if they deeply reflect on their error, it may lead to feelings of remorse, humility, and repentance. These feelings can bring the sinner closer to Allāh, as they recognize their weakness and need for divine mercy. In this sense, the sin becomes a turning point, a catalyst for spiritual growth and proximity to Allāh. This challenges the simplistic notion that sin is purely destructive. While it may cause harm, it can also serve as a moment of spiritual enlightenment if it leads to a renewed awareness of one's dependence on Allāh's grace.

One must understand that the inner state that results from an action is more important than the action itself. A sin that leads to feelings of humility and a recognition of one's spiritual poverty before Allāh can ultimately be more beneficial than an act of obedience that leads to pride and arrogance. True spiritual progress depends on the heart's condition. If obedience leads one to feel superior, proud, or self-sufficient, it has failed to achieve its true purpose. And if sin humbles the person and makes them realize their weakness and reliance upon Allāh, it has succeeded in its true purpose.

نِعْمَتَانِ مَا خَرَجَ مَوْجُودٌ عَنْهُمَا، وَلَا بُدَّ لِكُلِّ مُكَوَّنٍ مِنْهُمَا... نِعْمَةُ الْإِيْجَادِ، وَنِعْمَةُ الْإِمْدَادِ

Two blessings no being can exist without, and not a single creation can BE without... The blessing of existence, and the blessing of sustenance.

أَنْعَمَ عَلَيْكَ أَوَّلًا بِالْإِيْجَادِ ، وَثَانِيًا بِتَوَالِيَ الْإِمْدَادِ

He has bestowed blessing upon you, first by giving you existence and second by continued sustenance.

A 'being' cannot 'be' unless it is existent. And it cannot exist unless it is brought into existence. To be brought into existence from non-existence necessitates the act of 'bringing' as belonging to other than the being, for how can a non-existent being will itself into existence if it and its will were non-existent to begin with?

It is the benevolence of the Creator and Originator to bring into being that which is non-existent. It is also an attribute solely His. This is the prime gift that the created being must be eternally grateful for, and is followed immediately by the second gift, the gift of sustenance.

A being that can bring itself into existence should be more than capable of sustaining itself, for the first act is more demanding than the second. Both notions are hypothetical, and hence impossible in reality, but they shall serve our purpose of illustrating this most vital concept. Which is to say that since the being did not, and cannot bring itself into existence, it certainly cannot sustain itself. If its existence is contingent upon the One who brought it into existence, then its sustenance is also contingent upon Him.

These two are not the rights of the created being, and cannot be demanded by the being. They are essential aspects of existence, given freely by Allāh, without which nothing could exist nor continue to exist. The idea that no created entity can escape these blessings positions the Creator as the sole source of life and sustainer of all things. The first blessing (existence) brings something into being, while the second blessing (sustenance) keeps it existent.

One must understand that creation is an act of Divine Grace. The realms, both material and spiritual, and all that is within them exist not out of necessity or by their own power, but because Allāh *willed* them to exist. Existence itself is hence a gift, one that no created being has earned or can claim by right. It is purely an expression of Divine Generosity. Existence is not a static state but a dynamic process. Beings are not just created once and left to exist on their own; rather, they are constantly dependent on Divine Sustenance, meaning that the Creator continuously emanates existence and sustenance to the created world. For the human being, Allāh provides not only the material necessities for survival, such as food, water, and air, but also the spiritual and intellectual resources needed for growth, knowledge, and enlightenment.

This is the 'Islāmic Worldview' where Allāh is intimately involved in every aspect of creation. He is not a 'distant creator' who simply sets the universe in motion and 'steps back.' Rather, He is actively engaged in every moment of existence, ensuring that all things are sustained and provided for, as He is *Al-Muhyī* المحي The Giver of Life, and *Ar-Razzāq* الرزاق The Provider.

٩٩

فَاقَتُكَ لَكَ ذَاتِيَّةٌ، وَوُرُودُ الْأَسْبَابِ مُذَكِّرَاتٌ لَكَ بِمَا خَفِيَ عَلَيْكَ مِنْهَا،

وَالْفَاقَةُ الذَّاتِيَّةُ لَا تَرْفَعُهَا الْعَوَارِضُ

Your poverty is intrinsic (essential of you). And the arrival of means are reminders to you of what is concealed from you of it. But the intrinsic (aspect of) indigence cannot be alienated by (simply correcting) the symptoms.

١٠٠

خَيْرُ أَوْقَاتِكَ وَقْتٌ تَشْهَدُ فِيهِ وُجُودَ فَاقَتِكَ وَتُرَدُّ فِيهِ إِلَى وُجُودِ ذِلَّتِكَ

Your finest moment is a moment in which you witness your indigence and through it you fall into the state of your submissiveness.

This is the poverty of the soul and the heart, a spiritual impoverishment. Though one may be grown in body, strong and able, they remain a child in spirit, needy and weak. Though they may possess mountains of wealth and far-reached fame, they remain dire and depressed. It is the essential nature of man, an intrinsic quality, created to be spiritually needy and impoverished, yet not altogether forsaken.

Means and opportunities to serve and obey wherewith one nourishes their spiritual states are but reminders of what is truly hidden from them—the enlightenment that would nourish them from their impoverished states. These means and opportunities are extrinsic to the being. They emanate from the being. They are the accidents arising from the essence, and the accident cannot rectify or alter the essence. If the essence is sound, the means will be sound. They will guide the being rightly upon the path. If the essence is corrupt, the means will be corrupt, and will sway him away from the path. Thus, the being's finest moment is in realizing his destitution with which he may beseech the aid of the Almighty, and from which he may be rescued.

---

(١٠١)

مَتَى أَوْحَشَكَ مِنْ خَلْقِهِ... فَاعْلَمْ أَنَّهُ يُرِيدُ أَنْ يَفْتَحَ لَكَ بَابَ الأُنْسِ بِهِ

When He isolates you from His creation... Know that He wants to open for you the door of affection.

(١٠٢)

مَتَى أَطْلَقَ لِسَانَكَ بِالطَّلَبِ... فَاعْلَمْ أَنَّهُ يُرِيدُ أَنْ يُعْطِيَكَ

When He releases your tongue to ask... Know that He wants to give you what you seek.

This is an inescapable condition of embarking the spiritual path. One often encounters moments of estrangement or alienation, which can induce a sense of loneliness. This state, while often interpreted negatively by society, is in truth a deliberate act of Divine Intervention. Allāh is removing the individual's comfort in creation and suspending him from worldly ties, to redirect his attention inward. And what may be perceived as a withdrawal from society or a sense of abandonment is, in fact, an opportunity for spiritual awakening.

This alienation serves a higher purpose. It is the opening of the door to Divine Intimacy الأُنْس بالله, fulfilling the innermost essence and meaning of mankind as إِنْسَان. Man is, by his nature, أُنْس, a sociable and companionable creature, but true intimacy and companionship are found not in the transient, finite world, rather in the eternal presence of Allāh. These gifted periods of isolation, trial, or social emptiness are necessary stages for reaching that transcendence. The experience of feeling disconnected from worldly matters pushes the individual to confront the deeper reality of their existence, that ultimate fulfillment lies not in creation but in the Creator.

The heart is ultimately designed to seek intimacy with the Divine, and worldly connections, though necessary, can often obscure this deeper relationship, which is fulfilled only through supplication. The very act of being able to ask Allāh for something is itself an indication that Divine Grace is near. The loosening of the tongue is not merely the motion of the fleshy organ, but the internal movement within the individual that compels them to turn to Allāh in prayer. This is not just a random occurrence but a prompt from Allāh, signaling His intention to give. The believer who feels inclined to pray, to ask, or to seek something from Allāh, should understand this an indication that Allāh has already set the process of Divine Response in motion. It is not a human attempt to influence the Divine, rather it is a gift from Allāh, a means by which He is preparing the believer to receive His bounty.

(١٠٣)

الْعَارِفُ لَا يَزُولُ اضْطِرَارُهُ وَلَا يَكُونُ مَعَ غَيْرِ اللهِ قَرَارُهُ

The 'ārif's sense of urgency does not part, nor is his resolution with other than Allāh, Exalted be He.

This is the epitome of an *'ārif.* He is never parted from his sense of absolute need and reliance, his unceasing awareness of dependency on Divine Sustenance. Because he knows that the highest form of knowing is in realizing the True Unity of the Divine, and this itself necessitates a non-being of self-sufficiency and independence. It leads to a deepening of one's recognition of human frailty, and the more one knows, the more one understands their existential poverty in the face of Allāh's Majesty. This is the true journey toward the Divine, a journey into greater humility and consciousness of one's limitations.

This perpetual need from which the *'ārif* is never parted stems from the realization that all existence, sustenance, and spiritual progression are entirely contingent upon Allāh. The *'ārif* understands that even their spiritual knowledge and states of closeness to the Divine Presence are not achievements born of their own efforts but are the result of His grace and gifting. In this regard, the state of necessity is not a sign of spiritual deficiency but a mark of profound spiritual maturity.

From this rises an inability to find rest or stability in anything other than the Divine Presence. The term قرار (rest, resolution, settlement) implies a state of permanence or contentment, in that the heart of the *'ārif* is in a constant state of movement, driven by dire longing to find its rest and contentment in the presence of Allāh alone. The *'ārif* only experiences this state after understanding the illusionary nature of the material world and its transient pleasures, and realizing that he cannot find lasting satisfaction in anything that is not the Absolute. As a result, his heart is always in search of the eternal, the unchanging, and the infinite, qualities found only in the Divine. For once he has glimpsed that higher reality, he will never find contentment in the shadows and reflections of the material world. Once he has tasted the intimacy with Allāh, he will never be satisfied with lesser realities.

For Almighty Allāh is the only true source of peace and satisfaction. The believer's relationship with Him is one of continuous seeking and unwavering reliance, recognizing that all good, all stability, and all fulfillment come solely from Him. It is not a weakness but a mark of spiritual elevation, for it signifies a profound understanding of the nature of reality. This is why the true believer's journey is one of constant spiritual strife, fueled by the understanding that all that is created is contingent, and all that is contingent can never satisfy the heart's longing for the Absolute and the Eternal.

(١٠٤)

أَنَارَ الظَّوَاهِرَ بِأَنْوَارِ آثَارِهِ وَأَنَارَ السَّرَائِرَ بِأَنْوَارِ أَوْصَافِهِ، لِأَجْلِ ذَلِكَ أَفَلَتِ الْأَنْوَارُ الظَّاهِرَةُ وَلَمْ

تَأْفُلِ الْأَنْوَارُ الْقُلُوبِ وَالسَّرَائِرِ، وَلِذَلِكَ قِيلَ

~ طَلَعَتِ شَمْسُ مَنْ أُحِبُّ بِلَيْلٍ فَاسْتَضَائَتْ فَمَا لَهَا مِنْ غُرُوبِ ~

~ إِنَّ شَمْسَ النَّهَارِ تَغْرُبُ بِاللَّيْلِ وَشَمْسُ الْقُلُوبِ لَيْسَتْ تَغِيبُ ~

He has illuminated the manifest with the lights of His traces and He has illuminated the innermost with the lights of His Attributes. Due to this, the outward lights fade, and lights of the hearts and the innermost do not fade. And thus it was said,
'By night rose the sun of One whom I love, illuminated, and was not for it a setting... Indeed the sun of the day sets by night, but the sun of the hearts has no setting...'

The outward world of phenomena ظاهر is illuminated by Divine Signs آثار, which are manifestations of Allāh's presence. These signs are tangible, observable in nature, in the order of the cosmos, and in the events of life. The physical world serves as a trace indication of the Divine, pointing the mind toward the ultimate source of all things.

In contrast, the inner realm of secrets and mysteries السرائر is illuminated not by signs, but by the Divine Attributes أوصاف, which are intangible and direct reflections of His essence. The heart or the inner self, through contemplation and spiritual purification, becomes a vessel for these Divine Attributes. Attributes like mercy, wisdom, and love shine inwardly, guiding the soul to higher understanding and spiritual proximity to Allāh.

This distinction echoes the difference between empirical knowledge (gained through sensory experience) and intuitive or inward knowledge (gained through spiritual realization). The external world may teach us about God's existence, but His reality is realized through direct spiritual experience. For the outward lights are bound by time and space. They appear and disappear, rise and set. They are finite and transient.

But the lights of the hearts, those illuminated by the Divine Attributes, are not subject to such limitations. They represent timeless knowledge and spiritual insight that transcends the physical world. They are a form of illumination that remains constant and unshakable. As the physical world is bound to perish and decay, so too are its lights. But the heart's illumination by the Divine endures beyond time. This permanent light is the realization of Allāh's Eternal Majesty, which does not wane like the light of the sun. The darkness of night, of ignorance, of separation from the Beloved, is dispelled by the Light of Love, a sun that never sets.

(١٠٥)

لِيُخَفِّفَنْ أَلَمَ الْبَلَاءِ عَلَيْكَ عِلْمُكَ بِأَنَّهُ سُبْحَانَهُ هُوَ الْمُبْتَلِي لَكَ، فَالَّذِي وَاجَهَتْكَ مِنْهُ
الْأَقْدَارُ هُوَ الَّذِي عَوَّدَكَ حُسْنَ الْإِخْتِيَارِ

To ease the suffering of affliction upon you, know that it is by Him, Glory unto Him, that He has set the affliction upon you. And that which you encounter from Him of fate is that which accustoms you to good decisions.

The pain of trials and suffering is an inseparable part of your humanness, but knowing the source origin of the trial can alleviate its burden and transform its experience. Knowing that Allāh is the one testing you implies that the trial is not arbitrary or meaningless, but rather part of His Divine Plan for you. This transforms the suffering from something chaotic and unbearable into something purposeful and meaningful, and strengthens your faith in His wisdom and justice to alleviate the emotional and psychological pain that might otherwise accompany trials. You are being trained to see beyond the immediate pain and to trust the unfolding process as it strengthens you towards your purpose. Suffering is not to be framed as a sign of neglect or punishment, but as an opportunity to deepen one's reliance on Allāh and trust in Him. The affliction thus becomes a spiritual tool for drawing the believer closer to the Divine, making the burden of suffering lighter through the realization that it comes from a source of wisdom and mercy. For He who tests you with the trials is also the One who has and will guide you through life with beneficial choices. There is a clear continuity in Divine Wisdom. The trials and tests are orchestrated by the same Hand that has brought good into your life, such that all events, whether seemingly positive or negative, are part of a holistic wisdom that consistently aims for the ultimate good of the believer.

---

(١٠٦)

مَنْ ظَنَّ انْفِكَاكَ لُطْفِهِ عَنْ قَدَرِهِ فَذَلِكَ لِقُصُورِ نَظَرِهِ

Whoever thinks that Allāh's gentleness is separated from His ordainment, then that is due to a fault in his perception.

Allāh's grace لطف and His decree قدر are inseparable. It is false to assume that when one encounters difficulty or hardship, Allāh's grace is absent or withdrawn, as false as to assume that Divine Decree and Divine Benevolence are at odds with each other. The believer must acknowledge that Allāh's care and providence is ever present in His ordainment.

لَا يُخَافُ عَلَيْكَ أَنْ تَلْتَبِسَ الطُّرُقُ عَلَيْكَ، وَإِنَّمَا يُخَافُ عَلَيْكَ مِنْ غَلَبَةِ الْهَوَى عَلَيْكَ

*He does not fear for you that the paths will confound you, rather He only fears
for you that your whims will defeat you.*

The danger does not lie in the confusion of choices or the difficulty in
discerning the right path. The fear is not that the believer will become lost
in a maze of decisions or become disoriented in their spiritual or moral
journey. Clarity of guidance is ever available and accessible. The paths to
righteousness, virtue, and truth are ever illuminated for those who seek
them sincerely. Moral truths and the principles of upright conduct are
not inherently hidden or inaccessible. The knowledge of right and wrong
is embedded in both human reason and in Revelation, and those who
seek guidance with sincerity will always find the right path.

Hence, there is no fear of getting lost due to external factors or
complexities, for the human capacity for discernment, when aligned with
right intention, will always be drawn to the truth. This is what moral
clarity dictates, that while life presents many choices, it is within the
power of the individual to choose rightly when they are guided by sound
principles, ethical reasoning, and spiritual insight.

The true danger for the believer lies in the overpowering influence
of base desires and inclinations. The real obstacle upon the right path is
not a lack of guidance but the dominance of one's lower self, which leads
to moral blindness and error, despite the availability of clear guidance.
These whims and desires cloud judgment, distort perception, and steer
one away from the path of virtue, even when the right course of action
is evident. The battle against the self is therefore central to maintaining
moral clarity, as unquestioned desires sow the seeds of self-deception,
rationalizing wrong choices, and ignoring the guidance that is present.

True freedom and moral agency come not from the absence of external
obstacles, but from the mastery of one's own passions. The challenge
for the moral agent is less about external confusion and more about
maintaining self-discipline and inner clarity in the face of conflicting
impulses. The human struggle lies in resisting the temptations of the ego
and maintaining a state of inner humility and receptivity to higher truths.
In this manner, the haze of confounding choices and decisions is lifted
and clarity is granted with which the course is maintained. All else that is
external becomes a semantic and logistical matter.

If the internal state of the being is sound and clear, both spiritually
and intellectually, all external obstacles of worldly life are easily resolvable
and the path becomes clear. However, if the internal aspect is itself
confounded, the blame lies not with a lack of guidance, but with the self
that could not prevent itself from self-delusion.

(١٠٨)

سُبْحَانَ مَنْ سَتَرَ سِرَّ الْخُصُوصِيَّةِ بِظُهُورِ الْبَشَرِيَّةِ، وَظَهَرَ بِعَظَمَةِ الرُّبُوبِيَّةِ فِي إِظْهَارِ الْعُبُودِيَّةِ

Glorified is the One who has veiled the secrets of eliteness in the manifestation of humanness, and has revealed the greatness of Divinity in manifest servitude.

Khūsus خصوص, the status of eliteness with the Divine is hidden beneath the veil of ordinary human existence and is embedded in the subtlety of humanity. These elite are not of great power and status, fame or wealth. They are not among the notables and noteworthy. It is not by great heroic acts that they are granted this eliteness. Rather it is the small acts of kindness and mercy, of humanity, whose most profound aspects remain concealed to the casual observer, as one of the scholars said;

... خفية عن أبصار المستمسكين بالأسباب العادية ...

...hidden from the sights of those who cling to causal reasons...[61]

The human form, with all its limitations and imperfections, is as a veil cast over the deeper spiritual potential within. The body and the material realm, while visible, obscure the inner reality and profound ability that the human being possesses, that allows him to rise above the rest of creation to an elite station with the Creator. Those of this elite status may appear as ordinary or even limited creatures, yet within them lies the secret of divine love that is never seen on the surface, not even to themselves, and is uncovered only through spiritual insight and a conscious inner awakening.

The path to attaining that status lies in worship and servitude. Only through salvation can one attain sanctification. Lordship ربوبية is made manifest through servitude عبودية. While Allāh is exalted in His majesty and transcendence, His grandeur becomes most apparent in the submission and devotion of His creation. Servitude, then, is not a sign of human weakness but a reflection of the Divine's Greatness.

True power and majesty are revealed not in control and domination, as is oft expressed in the human projection of sovereignty, but in mercy and kindness, as is expressed in the relationship between the Lord and the servant. The human role of servitude is expressed in humility, obedience, and devotion, and it becomes the context in which Allāh's transcendence and power is manifested. Humanity, through its submission and acknowledgment of dependence on the Divine, acts as a mirror reflecting the greatness of the Creator, and it is through that greatness that He, in his mercy and kindness, guides, nurtures, and grants His most devout, pious, and righteous to an elite status. Though they may seem deprived and impoverished in the outward, they are beyond wealth in the inward.

---

61   Ibn 'Ajībah's *Bahr al-Madīd*, in his commentary on Sūrah al-Kahf

(۱۰۹)

لَا تُطَالِبْ رَبَّكَ بِتَأَخُّرِ مَطْلَبِكَ وَلٰكِنْ طَالِبْ نَفْسَكَ بِتَأَخُّرِ أَدَبِكَ

Do not demand of your Lord to the delay of your quest, rather demand of
yourself to the delay of your discipline.

The distinction between the elite and the lesser is best found in
their approach to the Divine. When the reward or the response of the
supplication is delayed, the lesser tend to demand from their Lord
immediate recompense for their deed, assaulting Him with blame for
not fulfilling His 'end of the bargain.' The elite, on the other hand, tend
to become concerned, suspecting that the delay might be caused by a
shortcoming on their part.

To be among the elite, one must avoid placing demands or complaints
upon Allāh when their desires or requests are not immediately granted.
Patience and trust in His wisdom are essential components of the spiritual
journey and are defining attributes of being among His elite. It is to
understand that Divine timing operates according to a higher wisdom,
one that may not always align with human expectations or desires.

Rather one must reflect on themselves, on their own behavior and
spiritual development, as the delay in receiving what one desires may be
due to a lack of proper conduct or spiritual discipline. Instead of projecting
dissatisfaction outwardly onto Divine Action, one is called to examine
the state of their own character, as spiritual growth is intricately tied to
the cultivation of virtues such as patience, humility, and sincerity.

⋅⋅◦◦●◦◦⋅⋅

(۱۱۰)

مَتَى جَعَلَكَ فِي الظَّاهِرِ مُمْتَثِلًا لِأَمْرِهِ وَرَزَقَكَ فِي الْبَاطِنِ الْاِسْتِسْلَامَ لِقَهْرِهِ...

فَقَدْ أَعْظَمَ الْمِنَّةَ عَلَيْكَ

When He places you, in the outward, obedient to His command, and endows
you, in the inward, submission to His power... Such a thing is an immense
blessing upon you.

Outward conformity to Allāh's commands is reflected in an individual's
actions and behaviors. Obedience means to align one's outward life with
the Divine Will, manifested in following religious duties, ethical practices,
and social responsibilities. Inner submission means to develop a state of
inner acceptance and surrender to Allāh's decree, even when faced with
adversity, hardship, or challenges beyond one's control. The believer must
understand that true spiritual attainment is impossible without both the
outward conformity and the inward submission.

This inward surrender involves a submission of the heart, where the individual not only accepts but also finds peace in the fact that certain aspects of life are governed by forces beyond his understanding or control, and that one must obey the command and perform the duty whether or not they can rationalize the outcomes.

When Allāh grants the believer both the ability for outward obedience and the realization of inward submission, He has indeed given the individual the greatest gift. For true spiritual fulfillment is not achieved merely through external compliance, nor through passive acceptance alone, but through the harmony of both. When one is able to outwardly act in alignment with Divine Guidance while inwardly accepting all aspects of life, including the hardships imposed by Allāh's decree, and this represents the highest form of spiritual favour.

✻ ⊰◆⊱ ✻

(١١١)

$$ لَيْسَ كُلُّ مَنْ ثَبَتَ تَخْصِيصُهُ كَمُلَ تَخْلِيصُهُ $$

Not everyone proven (established) as His elect is perfect in his cleansing.

Being among the elite does not grant one immunity from the process of purification. Those who have been blessed with unique spiritual opportunities or given a certain position of influence, knowledge, or responsibility are not without their own shortcomings. Just because one has been chosen or favoured in some way, it does not necessarily imply that they have reached the peak of spiritual perfection.

This is the prime distinction between potential and actualization. Being chosen for a special purpose or receiving Divine Favour is an acknowledgment of one's potential, but potential alone does not guarantee that one will actualize the highest form of spiritual realization. The gift of being chosen may be a starting point, but it does not automatically equate to spiritual completion or moral superiority.

So long as the individual is in the living world, they are bound to a continual process of self-discipline, humility, and purification, a path that grows evermore challenging and demands self-awareness and vigilance. Rather, should one assume themselves to be among the favoured, they would cripple themselves of self-vigilance, and regress from that higher status. Even the sanctified are ever engaged in self-rectification. Did not the Prophet ﷺ himself, when asked about standing in nightly prayers until his feet swelled, though he was forgiven all his sins, say;

$$ ۞ أَفَلَا أَكُونُ عَبْدًا شَكُورًا ۞ $$

Should I not be a grateful servant? [62]

✻ ⊰◆⊱ ✻

---

62 متفق عليه

（۱۱۲）

لَا يَسْتَحْقِرُ الوِرْدَ إِلَّا جَهُولٌ ؛

الوَارِدُ يُوْجَدُ فِي الدَّارِ الآخِرَةِ... وَالوِرْدُ يَنْطَوِي بِانْطِوَاءِ هذِهِ الدَّارِ،

وَأَوْلَى مَا يُعْتَنَى بِهِ مَا لَا يُخْلَفُ عَنْكَ وُجُودُهُ،

الوِرْدُ... هُوَ طَالِبُهُ مِنْكَ، وَالوَارِدُ... أَنْتَ تَطْلُبُهُ مِنْهُ،

وَأَيْنَ مَا هُوَ طَالِبُهُ مِنْكَ مِمَّا هُوَ مَطْلَبُكَ مِنْهُ؟

None, but the ignorant, despise (undermine/oppose/reject) the Wird (invocation/recitation/supplication).
The Warid (blossom/bloom/inspiration from the Wird) is in the Realm of the HereAfter, while the Wird vanishes with the vanishing of this realm.
The primary (necessity) is to be concerned with what does not cease to exist.
The Wird is what He requests from you. The Warid is what you seek from Him. And where is what He requests from you and what you seek from Him?

To belittle or disregard the *Wird* is to lack an understanding of its significance in the journey towards spiritual refinement. Sustained regular effort in any spiritual or moral pursuit, however small, is the cornerstone of true inner transformation. Disciplined practice in devotion is the very foundation for aligning one's inner self with higher virtue. Only he who lacks understanding would undervalue something so essential to spiritual growth and stability.

In this world, these practices like daily prayers or rituals are bound by time, fleeting and confined to one's lifetime. However, the fruits of these practices, the subtle inspirations and spiritual gifts, are realized in the Hereafter. The emphasis here is on establishing these practices and qualities as the foundation of one's existence that they may serve as the stepping stones upon which one can transcend their mortal existence. Material gains or worldly achievements will be left behind, but the fruits borne of one's spiritual dedication endure beyond this life, carrying into the next as an everlasting part of the soul's journey.

It is human nature to seek the permanent over the impermanent. However, what one seeks is not a demanded right. It is a gift, granted in exchange of what one delivers from what is sought from them. Almighty Allāh has established the *Wird* and through it He expects daily devotion from His servant. In return, through dedication in the *Wird*, the servant aspires to receive spiritual insights as lofty gifts.

The implication is that while these gifts are dependent on Allāh's grace, devotion is a human responsibility, requiring active engagement. His Benevolence is not granted to the passive recipient, else there would be no need for the law, for the decree, or for worship entirely.

The servant seeks inspiration and enlightenment, but will receive nothing without the active effort of his devotion. Even so, the act of devotion, while meaningful and essential, pales in comparison to the immense value of the gifted inspiration, which in itself is beyond human capacity to earn through effort alone. For how can we even begin to compare what we offer to Him, and what He gifts to us? [63]

This demonstrates the true value of the *Wird* and the immense foolishness of the ignorant who belittle it.

⟨١١٣⟩

وُرُودُ الأَمْدَادِ عَلَى حَسَبِ الاِسْتِعْدَادِ، شُرُوقُ الأَنْوَارِ عَلَى حَسَبِ صَفَاءِ الأَسْرَارِ

The arrival of aid is dependent upon the readiness (aptitude/preparedness).
The rising of the lights is dependent upon the purification of the innermost.

There is a profound relationship between inner readiness of the believer and the Divine Blessings from Allāh, in that the inflow of support and enlightenment depends on one's inner state of preparedness and purity of heart. The measure of Divine Aid one receives is proportional to the individual's state of spiritual preparedness, and the heart is the vessel that receives. The more prepared and expanded it is, the more it can receive. The believer must understand here that Divine Support does not merely descend upon anyone and everyone, rather, it seeks out those who have cultivated an open and receptive heart. This means that spiritual transformation and growth depend entirely on active preparation, as Almighty Allāh declares;

﴿...إِنَّ اللَّهَ لَا يُغَيِّرُ مَا بِقَوْمٍ حَتَّىٰ يُغَيِّرُوا مَا بِأَنْفُسِهِمْ...﴾

...Indeed, Allāh does not change [the state/condition of] a people, until they change themselves... [64]

Until they prepare themselves to receive guidance, no matter the measure of guidance showered upon them, it serves no benefit, just as the medicine will not heal if the patient does not want to heal. And just as knowledge requires intellectual readiness, spiritual support requires inner attunement and discipline. Only when the heart is aligned with Divine purposes, free from worldly influences, can it become a true recipient of Divine assistance. The attainment of true knowledge and enlightenment is contingent upon the individual's readiness for intellectual and moral clarity, paired with the willingness to act as is required of them.

---

63 See Hikam 8

64 Sūrah Ra'd 13:11

(١١٤)

الْغَافِلُ إِذَا أَصْبَحَ نَظَرَ فِي مَاذَا يَفْعَلُ، وَالْعَاقِلُ إِذَا أَصْبَحَ نَظَرَ فِي مَاذَا يَفْعَلُ اللهُ بِهِ

The fool... when he wakes, looks at what he will do,
The wise... when he wakes, looks at what Allāh will do with him.

The fool sees what he does, the wise sees what Allāh is doing with him. While the wise focus on Divine purpose and intention, the heedless focus on personal plans, because, as fools, they are self-centered and occupied with individual agendas. The fool is heedless because he measures life by his own volitions, ambitions, and tasks, often detached from a higher purpose or a deeper contemplation of meaning. He is so much absorbed in material concerns and self-driven motives that he fails to recognize any context larger than himself. This is the mindset of someone preoccupied with the surface of life, an individual oriented toward immediate and tangible outcomes. His heedless perspective is shaped by the ego's priorities, lacking in self-reflection, and doing good, if at all, only when it serves those priorities.

In contrast, the wise are marked by the attribute of reflection on Divine intentions, seeking to understand what role they are meant to play in Allāh's plan. Their contemplative outlook entails humility and surrender, acknowledging that one's life is shaped not solely by personal will but by a higher, guiding force. The wise approach each day with an openness to Divine direction, perceiving life's events as expressions of Allāh's Will. They acknowledge that wisdom involves an understanding of oneself as part of a greater narrative, and through this understanding they embody the essence of *Tawakkul*, trust in Allāh.

(١١٥)

إِنَّمَا اسْتَوْحَشَ الْعُبَّادُ وَالزُّهَّادُ مِنْ كُلِّ شَيْءٍ لِغَيْبَتِهِمْ عَنِ اللهِ فِي كُلِّ شَيْءٍ،

فَلَوْ شَهِدُوهُ فِي كُلِّ شَيْءٍ لَمْ يَسْتَوْحِشُوا مِنْ شِيْءٍ

The servants and ascetics only feel lonely (alienated/deserted) from everything because of their absence (in realizing) Allāh in everything. Would they witness Him in everything, they would not feel alienated from a single thing.

The sense of estrangement or loneliness they may feel arises not due to withdrawal from the world but from a lack of awareness, an incomplete perception of the Divine Presence. Despite their devotion, these individuals feel isolated or detached because their focus is often narrowly directed toward practices and abstinence rather than a continual, expansive awareness of Allāh's manifested presence in all things.

101

True closeness to Allāh involves seeing His presence in all things, not just in specific acts of worship or ascetic practices. It entails the belief that the Divine permeates all aspects of existence. Without this awareness, worship and asceticism become practices that paradoxically lead to a sense of separation, rather than union, with the Divine. The limitation lies in perceiving spirituality as limited to specific settings or actions rather than an ongoing relationship with reality. The human being is of a spiritual origin, and his very experience of existence is a spiritual one, albeit bound to a material form. Being aware of Allāh's presence, regardless of one's physical occupation, eliminates all sense of isolation. In this state of awareness, everything in existence becomes a reminder of the Divine, transforming the world from a place of potential distraction into one of continual connection and presence.

This requires adapting the ideal of continuous mindfulness of the Divine, by cultivating a state where one sees Divinity manifest in every occurrence and situation, such that the world no longer seems a barrier to spirituality but an ever-present field of higher realization. It is to see the unity in multiplicity, the essence in the form, the meaning in the symbol, and universality in the particulars.

(١١٦)

أَمَرَكَ فِي هَذِهِ الدَّارِ بِالنَّظَرِ فِي مُكَوَّنَاتِهِ، وَسَيَكْشِفُ لَكَ فِي تِلْكَ الدَّارِ عَنْ كَمَالِ ذَاتِهِ

He has commanded you, in this realm, to reflect upon His creations, and He will unveil for you, in that realm (HereAfter), the perfection of His essence.

The rationality of this world axiomatically involves recognizing God through His creations, for the human being is veiled from seeing his Lord, first by his senses, then his imagination, then the veil of life itself. Only in the Hereafter, when all veils are removed, is he promised a direct and profound unveiling of Allāh's essence. Thus does Allāh say;

﴿...فَكَشَفْنَا عَنكَ غِطَاءَكَ فَبَصَرُكَ ٱلْيَوْمَ حَدِيدٌ﴾

... Thus We have removed from you the veil, and your gaze on this day is piercing! [65]

Allāh's command, therefore, is to reflect on His creation as means of gaining insight into who He is. For the natural world, with its beauty, complexity, and order, are but a trace of His Divine Attributes. The world is a means of spiritual training, guiding one toward a contemplative awareness of the Creator's majesty. His true nature and essence has been promised in the HereAfter, when the veils of life have been lifted.

---

[65] Sūrah Qāf 50:22

عَلِمَ مِنْكَ أَنَّكَ لَا تَصْبِرُ عَنْهُ، فَأَشْهَدَكَ مَا بَرَزَ مِنْهُ

Knowing from you that you would not be patient with Him, He made you witness what emanates from Him.

The human being, regardless of his disposition, possesses an innate spiritual yearning for connection with the Divine. He has been created for the sole purpose of acknowledging the One and True with a desire that cannot be expressed in words. It is the heart's intense love, yearning, and incapacity to bear separation, that makes it impatient to meet the Beloved. This is a longing that transcends mere intellectual desire and is woven into the very fabric of the human essence, becoming a fundamental need, a necessity for the being's survival. And He Almighty understands this fundamental need and recognizes the heart's inability to be at peace when distanced from its source, and for that reason the heart is granted glimpses of the Divine Presence through manifestations in the created world.

By our very nature, we seek fulfillment and ultimate truth above all else, which can only be realized in Divine proximity. Such a yearning is an essential part of the human condition, driving us to search for meaning and understanding beyond the material world. In response to this yearning, Allāh reveals aspects and attributes of Himself through signs, experiences, or insights, that serve as reminders and windows into His presence. By allowing the heart to perceive these manifestations, Allāh satisfies the yearning for closeness while still maintaining Divine Transcendence. These signs in the world are profound expressions of His Divine Attributes and Qualities, granting a sense of connection that reassures and fortifies the heart, as He says;

﴿ ٱلَّذِينَ ءَامَنُوا۟ وَتَطْمَئِنُّ قُلُوبُهُم بِذِكْرِ ٱللَّهِ أَلَا بِذِكْرِ ٱللَّهِ تَطْمَئِنُّ ٱلْقُلُوبُ ﴾

Those who believe and their hearts are reassured by the remembrance of Allāh. Undoubtedly, by the remembrance of Allāh are the hearts reassured. [66]

This does not propagate the idea of theophany or the idea of an anthropomorphic manifestation of a deity in an observable or tangible form. Rather it means that the traces of Divine Reality are partially revealed through symbolic representations or phenomena in the world. Reflection upon the world, upon nature, events, or even moments of spiritual clarity are reminders of the greater reality beyond. They assure the heart of a higher power upon which it can place trust and conviction, offering comfort to the being while maintaining the balance between revelation and Divine mystery.

66 Sūrah ar-Ra'd 13:28

(١١٨)

لَمَّا عَلِمَ الْحَقُّ مِنْكَ وُجُودُ الْمَلَلِ لَوَّنَ لَكَ الطَّاعَاتِ،

وَعَلِمَ مَا فِيكَ مِنْ وُجُودِ الشَّرَهِ فَحَجَرَهَا عَلَيْكَ فِي بَعْضِ الْأَوْقَاتِ،

لِيَكُونَ هَمُّكَ إِقَامَةَ الصَّلَاةِ لَا وُجُودَ الصَّلَاةِ... فَمَا كُلُّ مُصَلٍّ مُقِيمٌ

Since He knows from you the presence of lethargy (boredom/weariness in actions) He has diversified the acts of obedience for you. And He knows of the presence of gluttony (greed/desire) in you, so He has restricted it upon you in certain times. That your concern be the establishment of prayer, not the mere presence of it... For not every worshiper who prays is an establisher of prayer.

Having known the impatience of the human being, driven by his longing desire to be in the Divine Presence, Almighty Allāh is also knowing of the human limitations, particularly the tendency of breeding fatigue through repetition. To safeguard the soul from overzealousness, overwhelming passion in acts of worship, in prayer, fasting, charity, and reflection, He Allāh maintains the soul's engagement by diversifying the being's servitude, thereby protecting spiritual practice from becoming monotonous. This diversity ensures that devotion remains ever fresh and engaging, enabling the soul to continually find new depths in worship rather than falling into mechanical habit. It maintains a psychological balance and prevents obsessiveness and compulsion.

Because human psychology is dynamic, true spiritual growth requires variation. It acknowledges the natural ebb and flow of human focus and energy, ensuring that religion is complementary to sound psychological states, and that the journey to the Divine is harmonious and rhythmic, as opposed to chaotic and burdensome. As a result, religious obligations are not merely ritualistic but are carefully designed to cater to the needs of the soul and the heart, drawing it closer to the Divine Presence through multiple dimensions.

This diversification is implemented both in space and time. The physical acts and their multitudes have been regulated to consume just enough effort and energy so as not to deplete the human being. Likewise, the duration of the acts and the intervals between them have been set at precise markers so as not to consume the entirety of the human being's limited life, thereby granting periods of respite between devotion.

The 'greed' pertains to impulsiveness and overzealousness in worship, often resulting in doing things haphazardly or simply for the sake of doing it. The commandment, after all, is to *establish* prayer, not simply to pray. It is to embody it and be fully involved in it, engaging mind, heart, and soul, rather than performing it as a mere formality.

(١١٩)

الصَّلَاةُ طُهْرَةُ الْقُلُوبِ مِنْ أَدْنَاسِ الذُّنُوبِ، وَاسْتِفْتَاحٌ لِبَابِ الغُيُوبِ؛

الصَّلَاةُ مَحَلُّ المُنَاجَاةِ وَمَعْدِنُ المُصَافَاةِ؛ تَتَّسِعُ فِيهَا مَيَادِينُ الأَسْرَارِ، وَتُشْرِقُ فِيهَا شَوَارِقُ

الأَنْوَارِ، عَلِمَ مِنْكَ الضَّعْفِ فَقَلَّلَ أَعْدَادَهَا، وَعَلِمَ احْتِيَاجَكَ إِلَى فَضْلِهِ فَكَثَّرَ أَمْدَادَهَا

Prayer is a purifier of hearts from the stains of sins, and is an opening of doors to the unseen. Prayer is a sanctuary of intimate conversation and a repository of purities. Expanded therein are regions of the innermost, and arise therein the rays of lights. He knows of the weakness in you, so He lessened their number, and He knows of your dire need for His grace, so He increased their yield.

Why is there an emphasis on the establishment of prayer by being consciously involved and engaged, rather than simply fulfilling the obligation? Why is it not enough to perform the deed and have it accepted? In truth, the deed may or may not be accepted, and upon its acceptance, may or may not be rewarded. But the performance and the recompense are mere contractual obligations between the servant and his Lord. In the end, prayer is prescribed not for the Lord's benefit. It does not affect Him whether the servant prays or not. Rather it was prescribed for the servant's benefit. There is more to it than the physical motions, serving a multi-dimensional role the servant's life. In its entirety, and not just its ritualistic aspects, it not merely a contractual obligation, but an intimate and profound act that purifies, illuminates, and strengthens the spirit through Divine Grace and Mercy.

Prayer has been prescribed as a spiritual cleansing that frees the heart from the weight and residue of moral lapses. This purification is not simply a reprieve from guilt but a medicinal process that restores clarity and peace within, allowing the believer to approach life with renewed integrity and focus. For this to bear fruit, there is an inner alignment that must take place between the physical act and the conscious awareness of performing the act. Once this alignment is realized, the prayer becomes as a gateway to Divine mysteries; inviting the worshipper into realms of insight; understandings that lie beyond the material and rational world; granting access to spiritual knowledge and intuition; realizing truths that transcend ordinary perception.

As upon initiating the prayer, one shuts themselves away from the world, and enters into a sanctuary of intimate conversation with their Creator, a private dialogue that is sincere, uninterrupted, and deeply personal. This communion turns into a profound purification process, where the individual's spiritual intentions and thoughts are refined and clarified. Such intimate moments with the Divine facilitate the stripping away of superficiality and allow the individual to confront and purify their true inner state.

Within the sanctuary of prayer are expanded realms of innermost secrets and mysteries, and therein arise the shining lights that illuminate the pathways leading to the furthest horizons. This is the expansion of one's consciousness; an expansion that allows the human being to encompass greater realizations and meanings of higher truths and insights; an expansion of awareness and understanding of reality. This experience goes beyond mere rational comprehension, an intelligence that transcends logic and reason, allowing the heart to intuitively grasp aspects of Divine Wisdom that cannot be expressed in words and symbols.

The blessing of prayer upon the human being is further layered with two more blessings. Knowing human limitations, Allāh has set prayer in manageable quantities, intervals, and durations, so as not to overwhelm the believer with the physical acts. To compensate for the reduction in the quantifiable measure, He has greatly expanded the prayer's qualitative yields, ensuring that its spiritual benefits remain abundant. This consideration reflects His Divine Compassion, recognizing human frailty while providing endless opportunities for His bounty. So which of the favours of your Lord will then you deny?

◆ ──────◈⊙◼◧◼⊙◈──── ◆

(١٢٠)

مَتَى طَلَبْتَ عِوَضًا عَنْ عَمَلٍ، طُولِبْتَ بِوُجُودِ الصِّدْقِ فِيهِ وَيَكْفِي الْمُرِيدَ وِجْدَانُ السَّلَامَةِ

When you demand compensation for a deed, demanded is sincerity in the deed from you. And (in any case) it is enough for the disciple, the sense of tranquility (safety).

Demanding fair compensation for your deed is your right, by Divine Law. It was, after all, your time and effort spent in performing the deed, and it was certainly recorded that you acted in accordance with His command and did as you were commanded. However, forget not that your deed serves Him no benefit nor harm. Ultimately it is not a favour or obligation you are doing on Him. What He truly sought from you was not the deed itself, but your sincerity in it. This is the nature of spiritual sincerity and the pitfalls of seeking recompense for good actions that most become ensnared in.

The underlying message urges the believer to pursue spiritual acts not for reward or to avoid retribution, but for the purification and harmony that those acts bring. As the desire for compensation undermines the sincerity of the action itself. When one seeks reward for a deed, whether material or spiritual, they are implicitly tested on their authenticity and integrity. True sincerity in action is devoid of expectation, as genuine devotion flows from a place of humility and love for the Divine, untainted by personal gain. The believer must understand that actions motivated by anticipated rewards introduce an external element that compromises the purity of their intentions.

106

One must learn to distinguish between intrinsic and extrinsic motivations and incentives. The highest spiritual acts are those done purely for the sake of goodness or devotion, without desire for outcome or recognition. Such actions are valued for their inherent goodness and not because they are outwardly pleasing. They prevent the believer from falling into the pitfalls of pride and arrogance, which once activated, incinerate the deeds altogether, instantly diminishing their value, regardless of how praiseworthy they are.

One must further learn to distinguish between values and virtues. A deed of value is a deed with an extrinsic measure whose recompense is equal in measure. A virtuous deed is a deed with intrinsic quality, whose worth is not measured by external factors but by the deed itself and what it yields in the inward. For the one who sincerely seeks Divine Pleasure, the true reward lies in *salām*, سَلَام, inner peace and harmony, free from the disturbances of ego or material desire. Inner tranquility is the highest form of compensation, as it reflects a state of contentment and alignment with Divine Will. This state of peace is both the outcome and validation of sincere spiritual practice.

If you should find, in the performance of your deeds, a sense of peace and tranquility, then this should suffice as their reward. It means that you have attained self-sufficiency in your ethical and spiritual practices. Rather than seeking external affirmation or reward, the highest aim of your practice should be to achieve inner equanimity and contentment.

(١٢١)

لَا تَطْلُبْ عِوَضًا عَلَى عَمَلٍ لَسْتَ لَهُ فَاعِلًا،

فَكَفَى مِنَ الْجَزَاءِ لَكَ عَلَى الْعَمَلِ أَنْ كَانَ لَهُ قَابِلًا

Do not seek compensation for a deed for which you were not the doer. It suffices from compensation for you upon the deed that He accepts it.

(١٢٢)

إِذَا أَرَادَ أَنْ يُظْهِرَ فَضْلَهُ عَلَيْكَ خَلَقَ وَنَسَبَ إِلَيْكَ

When He wants to bestow His favour upon you, He creates and attributes to you.

This two aphorisms reflect a profound perspective on the nature of action, agency, and Divine Will. We are offered here a perspective that challenges us to reconsider our sense of ownership over our actions, redirecting recognition to a higher source of power.

Though an individual might physically perform an action, the ultimate originator and manifester of that action and its outcomes is Allāh Almighty. We must ultimately acknowledge that we are not the primary doers; rather, we are mere instruments through which Divine Will is manifested. This is a reframing of social agency that reminds the believer not to demand compensation or acknowledgment for the deeds he performs, as he himself is not the ultimate author of those actions. It is that he was granted the will, the ability, the capacity and potentiality, and ultimately the means to perform the deed.

Hence the Prophet himself was told;

$$\text{﴿ فَلَمْ تَقْتُلُوهُمْ وَلَٰكِنَّ ٱللَّهَ قَتَلَهُمْ وَمَا رَمَيْتَ إِذْ رَمَيْتَ وَلَٰكِنَّ ٱللَّهَ رَمَىٰ}$$
$$\text{وَلِيُبْلِيَ ٱلْمُؤْمِنِينَ مِنْهُ بَلَاءً حَسَنًا إِنَّ ٱللَّهَ سَمِيعٌ عَلِيمٌ ﴾}$$

And you did not defeat them, rather Allāh defeated them. And you did not cast (the sands) when you casted, rather it was Allāh who casted, that He might test the believers with the ultimate test. Indeed, Allāh is All-Hearing, All-Knowing.[67]

The reminder to the believers is that though the physical act is performed by creation, the manifested Will is not of creation's. All of creation is but a means to manifest Divine Will. The believer thus understands that true freedom comes when one no longer seeks credit or reward, recognizing their deeds as part of a greater, divinely orchestrated plan. Here, the reward is redefined not as some external benefit or acknowledgment but as the privilege of simply being 'chosen' or 'accepted' to carry out a particular action. Being given the means and ability to perform the deed is an honour, and enough of a reward. When you feed the hungry, you are but a means of delivering Divine Providence. When you protect the innocent, you are but a means for delivering Allāh's Protection. In a spiritual context, this acceptance by the Divine is the highest form of grace, implying that being chosen to serve or to perform any virtuous act is, in itself, a profound honour and blessing.

In that regard, the opportunity to serve is the true reward. Realizing this shifts one's entire focus from seeking results or compensation toward gratitude for the opportunity to participate in Divine Will. It decentralizes the ego from spiritual practice, urging the believers to recognize themselves as vehicles of a greater power. The true reward lies not in material or worldly gain but in the acceptance and opportunity to serve a higher purpose. The saying thus invites humility, encouraging a view of life where fulfillment arises from alignment with divine will and where the act of service itself is the ultimate gift.

Yet, His Benevolence is unbound. Despite being the One to rightly claim all credit, He favours the sincere intentions and efforts of His servants, and attributes the goodness of His manifestations to them. So again, which of the favours of your Lord can you then deny?

---

67   Sūrah al-Anfāl 8:17

(۱۲۳)

لَا نِهَايَةَ لِمَذَامِّكَ إِنْ أَرْجَعَكَ إِلَيْكَ، وَلَا تَفْرُغُ مَدَائِحُكَ إِنْ أَظْهَرَ جُودَهُ عَلَيْكَ

There is no finality to your blame should He return you back to yourself (turn you away from Him); And there is no end to your acclamation should He manifest His Munificence upon you.

We established that there is indeed no success in *any* human endeavour without Divine Guidance. Though an intelligent species, it is axiomatically impossible for the human being to reach any degree of truth and enlightenment without being shown the way. Left solely to one's own devices, free from guidance or grace, human shortcomings become inexhaustible. This is due to the innate fallibility and limitations of the self. Guidance protects the self from endless desires, weaknesses, and ego-driven behaviors that are inherently flawed. The human being, by his very nature, is imperfect, prone to error, and has an utmost reliance on something greater than oneself to rise above base tendencies.

When Divine Grace is granted, it elevates the individual to a state where the expressions of praise and gratitude could be endless. When it is taken for granted, it is withdrawn, and when it is withdrawn, the individual is turned away from the Divine Presence and returned to himself. This is the fall of disgrace, as was the fate of the accursed;

﴿ قَالَ فَٱهْبِطْ مِنْهَا فَمَا يَكُونُ لَكَ أَن تَتَكَبَّرَ فِيهَا فَٱخْرُجْ إِنَّكَ مِنَ ٱلصَّغِرِينَ ﴾

He Allāh said, "Descend from it, not is it for you to be arrogant therein! So depart! Indeed, you are among the disgraced! [68]

The believer must understand that only through humility can the self be transformed to become a vessel of appreciation that continuously recognizes and praises the gifts bestowed upon it. This is the reciprocal relationship between Allāh's grace and human gratitude: as Allāh's generosity flows forth, human praise toward Him must flow in response. However, when the human being reciprocates ingratitude, Allāh's grace is withdrawn, and the resultant is damnation, no less, and there is no end to the blame upon him, for he has caused his own destruction.

———— ⚬❈⚬ ————

(۱۲٤)

كُنْ بِأَوْصَافِ رُبُوبِيَّتِهِ مُتَعَلِّقًا، وَبِأَوْصَافِ عُبُودِيَّتِكَ مُتَحَقِّقًا

Be with the attributes of His Lordship, inseparable, and with the attributes of your servitude, ascertained.

---

68   Sūrah al-A'rāf 7:31

The heart is purposed with two innate qualities that make it whole. The first is faith, conviction, something to cling to, something absolute that will not betray the heart. The second is knowledge, understanding, something to rely on, something also absolute that will continually illuminate the heart and guide it through darkness. Deficiency in either of these, or both, will cripple the heart and plunge it into depression.

The first, that is faith, can only be established in that which is absolute, that which will assure the heart of its pursuits and their outcomes. This is the heart's devotion and servitude to The Absolute. While recompense for one's deeds to others bears the possibility of suffering treachery and betrayal, recompense from Allāh is ever assured and guaranteed. There is no shortfall in His reward, and no treachery in His oath. Ascertaining oneself in their servitude to Him bears an absolute assurance that sustains the heart and gives it firm conviction.

The second, that is knowledge, can also only be established in that which is absolute, that which will assure the heart of the truth and only the truth. This is to be found only in the Divine Attributes, as they emanate only from The Absolute. While one may seek the truth in creation, they find only traces, subjective perspectives, facts that have the tendency to change. They find only those answers that avail what creation is and the mannerism of its existence, but do not avail the deeper meanings and mysteries of existence. Such knowledge comes only from the Divine, and becoming one with His attributes grants the seeker an understanding of *why* He has created.

(١٢٥)

مَنَعَكَ أَنْ تَدَّعِيَ مَا لَيْسَ لَكَ مِمَّا لِلْمَخْلُوقِينَ،

أَفَيُبِيحُ لَكَ أَنْ تَدَّعِيَ وَصْفَهَ وَهُوَ رَبُّ الْعَالَمِينَ؟

He prohibited that you claim what is not yours from what is created.
Would He then permit you that you claim His attributes, and He is the Lord of the realms?

No part of creation can be claimed by creation. Possession of property in the conventional sense is allowed, but only temporarily. Each individual, upon their death, must relinquish said ownership to be bequeathed to the next. Absolute ownership belongs only to Allāh. This is the existential prohibition upon creation, that no part of creation, intelligent or otherwise, can claim power and dominance. If such is the case regarding creation, mere traces of His majesty, can one even conceive a claim over His attributes? Can any part of creation claim to be innately merciful, truthful, powerful, majestic, benevolent, all-knowledgeable, save that they might embody mere authorized measures of those attributes?

(١٢٦)

كَيْفَ تُخْرَقُ لَكَ الْعَوَائِدُ وَأَنْتَ لَمْ تَخْرِقْ مِنْ نَفْسِكَ الْعَوَائِدَ

How can He break for you the customs (of causality) [to show you miracles],
while you cannot (even) break yourself from the customs (of your habits)

These words emphasize the internal transformation required for the individual seeking insight and spiritual unveiling. One must question their inner readiness for witnessing extraordinary manifestations or miracles. However, one must also remember that such experiences are a privilege granted to those who attain exclusivity with Allāh. They do not appear as mere phenomena, rather, they manifest as meanings to the signs of Allāh's favour, bestowed only upon those who have transcended their attachment to worldly norms and habits. To attain spiritual insight, one must break free from the ordinary impulses, attachments, and comforts that bind the soul to the material realm, as these prevent the soul from embracing Divine intimacy.

There is caution here against yearning for the miraculous without sincere self-transformation. If one remains entangled in causality, in the routines and desires that reinforce the ego, one's inner state remains unprepared for the responsibilities that come with Divine signs or insights. Miracles, by their very nature, do not abide by cause and effect, which is to say they are not caused by phenomena. A mind that intellects within the phenomenal field is subject to the logics of cause and effect. A miracle is absolute proof that there exists a power capable of suspending causality. For this reason, it is beyond any rational capacity to grasp, for the very lens used to rationalize it is limited.

Rather, the occurrence of a miracle, beyond amazement, is not meant to be rationalized. It is meant to be appreciated, its meanings discerned, to be granted with an understanding of the Divine. This is impossible if the mind itself is ever operational only in the planar field of causality due to it being enchained by base desires. Unveilings are only granted to those whose inner landscapes are purified and detached, who seek not power or status, but closeness to God. The 'breaking of habit' referred to here is for the benefit of cultivating awareness, discipline, and self-accountability in one's daily life, such that the ego's influence diminishes, allowing the Divine light to shine through and into the heart.

The theme here is to encourage the seeker and believer to direct their efforts inward, to look for those aspects that are spiritually weakening, to dismantle their attachments to superficial routines, and thus allow themselves the freedom of true reliance on the Divine to take root. In doing so, one no longer seeks miracles for their own sake but instead embraces the subtler, inward signs of Allāh's presence, which offer a more lasting and profound intimacy than any outward miracle.

(۱۲۷)

مَا الشَّأْنُ وُجُودَ الطَّلَبِ ، إِنَّمَا الشَّأْنُ أَنْ تُرْزَقَ حُسْنَ الأَدَبِ

The issue is not the seeking. Indeed, the only issue is that you are granted provision for righteous discipline.

This can also be translated as, "The matter of concern is not in the mere existence of your seeking; rather, it is in being granted refined manners and righteous discipline to seek."

The means by which one may reach the Divine is not the chief concern. Which pathway one takes, which *madhab* or *'aqidah*, which scholar to follow, which supplications to do, all these are not the primary concern. These are all but a means, and some among them are the right means while others are arguably the wrong means. But these are not, as we say here, the primary concern. A lack of discipline, even upon the most righteous plan, is an alchemy for failure.

One must supplement their act of seeking the Divine with the mannerism in which one approaches their search. Seeking, while essential, is not the sole or even primary means of spiritual refinement. Rather, the quality of one's *'adab* أدب, their outward and inward manners, etiquettes, and discipline with Allāh is more crucial. *Adab*, in this context, does not only pertain to one's politeness and courtesy, it also extends to their consistency, perseverance, and discipline. Simply having the desire or ambition to seek the Divine in one's spiritual journey is insufficient if one's approach lacks the reverence and patience that true *adab* entails. Spiritual advancement requires not only sincerity but also a posture of humility and awareness of Allāh's majesty and mercy. In this way, *adab* becomes both the path and the goal, sustaining the journeyman however difficult the journey might be.

---

(۱۲۸)

مَا طَلَبَ لَكَ شَيْءٌ مِثْلُ الإِضْطِرَارِ، وَلَا أَسْرَعَ بِالمَوَاهِبِ إِلَيْكَ مِثْلُ الذِّلَّةِ والافْتِقَارِ

Nothing demands from you like compulsion, and nothing hastens by gifting to you such as lowliness and dire need.

Nothing brings you closer to Him like desperation, and nothing hastens His gifts to you like humility and neediness. *Idhtirār* اضطرار, desperation, is a unique and powerful force that drives one closer to Allāh. It is not merely hopelessness but an acute realization of the reality of one's utter dependence on Allāh's care and providence, a realization that He alone carries life and death in His Hands.

---

(١٢٩)

لَوْ أَنَّكَ لَا تَصِلُ إِلَيْهِ إِلَّا بَعْدَ مَحْوِ دَعَاوِيكَ وَفَنَاءِ مَسَاوِيكَ لَمْ تَصِلْ إِلَيْهِ أَبَدًا؛

وَلَكِنْ إِذَا أَرَادَ أَنْ يُوصِلَكَ إِلَيْهِ غَطَّى وَصْفَكَ بِوَصْفِهِ، وَ غَطَّى نَعْتَكَ بِنَعْتِهِ،

فَوَصَلَكَ إِلَيْهِ بِمَا مِنْهُ إِلَيْكَ، لَا بِمَا مِنْكَ إِلَيْهِ

If you do not reach Him save only after annulment (of your equals or competitions) and annihilation of your vices... You will never reach Him... Instead, when He wants you to reach Him, He conceals your attribute with His attribute, and He conceals your characteristic with His Characteristic. So you draw near to Him by what comes from Him to you. Not by what comes from you to Him.

Perfection for the human being is an abstract concept. Perfection belongs only to Allāh, and the most that the human being can do is to aspire it. If you assume to only reach Him after the complete obliteration of your spiritual competition and only after the utter annihilation of *all* your faults, you will never reach Him. It is impossible to be the best in righteousness and piety, for there will always be another to spirit ahead. It is impossible to completely annihilate the self, for the self is composite of your being, inseparable.

The idea that one must perfect their supplications and erase all faults before seeking closeness to Allāh suggests an impossible standard. If such were the case, no one could ever attain that lofty rank. The essence of one's journey toward the Divine is not about personal perfection and self-annihilation. Rather, it is an acknowledgment of our inherent imperfections and limitations in light of His perfection. By cloaking the seeker's faults with His attributes, He saves the seeker from trying to achieve a state of perfect purity on their own. Instead, He envelops them in His grace, allowing them to transcend their limitations. This is the essence of Divine love and compassion. He Almighty, Most Merciful, is well aware of human frailty and, in response, offers a path toward connection that is rooted in His own attributes rather than the seeker's efforts, such that true connection with Him comes not from the human side but as a gift from Allāh in recompense of the seeker's sincerity.

Understand then, that when He wants to bring you closer to Him, He veils your attribute, which is faulty and deficient, with *His* attribute, which is perfect and complete. And He covers your characteristic, which is flawed and weak, with *His* characteristic, which is whole and powerful. Thus, He brings you to Him through what comes from Him to you, not through what comes from you to Him. After all, whatever the human being does, no matter how sincere, will always be limited. And what can the limited offer to He who is limitless?

(۱۳۰)

لَوْلَا جَمِيلُ سَتْرِهِ لَمْ يَكُنْ عَمَلُكَ أَهْلًا لِلْقَبُولِ

Were it not for the beauty of His veil, no deed of yours would be worthy of acceptance.

His cloaking of your attribute, faulty and deficient, with *His* attribute, perfect and complete, and His covering of your characteristic, flawed and weak, with *His* characteristic, whole and powerful, is what makes your servitude worthy of His acceptance. This is the beauty of the covering and cloaking as it conceals the ugliness of one's shame and shortcoming.

Human actions, no matter how righteous or virtuous they may seem, are inherently imperfect because the human being is inherently imperfect. Every act of worship or deed carries the risk of shortcomings, insincerity, heedlessness, and attachment to praise. Left uncovered, these imperfections make our actions unworthy of Divine acceptance.

The believer must remember that our actions alone do not earn Divine favour; it is Allāh's merciful covering that grants them value. Without His covering over our faults, every deed would manifest error, and every doer would plunge into hopelessness.[69] The believer must remember that acceptance of our deeds is not a product of our personal merit and ability but rather of Divine mercy that He would deem them acceptable enough to conceal our faults in them.

———————————

(۱۳۱)

أَنْتَ إِلَى حِلْمِهِ إِذَا أَطَعْتَهُ أَحْوَجُ مِنْكَ إِلَى حِلْمِهِ إِذَا عَصَيْتَهُ

You are more in need of His forbearance when you obey Him than you are when you disobey Him.

Know then, that even in acts of obedience, the believer is in desperate need of Allāh's forbearance and mercy because of his inherent flaw and imperfection. While one might naturally think that His forbearance is primarily necessary in times of disobedience, for Him to forgive our shortcomings, we are more desperately in need of His mercy in overlooking our shortcomings when accepting our deeds. We are never fully parted from our pride, self-satisfaction, even a sense of entitlement for reward. These subtle flaws may pass unnoticed, but they quietly erode the sincerity of one's devotion, making even righteous actions susceptible to the ego's influence. Our acts of worship do not place us beyond the need for Divine grace. Rather, they heighten that need, as they also invite hidden pitfalls that may nullify all righteous intent.

———————————

69   Refer back to the first Hikam.

⟨١٣٢⟩

السَّتْرُ عَلَى قِسْمَيْنِ...

سَتْرٌ عَنِ المَعْصِيَةِ، وَسَتْرٌ فِيهَا؛

فَالعَامَّةُ يَطْلُبُونَ مِنَ اللهِ تَعَالَى السَّتْرَ فِيهَا خَشْيَةَ سُقُوطِ مَرَاتِبِهِمْ عِنْدَ الخَلْقِ،

وَالخَاصَّةُ يَطْلُبُونَ السَّتْرَ عَنْهَا خَشْيَةَ سُقُوطِهِم مِن نَظَرِ الْمَلِكِ الْحَقِّ

*Concealment is of two kinds; concealment from sinning, and concealment
in it. The commoners seek from Allāh concealment in it (the sin) for fear of
falling in rank among creation, while the elite seek concealment from it, for
fear of falling in rank in the sight of the Lord of the Truth.*

His concealment of your flaws comes in two forms. The first is a
concealment that protects one from sinning. The second is a concealment
in the sin itself, having committed it.

As for the first, this is a blessing that prevents one from acting sinfully
falling into error. The righteous desperately seek this type of covering,
while others tend to remain heedless of it. As for the second, this is a
covering within the sin itself, where Allāh conceals a person's misdeeds
from others. It prevents public shame but does not address the root of the
spiritual problem, and is thus the one most feared by the righteous. For
though it may protect one from falling in the eyes of the people, nothing
of it is concealed from Allāh's sights, and they fear most falling in the eyes
of their Lord. Those who often seek this second type of covering, hope
that their sins remain hidden to preserve their status or repute among
others, thus defining their focus on worldly concerns rather than their
relationship with Allāh.

The true concern for the righteous is not the opinions of others but
their standing before Allāh. For them, the real danger lies in the potential
estrangement from His grace that sin represents. Their fear is rooted in
a profound reverence for Allāh's gaze upon them and a sincere desire to
remain spiritually close to Him.

⟨١٣٣⟩

مَنْ أَكْرَمَكَ إِنَّمَا أَكْرَمَ فِيكَ جَمِيلَ سَتْرِهِ،

فَالْحَمْدُ لِمَنْ سَتَرَكَ لَيْسَ الْحَمْدُ لِمَنْ أَكْرَمَكَ وَشَكَرَكَ

*Whoever honoured you only honoured the beauty of His (Allāh's) concealment.
Thus, praise belongs to the One who concealed you, not to the one who honoured
and thanked you.*

115

Those who bestow honour upon others do so upon judgment of what is outwardly manifest. They see the material achievements of the individual, and they honour the individual accordingly. But the manifestation of good outcomes from one's deeds manifest only because of the concealment of their flaws. When others see goodness in us and show appreciation, it is not merely our own virtues they perceive, but rather the result of Allāh concealing our faults and presenting our better qualities. Hence, any honour or respect received from others is, in reality, a reflection of His gracious covering over our flaws and limitations.

The believer must be vigilant. Rather than feel pride or self-satisfaction when others honour him, he must remember that the true source of any respect is Allāh's covering over him. This must enable him to avoid becoming attached to people's praise or developing a sense of entitlement, and redirect his gratitude from those who praise and honour him, to Almighty Allāh who made such respect possible.

﴿١٣٤﴾

مَا صَحِبَكَ إِلَّا مَنْ صَحِبَكَ وَهُوَ بِعَيْبِكَ عَلِيمٌ، وَلَيْسَ ذَلِكَ إِلَّا مَوْلَاكَ الْكَرِيمُ،
خَيْرُ مَن تَصْحَبُ مَن يَطْلُبُكَ لَكَ لَا لِشَيْءٍ يَعُودُ مِنْكَ إِلَيْهِ

No one (truly) accompanies you save the one who accompanies you knowing your flaws, and none can be such, save your Noble Master. The best companion is one who seeks you for you, not for anything that returns from you to him.

Human relations are deeply sophisticated. No one truly knows who another is until they have known their innermost secrets, their concealed faults and flaws. In that sense, no one can ever truly know other than themselves, in what they present and what they conceal. Only He who is All-Knowing can encompass who each individual is. Thus, only He can truly accompany the individual, as He says;

﴿ ... وَأَعْلَمُ مَا تُبْدُونَ وَمَا كُنتُمْ تَكْتُمُونَ ﴾

... and I know what you reveal [make apparent of yourselves] and what you conceal [of your secrets] [70]

Meaning, He is well aware of all the good that we endeavour to present, and of all the faults that we strive to keep hidden of ourselves. Indeed, it is He alone who, from His mercy, chooses not to unveil our shortcomings and flaws, who keeps concealed our secrets, who is each individual's most Trusted Confidant, and loves us not for our deeds but for the sincerity in our hearts.

---

70   Sūrah al-Baqarah 2:33

(١٣٥)

لَوْ أَشْرَقَ لَكَ نُورُ الْيَقِينِ لَرَأَيْتَ الآخِرَةَ أَقْرَبَ إِلَيْكَ مِنْ أَنْ تَرْحَلَ إِلَيْهَا وَلَرَأَيْتَ مَحَاسِنَ الدُّنْيَا وَقَدْ ظَهَرَتْ كِسْفَةُ الْفَنَاءِ عَلَيْهَا

If the light of certainty shone upon you, you would see the Hereafter closer to you than your journey towards it. And you would see the beauty of the world as the eclipse of annihilation manifests upon it.

The beauty of this world, this life, albeit praiseworthy, is marked with signs of vanishing, and only the fool would deny and remain heedless of such a reality. Their denial and heedlessness is caused by doubt and uncertainty, a love for the worldly and a hatred for death, and were the light of certainty to be shined upon them, they would indeed see that other reality loom closer to them than their temporal and inevitable journey towards it.

When one truly attains this light of certainty, the reality of the Hereafter, the eternal life beyond this world, becomes vividly present. It is no longer a distant destination but an imminent truth, nearer than the steps of the journey. It makes one less consumed by worldly distractions and more focused on preparing for the inevitable return to Allāh. This light is so powerful, that when it shines upon the heart, all the overwhelming attractions of the world upon the soul, all its pleasures, achievements, and status, all appear as transitory, unveiling the marks of their impermanence.

Though the beauty of this world can still be appreciated, he who possesses certainty perceives it as a passing phase, a bridge to be crossed, rather than an ultimate reality or a place of permanent abode. This realization does not demand the rejection of the world but rather the awareness that it is inherently fleeting, which liberates the seeker from attachment and cultivates detachment from worldly desires. Such an individual finds beauty in creation while remembering its purpose as a signpost toward the Creator.

Certainty, *yaqīn* يقين, is arguably the highest level of spiritual insight that purifies the heart by clarifying what is real from what is illusory, or merely 'realistic'. It calms the heart and makes it steadfast in its desire for the eternal felicity of the HereAfter above and beyond the transient comforts of the world. It is with this light of certainty that one's actions are purified and aligned with the pursuit of the eternal rather than the temporary. This is an encouragement to the seeker, to strive toward the cultivation of this inner light, and transform their perspectives of both the world and the Hereafter, thereby allowing themselves to be guided toward living a life rooted in true purpose and spiritual vision.

(١٣٦)

$$مَا حَجَبَكَ عَنِ اللهِ وُجُودُ مَوْجُودٍ مَعَهُ ، إِذْ لَا شَيْءَ مَعَهُ،$$

$$وَلَكِنْ حَجَبَكَ عَنْهُ وَهُمْ وُجُودِ شَيْءٍ مَعَهُ$$

What veils you from Allāh is not the existence of another being alongside Him, for there is no thing alongside Him. Rather, what veils you from Him is the illusion of another thing alongside Him.

The notion of plurality and diversity in the Divine is an illusory notion. It has no basis in truth, no proof nor evidence existent, rational or otherwise. This illusion, that most are served with, is an artificial construct, designed to propagate the idea that felicity and contentment can be found in the world of created entities. There is nothing in existence besides Allāh, in power or majesty, that can possibly be confounded for Him, or that might veil us from recognizing Him as the One and True. He *is* the ultimate reality, the One whose existence is absolute and singular. Consequently, there is no real 'veil' between the Creator and His creation, and what actually prevents an individual from experiencing Allāh's presence is only an illusion of separation, a mistaken perception that there are independent entities or desires that exist apart from Him, or that can be called upon to facilitate or arbitrate a closeness to Him. If the individual believes that anything other than Allāh has intrinsic power or worth, when in reality, no such comparison exists, both the belief and the comparison made are illusory. Such an illusion, self-imposed, becomes the veil that distances the individual from His Presence.

(١٣٧)

$$لَوْلَا ظُهُورُهُ فِي المُكَوَّنَاتِ مَا وَقَعَ عَلَيْهَا وُجُودُ إِبْصَارٍ،$$

$$وَلَوْ ظَهَرَتْ صِفَاتُهُ اضْمَحَلَّتْ مُكَوَّنَاتُهُ$$

Were it not for His manifestation among creation, there would be no occurrence of vision upon them, and yet if His attributes manifested, His creation would be obliterated.

(١٣٨)

$$أَظْهَرَ كُلَّ شَيْءٍ لِأَنَّهُ البَاطِنُ، وَطَوَى وُجُودَ كُلِّ شَيْءٍ لِأَنَّهُ الظَّاهِرُ$$

He made everything manifest because He is the Concealed, and He folded the existence of everything because He is the Manifest.

118

Perception is a Divine gift, and its primus is to perceive Divine Manifestation. Despite this, what we perceive in creation is but a trace of the True, a Sign of His Majesty. Were His attributes to manifest in their true and original forms, creation itself would vanish and become imperceivable. For how can one look upon other than Him alongside Him? It is only His presence in creation that makes it perceivable to us, for every created thing serves as a sign of His existence, and without His Light and Will, there would be nothing for us to perceive. The concealment of His essence is necessary because the complete unveiling of His attributes would overwhelm creation such that it could not exist independently. Creation is not without deliberate measure of manifestation. It is carefully balanced so that it is visible to us, yet it remains a veil that protects us from being consumed by the limitless intensity of His reality.

(۱۳۹)

أَبَاحَ لَكَ أَنْ تَنْظُرَ مَا فِي الْمُكَوَّنَاتِ وَمَا أَذِنَ لَكَ أَنْ تَقِفَ مَعَ ذَوَاتِ الْمُكَوَّنَاتِ

﴿ قُلِ انْظُرُوا مَاذَا فِي السَّمَوَٰتِ وَالْأَرْضِ... ﴾

فَتَحَ لَكَ بَابَ الْإِفْهَامِ وَلَمْ يَقُلْ انْظُرُوا السَّمَوَاتِ؛ لِئَلَّا يَدُلَّكَ عَلَى وُجُودِ الْأَجْرَامِ

He allowed you to observe what is within the creation, but He did not permit you to stand (in likeness) with the entities of the creation.
"Say, 'Gaze upon what is in the heavens and the earth...'"[71]
He opened for you the door of understanding and did not say, 'Look at the heavens,' in that it lead you (only) to the existence of celestial bodies.

He did not give you the same rank, the same composition, the same powers and attributes, as He has given other entities in creation. Permission here means that by making you a distinct entity that can reason and judge, He has granted you the ability to observe and reflect upon the rest of creation by opening for you the doors to understanding, so that by saying to you *'Gaze upon the Heavens'* and the rest of creation, He has not limited you to only *looking* at the physical bodies and shells of creation, but to *see* and discern from them their essences. The emphasis is to *see* what is *in* the heavens and the earth, to discern unity from their multitudes, and not simply to *look* at the them. For it is not enough to be human and merely look and marvel upon creation without discerning their realities and to Whom those realities owe their existence. Knowledge is not the knowing of what things are and how they exist. It is to know why they are as they are, why they manifest a certain mannerism of being, and why they exist. Why was all this created?

71   Sūrah Yūnus 10:101

(١٤٠)

الأَكْوَانُ ثَابِتَةٌ بِإِثْبَاتِهِ، وَمَمْحُوَّةٌ بِأَحَدِيَّةِ ذَاتِه

The worlds are established by His affirmation, and yet they are obliterated by the singularity of His essence.

The worlds *akwān* أكوان (singular, *kawn* كون), are originated upon His *word*, an affirmative command, *kun* كن, Be. Then they are kept existent upon that affirmation, *fayakūn* فيكون, Become. All of existence and everything existent within is entirely dependent upon Allāh's will and continuous support. Nothing in creation possesses intrinsic reality; rather, it is His will alone that sustains and upholds reality, in that there *is* a reality solely because *He* is Real. Without this affirmation of 'Be' reality would simply cease *to be*.

No part of created existence has a singular reality. Each thing is either composite in and of itself, or a composite of other multitudes. An absolute singular entity does not exist in this created reality. Reality *is* because of its innate multiplicity, particularity, and diversity. It is the resultant outcome of the singular affirmation of Be, *kun* كن, from which comes the multiples of becoming *fayakūn* فيكون.

As such, all of created reality must necessarily exist in multiplicity. The most ideal state of existence is a unified state, and yet no such state among creation can exist. The universe must, by its very nature, contain multiplicity. In that regard, the presence of a singular unity obliterates all multiplicity, for that unity is absolute, and the absolute triumphs all else. In the face of Allāh's absolute oneness, *ahadiyya* أحدية, creation's apparent existence fades into insignificance. His oneness is so complete and singular that all multiplicity and separateness are illusions when measured against His transcendent reality. The created world, though real in a physical sense, is 'obliterated' in that it holds no independent existence apart from Allāh. For the seeker, this is an invitation to understand that while creation exists, it is not an end in itself but rather a means of perceiving and understanding the Ultimate Reality of the Divine.

This is among the deeper dimensions and meanings of;

﴿ ٱللَّهُ لَآ إِلَٰهَ إِلَّا هُوَ ٱلْحَىُّ ٱلْقَيُّومُ... ﴾

Allāh! There is no god save He, the Ever-Living, Self-Sustaining...[72]

It is to affirm that there was none, there is none, and there never will be, save for Him, Allāh, the Absolute One. When the individual truly realizes this, deep within their heart, they understand that nothing in this world, in this life, in all of reality, truly demands their conscious attention and awareness, save the Divine.

---

72 Sūrah al-Baqarah 2:255

(١٤١)

النَّاسُ يَمْدَحُونَكَ بِمَا يَظُنُّونَ فِيكَ، فَكُنْ أَنْتَ ذَامًّا لِنَفْسِكَ بِمَا تَعْلَمُهُ مِنْهَا

People praise you for what they assume about you, so be critical of your 'self'
for what you know about it.

(١٤٢)

الْمُؤْمِنُ إِذَا مُدِحَ اسْتَحْيَا مِنَ اللهِ تَعَالَى أَنْ يُثْنَى عَلَيْهِ بِوَصْفٍ لَا يَشْهَدُهُ مِنْ نَفْسِهِ

The believer, when he is praised, feels shy before Allāh that he might be lauded
with a quality which he does not witness of himself.

(١٤٣)

أَجْهَلُ النَّاسِ مَنْ تَرَكَ يَقِينَ مَا عِنْدَهُ لِظَنِّ مَا عِنْدَ النَّاسِ

The most ignorant of mankind is one who abandons the certainty of what is
with him, for the mere assumptions of other people.

(١٤٤)

إِذَا أَطْلَقَ الثَّنَاءَ عَلَيْكَ وَلَسْتَ بِأَهْلٍ فَأَثْنِ عَلَيْهِ بِمَا هُوَ أَهْلُهُ

When praise is bestowed upon you, though you are not worthy, praise Him
(Allāh) with what He is worthy.

Often, what is perceived of a person, and what is true of them are disparate. The human being is critical of what he presents to his fellow human beings, yet seldom critical of what he presents to himself, and more often in disregard of what might otherwise be deemed blameworthy. One may be praised or admired by the assumption of their virtues, strengths, or purity that may or may not align with their true nature. Such praise can be uplifting to one's self esteem, but poses grave danger by potentially inflating the ego or leading to self-complacency.

It is thus important to remain grounded by focusing on self-knowledge rather than external validation, for such validation is only partially true, if at all, of one's true inhibitions. Self-knowledge means to hold oneself accountable, to acknowledge shortcomings, and maintain humility even in the face of deserving praise. Herein lay the dangers of forsaking one's own inner truth and convictions in favour of the opinions, assumptions, or values of others. To abandon what is certain within oneself for the uncertain judgments and fleeting trends of others is a sign of profound ignorance. One risks being pulled into endless, conflicting directions, losing clarity and purpose along the way.

This wandering from one's inner truth, shifting focus from self-criticism and rectification, to self-praise by pursuing the opinions of others, erodes the heart's peace. The believer, in this regard, is truthful and honest. He does not conceal his true self from himself, and most importantly from Allāh. When he is praised, he is humble and gracious, but he is also shy before Allāh, fearful that he might be praised for a quality he does not truly possess.

How then does one protect themselves from falling into such a paradox, where praise may seem deserving yet not true to the individual's attributes that are being praised?

The believer understands that though it was by their doing that the praiseworthy deed was manifest, the ability, the potentiality, the opportunity, and the means to perform the deed all came from Allāh.[73] In staying true to this contingency, the believer carries forward all praise received and entrusts it, rightfully so, to the Divine. In doing so, he protects himself from his unworthiness, and gives Allāh the due right of all worthiness.

(١٤٥)

الزُّهَّادُ إِذَا مُدِحُوا... انْقَبَضُوا، لِشُهُودِهِمُ الثَّنَاءَ مِنَ الْخَلْقِ ،

وَالْعَارِفُونَ إِذَا مُدِحُوا... انْبَسَطُوا، لِشُهُودِهِمْ ذَلِكَ مِنَ الْمَلِكِ الْحَقِّ

The ascetics, when praised, contract due to their witnessing the praise from creation. And the knowers, when praised, expand due to their witnessing that (as being a blessing) from the True King.

The distinction is first made between an ascetic, *zāhid* زاهد, and a knower, *'ārif* عارف. Not every knower is an ascetic and not every ascetic is a knower. The ascetic is one who withdraws, physically, from material attachments and social indulgences, to isolate and devote himself entirely to worship. The knower is one who understands his Creator and the Ordinance upon him. Though he may opt for isolation, the knowledge granted to him removes the necessity of being an ascetic.

Both, when given praise, react differently. The ascetic, due to his withdrawal from the norms of praise and acclaim, finds little comfort when it comes. It causes them to withdraw further, frightful of its corruptive capabilities. The knower, due to the knowledge granted to him, acts in accordance to the understanding of الحمد لله رب العالمين, that *All* praise is due unto Allāh, Lord of the Worlds. They are not concerned for the corruptibility of praise unto them, for they knowingly forward all praise received to Allāh, without hesitation.

---

73 See Hikam 74 in connection with 110

(١٤٦)

مَتَى كُنْتَ إِذَا أُعْطِيْتَ بَسَطَكَ الْعَطَاءُ، وَإِذَا مُنِعْتَ قَبَضَكَ الْمَنْعُ،

فَاسْتَدِلَّ بِذَلِكَ عَلَى ثُبُوْتِ طُفُوْلِيَّتِكَ، وَعَدَمِ صِدْقِكَ فِيْ عُبُوْدِيَّتِكَ

When you are given, your generosity expands, and when you are denied, your
grasp tightens. Take that as evidence of your immaturity and lack of sincerity
in your servitude.

The nature of the soul is resonance, an oscillation between expansion
and contraction. Its delight is amplified in a state of expansion, such as
the long draw of fresh breath, invigorating and exhilarating that it feels
compelled to share such experiences with others. In a state of contraction,
its delight is withdrawn. It realizes how limited and precious its possession
is, and it tightens its grasp. When you are given, you feel expanded by the
gift, an incredible sense of exhilaration that might even compel you to
extend and share your delight with others. When you are denied, you feel
constrained by the denial, so much so that you would create protective
barriers around you lest someone take what little you think you have.

This is a profound sign of spiritual immaturity,[74] that one's emotional
state is overly influenced by material circumstances, feeling joy when
receiving blessings, and distress when deprived. This spiritual 'childishness,'
is where one's servitude to Allāh is conditional, dependent upon the flow
of worldly favours. Rather, true servanthood is not about reaching for the
Divine solely in times of ease but also maintaining steadfastness, patience,
and gratitude during times of hardship.

---

(١٤٧)

إِذَا وَقَعَ مِنْكَ ذَنْبٌ فَلاَ يَكُنْ سَبَبًا لِيَأْسِكَ مِنْ حُصُوْلِ الإِسْتِقَامَةِ مَعَ رَبِّكَ،

فَقَدْ يَكُوْنُ ذَلِكَ آخِرَ ذَنْبٍ قُدِّرَ عَلَيْكَ

Should there occur a sin from you, let it not be a cause for despair of attaining
uprightness with your Lord, for that may be the last sin decreed upon you.

The believer, should he fall into sin, must tread with care that they do
not also fall into despair. A single act of wrongdoing should not make one
lose hope in reaching a state of spiritual uprightness. Instead of allowing
a sin to drive one away from Allāh in shame or despondency, the believer
should use it as a means to increase their resolve for repentance and
reform, as each instance of self-correction brings one closer to a more
refined and upright state.

74 I strongly recommend Imām al-Ghazzālī's *'Ayyuhal Walad'*

Sin is not an irreversible breach. Rather, it is a test of one's dedication and sincerity in servanthood. Through each act of repentance, the heart grows stronger in humility. Herein lies a Divine Compassion for human fallibility. He *wants* to forgive, as through forgiveness, the bond between Him and His servant grows ever stronger. He *wants* you to admit fault, to turn to Him in sincerity and humility, and ask His guidance. For guidance is the greatest blessing awarded in this life, and He *wants* to award it to His most humble and appreciating servants. Not to those who would despair and lose hope. For how wretched is the one who loses hope knowing that the Lord of the Worlds is ever eager and ready to uplift?

(١٤٨)

إِذَا أَرَدْتَ أَنْ يَفْتَحَ لَكَ بَابَ الرَّجَاءِ فَاشْهَدْ مَا مِنْهُ إِلَيْكَ،

وَإِذَا أَرَدْتَ أَنْ يَفْتَحَ لَكَ بَابَ الْخَوْفِ فَاشْهَدْ مَا مِنْكَ إِلَيْهِ

If you want the door of hope to open for you, witness what comes from Him to you. And if you want the door of fear to open for you, witness what goes from you to Him.

There is a delicate balance between hope and fear, and both are essential qualities on the spiritual path. In one aspect, there is a cultivation of hope by reflecting on all that comes from Allāh, and all that is further promised. When one contemplates the boundless gifts of mercy and compassion, hope naturally takes root. It inspires confidence and motivates the seeker to continue striving, knowing that Allāh's kindness is always near. In another aspect, there is a cultivation of a healthy sense of fear by observing the flaws and mistakes within oneself that reveal the extent to which one falls short of fully receiving honour from Allāh. This recognition is not meant to lead to despair but to inspire humility and accountability. By seeing the gap between human imperfection and the Divine standard, the seeker develops an awareness of their actions and their need for mercy and guidance.

The balance between hope and fear is vital and must be diligently observed. That hope should not overtake fear, lest it result in laxity and a loss of vigilance, false sense of success, or the assumption that 'all will be well' regardless of the outcomes. And fear should not overtake hope, lest it result in overwhelming anxiety and a loss of trust, increased hesitation, or the assumption that one is 'not worthy of worship' leading them to abandonment and undeserving self-condemnation. Balancing oneself between the two prevents the pitfalls of arrogance and urges constant self-improvement. It reminds one that they are not alone upon the journey, that Allāh is always with them, so long as they trust and revere Him.

(١٤٩)

رُبَّمَا أَفَادَكَ فِي لَيْلِ القَبْضِ مَا لَمْ تَسْتَفِدْهُ فِي إِشْرَاقِ نَهَارِ البَسْطِ

﴿ ...لَا تَدْرُونَ أَيُّهُمْ أَقْرَبُ لَكُمْ نَفْعًا... ﴾

It may be that what benefited you during the night of restraint, you did not benefit from during the daylight brightness of expansion...
"Not do you know which is closer to you in benefit" [74]

There are symbolic aspects here, where the night represents periods of darkness, periods of sadness and suffering, periods of intense constriction, and where the day represents periods of joy, abundance, and expansion. The human being is inseparable from either of them, as such is the nature of the worldly life.

Periods of expansion have positive effects on one's psychology. They fuel ambition and passion, they grant clarity of mind and room to think, thereby enabling one to seek the bounty of Allāh. However, they do not always yield benefit, particularly upon the spiritual path, and what one gains in the constriction of night is more beneficial than what they gain in the expansion and radiance of day. For rather than expand one's thoughts in the outward, the constriction forces them to direct their thoughts inward. This is the true yield of trials and tribulations, of sorrow and suffering.

There is always hidden wisdom in life's trials, particularly in periods of spiritual constraint when the heart feels weighed, isolated, or distant from and sense of joy. These are periods of darkness, and in these moments, though they may feel like constricting 'nights,' they contain invaluable benefits. For such are the moments in which humility, sincerity, and resilience truly thrive, that are not as easily cultivated in times of ease and abundance. Though such states carry with them a sense of fear, they force the seeker to confront their own limitations and deepen their reliance on Allāh. They also encourage the seeker of the rising sun of hope with the coming dawn, a period of 'daylight,' of ease, joy, and energy.

Though difficult, periods of constraint reveal aspects of ourselves that need growth or healing. They reveal the innate weaknesses that one is often heedless of in their expansive states. They humble the heart, removing any false sense of self-sufficiency and reminding the believer that strength lies in turning to Allāh, even when His presence feels distant. It is an opportunity to cultivate inner resilience and humility, and to prepare oneself to handle ease and blessing with a greater sense of gratitude and balance. The wisdom gained from such times is more precious than what is learned from books. It teaches the soul the true meaning of purpose and existence in this world.

---

74 Sūrah an-Nisā'a 4:11

(١٥٠)

مَطَالِعُ الأَنْوَارِ القُلُوبُ وَالأَسْرَارُ

The sources of lights are the hearts and the secrets.

(١٥١)

نُورٌ مُسْتَوْدَعٌ فِي القُلُوبِ... مَدَدُهُ مِنَ النُّورِ الوَارِدِ مِنْ خَزَائِنِ الغُيُوبِ

Light entrusted in the hearts... its extension is from the light of inspiration from the treasures of the unseen.

(١٥٢)

نُورٌ يَكْشِفُ لَكَ بِهِ عَنْ آثَارِهِ، وَنُورٌ يَكْشِفُ لَكَ بِهِ عَنْ أَوْصَافِهِ

There is a light by which He unveils for you His traces, and a light by which He unveils for you His attributes.

(١٥٣)

رُبَّمَا وَقَفَتِ القُلُوبُ مَعَ الأَنْوَارِ... كَمَا حُجِبَتِ النُّفُوسُ بِكَثَائِفِ الأَغْيَارِ

The hearts may cease with the lights... just as the selves are covered by veils of otherness.

The inroads to the soul are in the senses, and the inroads to the heart are in the soul. Much of what comes to the Heart comes through the soul, and is pure if the soul is pure, corrupt if the soul is corrupt. Along this passage, the lights destined for the heart and the secrets are often prevented from reaching it due to the soul being transfixed on the otherness of creation.

The hearts and inner secrets are the rising points of lights, meaning that spiritual illumination starts from within. These lights are not simple intellectual understandings but inspirations that descend from the 'hidden treasures' of the unseen realm. They are sacred, granted from beyond worldly knowledge, and they illuminate true reality from within. Among them is a light placed in the heart by which it is enlivened, which is sustained by another light that comes from the hidden mysteries of the Divine. Then there is a light through which He unveils His traces for you, which makes known what is unknown and reveals what is concealed. And finally, there is a light through which He unveils His attributes for you, through which the heart realizes His manifestation in reality. These three lights provide for the being an understanding of himself, an understanding of reality, and an understanding of the Creator.

These are the three dimensions of true knowledge; to know oneself and their place in reality, to know reality and the places of all things in reality, and to know Allāh and the relationship between Him and all that He creates.

The only barrier to these three dimensions of higher knowledge is the self. The lights are prevented from penetrating the heart when the soul is veiled by the densities of otherness. And this may delude the heart into forgetting that these lights are but the means and not the ends in themselves. Just as worldly distractions can veil and entrap the soul, spiritual experiences can transfix the heart as it witnesses their marvels.

For this reason, He Allāh veils the lights, thus explained...

(١٥٤)

سَتَرَ أَنْوَارَ السَّرَائِرِ بِكَثَائِفِ الظَّوَاهِرِ؛ إِجْلَالًا لَهَا أَنْ تُبْتَذَلَ بِوُجُودِ الإِظْهَارِ وَأَنْ يُنَادَى عَلَيْهَا بِلِسَانِ الاِشْتِهَارِ

He concealed the lights of secrets with veils of outward appearances; out of reverence for them lest they are degraded with the presence of the apparent, and are invoked by the tongue (language) of fame.

The lights of the inner secrets are concealed by the veils of outward appearances, out of reverence for them, to protected them from being cheapened by apparent and literal derivations, and from being proclaimed by tongues of fame. They are not spoken of far and wide, their meanings are not plain and apparent, for if they were so, they would lose their value and purpose. These lights are reserved for the elite, those who would strive and struggle toward them. They are too previous to be left in the open for all to indulge in.

This concealment is not an act of denial but a protective grace. The wisdom here emphasizes that the sanctity and profound beauty of spiritual truths are preserved when hidden from the casual gaze. Just as rare treasures are guarded from public view to protect their value, so too are these inner lights shielded, allowing the heart to experience and nurture its insights in a private communion with Allāh rather than exposing them to superficial interpretation or unworthy scrutiny.

Outward simplicity or even ordinary behavior might be used to mask profound inner awareness. This balance maintains the purity of spiritual knowledge, as genuine insights are not meant for display. When the heart is illuminated by these Divine Lights, they remain secret between the seeker and Allāh. In doing so, the seeker is saved from falling into vanity and pride, knowing that true wisdom is found in quiet humility and not in the pursuit of recognition or fame.

(١٥٥)

سُبْحَانَ مَنْ لَمْ يَجْعَلِ الدَّلِيلَ عَلَى أَوْلِيَائِهِ إِلَّا مِنْ حَيْثُ الدَّلِيلُ عَلَيْهِ

وَلَمْ يُوصِلْ إِلَيْهِمْ إِلَّا مَنْ أَرَادَ أَنْ يُوصِلَهُ إِلَيْهِ

*Glory be to Him who did not establish proof for His select except where the
evidence is for Him, and did not convey it to them except for those who desired
to convey it to Him.*

(١٥٦)

رُبَّمَا أَطْلَعَكَ عَلَى غَيْبِ مَلَكُوتِهِ، وَحَجَبَ عَنْكَ الِاسْتِشْرَافَ عَلَى أَسْرَارِ العِبَادِ

*He may have revealed to you the unseen of His dominion, and veiled from you
the probing into the secrets of His servants.*

(١٥٧)

مَنِ اطَّلَعَ عَلَى أَسْرَارِ العِبَادِ وَلَمْ يَتَخَلَّقْ بِالرَّحْمَةِ الإِلَهِيَّةِ...

كَانَ اطِّلَاعُهُ فِتْنَةً عَلَيْهِ وَسَبَبًا لِجَرِّ الْوَبَالِ إِلَيْهِ

*Whoever probes into the secrets of the servants and does not embody Divine
Mercy, his probing becomes a temptation for him and a cause for drawing
calamity towards him.*

The true *awliyā'* أولياء are not apparent. They are concealed in plain
sight. They do not carry the marks and signs accustomed to saints. Their
acts and manifestations are not for the public, rather they are for Allāh,
and He does not need signs to know them. This is His Glory, that He has
concealed them among His servants, and makes them known only when
they are deemed to serve as means, for others, to Him.

These individuals, whose lives are enriched by spiritual closeness to
Allāh, are not necessarily recognized by visible signs or markers; rather,
their proof lies in the same subtlety by which Allāh Himself is known.
This means that just as His essence is hidden from plain sight and only
perceivable to those who seek sincerely, His *awliyā'* are also hidden under
the veil of ordinary appearances. They are recognized not by outward
indicators but by an inner connection that resonates only with those
whose hearts are attuned to a higher reality.

The wisdom is in guiding only specific individuals to recognize and
benefit from the *awliyā'*. This recognition is not a matter of chance but a
part of Allāh's guidance, reserved for those whom He wills to bring close.
Those who are meant to find and learn from the *awliyā'* will do so because
Allāh has opened their hearts and granted them insight to finding them.

This is part of the mannerisms of spiritual seeking and guidance. While people often search for outward signs of righteousness, only those who are sincere are directed to Allāh's *awliyā'* through an inwardly inspired understanding. This mystery keeps the relationship with the *awliyā'* pure and untouched by worldly measures of fame or status.

Such is the protection placed upon the *awliyā'* that He Allāh may choose to unveil all the mysteries of creation and yet keep the *awliyā'* concealed. The seeker may be granted insight into the vast mysteries of Allāh's dominion, encompassing all the knowledge of creation, the signs, and the cosmic order, and yet, even with this spiritual privilege, they remain veiled from knowing the hidden states and secrets of Allāh's true servants. This is the sanctity of each individual's inner life, protected from the gazes of others.

To be given awareness of someone else's hidden states or struggles is, in essence, a trust that calls for profound compassion and mercy. One who has not realized mercy in their heart, their probing turns upon themselves, becoming temptation and driving them into self-destruction. They become obsessed with unraveling the secrets of others, an impossible feat given that they are attempting to breach Divine Protection, and their obsessions consume them.

---

(١٥٨)

حَظُّ النَّفْسِ فِي الْمَعْصِيَةِ ظَاهِرٌ جَلِيٌّ، وَحَظُّهَا فِي الطَّاعَةِ بَاطِنٌ خَفِيٌّ، وَمُدَاوَاةُ مَا يَخْفَى صَعْبٌ عِلَاجُهُ

The share of the self in disobedience is apparent and clear, while its share in obedience is hidden and subtle. Treating what is hidden is difficult to remedy.

When one commits a sin, it is often evident that the act originates from the volitions of the self. Sin is defined as 'missing the mark' of good intent, where the heart intends righteous action, and executes it for a goodly outcome, but the projection of the intent is deviated from the path thus becoming a sin. The entity that causes the deviation is the ego, and hence sin typically manifests in immediate, self-centered, or worldly gains, all of which serve the volitions of the ego. However, in acts of worship or obedience, the ego's involvement can be subtler and harder to detect. Though the intention is sincere, the act itself may not be entirely free from the motives of the self. The believer may, for instance, perform a righteous act outwardly but harbor hidden motivations, such as pride, self-satisfaction, or the desire for praise. The challenge lies in recognizing that even obedience can be tainted by the ego's hidden influence, and such hidden influences are most difficult to remedy.

---

(١٥٩)

رُبَّمَا دَخَلَ الرِّيَاءُ عَلَيْكَ مِنْ حَيْثُ لَا يَنْظُرُ الْخَلْقُ إِلَيْكَ

Showing off may enter upon you from where creation does not see you.

(١٦٠)

اسْتِشْرَافُكَ أَنْ يَعْلَمَ الْخَلْقُ بِخُصُوصِيَّتِكَ دَلِيلٌ عَلَى عَدَمِ صِدْقِكَ فِي عُبُودِيَّتِكَ

Your desire for creation to know your special qualities is evidence of the lack of sincerity in your servitude.

(١٦١)

غَيِّبْ نَظَرَ الْخَلْقِ إِلَيْكَ بِنَظَرِ اللهِ إِلَيْكَ، وَغِبْ عَنْ إِقْبَالِهِمْ عَلَيْكَ بِشُهُودِ إِقْبَالِهِ عَلَيْكَ

Conceal yourself from the gaze of creation with the gaze of Allāh upon you, and be absent from their attention towards you with the awareness of His attention towards you.

From among the interventions of the ego that cause the deviations of righteous intent is an innate attribute of the ego that seeks to claim praise by presenting itself as the doer of the deed, when in reality it is the deed that deserves recognition and not the doer. This bid to claim praise and recognition is called *riya'a* رياء, 'showing off.' It is incredibly subtle and nuanced, often undetectable and sometimes indistinguishable from sincerity and modesty. It is connoted as the *'Lesser Shirk'* الشرك الأصغر,[75] and the *'Hidden Shirk'* الشرك الخفي,[76] and described as أخفى من ديب النمل 'subtler than the crawling of ants.'[77]

It can sometimes take apparent forms and be immediately realized, but its most dangerous forms are those that pass unchecked, often through heedlessness, that can occur so frequently as to become habitual and instinctive. This is where utmost vigilance is demanded, as the desire to have the gaze of others upon you is a sign of your lack of sincerity. It nullifies the deed as being for Allāh, becoming but a performance and entertainment to be lauded. One should be more keen to conceal themselves from the gaze of others by being mindful of Allāh's gaze, and deprive themselves of outward attention in readiness for Allāh's attention.

---

75 Musnad Imām Ahmad 23630

76 Sunan Ibn Mājah 4204

77 Recorded in Al-Bukhārī's *Adab al-Mufrad* on the authorities of AbuBakr, A'isha, and Ibn Abbās, ﷺ, who is also reported to have said that it is *'subtler than the crawling of a black ant on a black stone on a dark night,'* or something to that effect.

(١٦٢)

مَنْ عَرَفَ الْحَقَّ شَهِدَهُ فِي كُلِّ شَيْءٍ ، وَمَنْ فَنِيَ بِهِ غَابَ عَنْ كُلِّ شَيْءٍ،
وَمَنْ أَحَبَّهُ لَمْ يُؤْثِرْ عَلَيْهِ شَيْئًا

Whoever knows Al-Haqq, witnesses Him in everything. And whoever is annihilated in Him is absent from everything. And whoever loves Him, prefers nothing over Him.

(١٦٣)

إِنَّمَا حَجَبَ الْحَقَّ عَنْكَ شِدَّةُ قُرْبِهِ مِنْكَ

Indeed, Al-Haqq is only veiled from you due to the intensity of His nearness to you.

(١٦٤)

إِنَّمَا احْتَجَبَ لِشِدَّةِ ظُهُورِهِ ، وَخَفِيَ عَنِ الْأَبْصَارِ لِعِظَمِ نُورِهِ

Indeed, He is only veiled due to the intensity of His manifestation, and is concealed from sight due to the magnitude of His Light.

Knowing the truth and knowing *The Truth* are distinct. *The* Truth does not encompass facts and figures. *The* Truth is not found in words and expressions. *The* Truth is One with the One, the Absolute, the True, *Al-Haqq* الحق. Whoever knows *Al-Haqq* witnesses Him in everything. It means to understand and realize, not from one's own intellectual reasonings, but from what is revealed from *Al-Haqq*. Whoever is absorbed in that revelation becomes absent from everything, and whoever loves it prefers nothing else over it.

There are three stages to achieving this. The first is in knowing *Al-Haqq* such that one perceives His presence manifested in all things, as everything in creation speaks of its Creator. The second is to be in a state of total absorption, where a person becomes so immersed in Divine revelation that worldly distractions fade away. The third is cultivating a love for the Divine, an intense preference for Him, leaving no desire or attachment that could rival this love.

Know then, that His closeness is so profound that it becomes a veil itself. His presence is so deeply entwined with our being that we fail to see Him, just as a fish may not perceive the water in which it swims. His manifestation is so pervasive that it appears hidden, and His light so intense that our limited sight cannot bear it, much like the sun's brilliance when it overwhelms our vision. The obstacles to witnessing the Divine lie not in distance but in our perception.

True witnessing arises not from seeing *Al-Haqq* externally but from perceiving Him inwardly, as one's reality becomes so intertwined with His Divine Presence that no barrier exists in between. It entails cultivating a heart attuned to His ordinance, for He is *Al-Haqq, the True and Absolute,* and His Word is *Al-Haqq*. This nurtures inner clarity and humility to perceive the Divine Nearness that permeates all existence, even if it defies ordinary sight. In such recognition, one will naturally be compelled to experience a love that overshadows all else, revealing that Allāh's supposed absence is, in reality, the deepest and most manifest of all presence.

(١٦٥)

لَا يَكُنْ طَلَبُكَ سَبَبًا إِلَى الْعَطَاءِ مِنْهُ فَيَقِلَّ فَهْمُكَ عَنْهُ ، وَلْيَكُنْ طَلَبُكَ لِإِظْهَارِ الْعُبُودِيَّةِ

وَقِيَامًا بِحُقُوقِ الرُّبُوبِيَّةِ

Let not your seeking be a cause for the giving from Him, that it lessens your understanding of Him, but let your seeking be for the sake of manifesting servitude and fulfilling the rights of Lordship.

(١٦٦)

كَيْفَ يَكُونُ طَلَبُكَ اللَّاحِقُ سَبَبًا فِي عَطَائِهِ السَّابِقِ ؟

How can your later seeking be a cause for His prior bestowal?

(١٦٧)

جَلَّ حُكْمُ الْأَزَلِ أَنْ يَنْضَافَ إِلَى الْعِلَلِ

Too majestic is the eternal decree that it should be added to the nominal causes.

Do not let your search for *Al-Haqq* become a cause that prompts something from Him, only to reduce your understanding of who He truly is. You risk becoming a servant who only does if there is reciprocation, and withdraws when there is none. You risk being a servant who is compensated in precise measure of your actions, and upon judgment, should your deeds fall short of earning paradise, you find lacking that Mercy from Him that would grant you the eternal bounty. You risk being dubbed the merchant who demands his pound of flesh, who assumes that it is not by the Mercy of Allāh that you are bountiful, but by your own strength and ability, such that when your strength and ability inevitably fails, you find yourself humiliated and in dire need of His mercy. Look to the frail and weak, the crippled and old, and testify that Allāh's mercy upon them is not due to what they put forth, but purely due to His love, His care, and His providence upon them.

So, let your search for enlightenment be guided by an expression of servitude and a fulfillment of the rights of His Lordship, rather than a quest to fulfill your own presumed rights. For you came *from* Him. Your existence is a gift *from* Him. How then can your search for Him precede what He has already given you?

The believer must shift their focus from a transactional approach of worship toward a more genuine sense of servanthood. To seek out the Divine only to attain something implies that one sees their own actions as a driving force behind Allāh's grace. That you are in His favour because of what you put forth from your intentions and actions, when in reality, Allāh's mercy and provision are not bound by your requests. They are an ever-present reality preceding our desires and efforts. When one believes their request is what prompts Allāh's response, they narrow their understanding of His boundless generosity, forgetting that His giving is rooted in His own Will and Wisdom, not contingent upon human actions. Rather, seeking from Allāh should be a demonstration of one's servitude, not an expectation for reward. Such an approach respects the rights of Allāh's absolute Lordship and Autonomy.

By seeking solely out of a desire to fulfill the duties of servanthood, one acknowledges Allāh as the ultimate source of all blessings, acting not out of self-interest but out of deep reverence and recognition of His pre-existing grace. His generosity and provision are timeless, existing before any human thought or action. Thus, one's worship, while cherished, does not 'cause' Allāh's favour but rather is a response to the endless favours already bestowed. By embracing this understanding, the seeker learns to approach the Divine Presence with a heart free from expectations, focused instead on loving and serving for the sake of His Love itself, rather than as a means to an end.

You realize then that your seeking from Him cannot precede what He has already destined for you. You can only accept and embrace what He has ordained, and show gratitude for it. The ordainment is too majestic to be compared and appreciated on the horizontal plane of cause and effect. His will and decree are above and beyond any reliance on worldly causes and conditions, independent from the chain of causality that governs the logics and rationales of creation. Where from our limited perception the unfolding of reality seems to follow a series of interconnected causes and effects, Allāh's decree manifests from beyond any plane, unbound by the constraints of time, place, or causation.

When one truly understands this distinction, they learn to accept life's events, whether joyous or painful, with submission and humility, knowing that these events stem from a wisdom beyond their comprehension, and beyond their control. It frees the seeker from reliance on worldly causes or attributing importance to human plans. It places the being in a state of submission, to realize their purpose as not one that entails controlling their lives and outcomes, but to correct their lives in readiness of a higher, otherworldly purpose.

(١٦٨)

عِنَايَتُهُ فِيكَ لَا لِشَيْءٍ مِنْكَ؛

وَأَيْنَ كُنْتَ حِينَ وَاجَهَتْكَ عِنَايَتُهُ وَقَابَلَتْكَ؟

رِعَايَتُهُ لَمْ يَكُنْ فِي أَزَلِهِ إِخْلَاصُ أَعْمَالٍ وَلَا وُجُودُ أَحْوَالٍ؛

بَلْ لَمْ يَكُنْ هُنَاكَ إِلَّا مَحْضُ الْإِفْضَالِ وَعَظِيمُ النَّوَالِ

His care for you is not due to anything from you. Where were you when His care faced you and His protection met you? In His eternity, there was no sincerity of deeds, nor the existence of states. Rather, naught was there save for pure grace and immense favour.

His grace, providence, care, and mercy upon you, that sustains you and keeps you existent, is not due to anything from you. For one might ask, where were you when His grace reached and embraced you to bring you into existence? Where were you when the flesh and bones were assembled in your mother's womb? When the Divine Breath of Life brought you into this world? Was it by *your* doing that it all came to be? Or some spontaneous causes of events? In the eternity of His being, He did not need from you the sincerity of intentions or the ranks of sainthood to bring you into being. It was all owed purely to His Grace and Mercy that He chose to bring each individual into existence, grant them provision, sustenance, shelter, and above all, guidance upon the path to His Presence and Eternal Love.

Even as we exist, Allāh's kindness and care for His servants is neither earned nor dependent on any prior action. His grace reaches us not because of something we offer, but because of His boundless mercy. This teaches humility, as it dispels any notion that we can *earn* Allāh's care or that it is contingent upon our deeds or intentions. Rather, His generosity is purely out of goodness, beyond human calculation or reciprocation. His favour is present long before we are aware of it. It existed even before we came into being, not because of our actions or qualities, but out of His infinite kindness. It is He Who saves us from destitution; Who uplifts us at our lowest; Who grants respite in difficulty. Our very existence, and all the good that we experience, is a result of His will.

Understand the depth of this truth, and respond with love and reverence rather than entitlement. *Realize* that everything, from your creation to your sustenance, comes from Allāh's generosity, until it becomes clear to you that your role should be one of humble gratitude and acknowledgment of His benevolence. So that you shift your focus from seeking reward to appreciating the gifts you constantly receive, drawing you nearer to the sincerity and devotion that pleases your Creator.

(١٦٩)

عَلِمَ أَنَّ الْعِبَادَ يَتَشَوَّفُونَ إِلَى ظُهُورِ سِرِّ الْعِنَايَةِ فَقَالَ

﴿ ... يَخْتَصُّ بِرَحْمَتِهِ مَن يَشَآءُ ﴾

وَعَلِمَ أَنَّهُ لَوْ خَلَّاهُمْ وَذَلِكَ لَتَرَكُوا الْعَمَلَ اعْتِمَادًا عَلَى الْأَزَلِ فَقَالَ

﴿ ... إِنَّ رَحْمَتَ اللَّهِ قَرِيبٌ مِّنَ الْمُحْسِنِينَ ﴾

He knew that the servants anticipate the manifestation of the secret of care, so
He said, 'He chooses for His mercy whom He wills.'[78]
And He knew that if He left them, they would abandon action to depend on
predestination, so He said, 'Indeed, the Allāh's mercy is near to the doers of good.'[79]

These are the two extremities of one's servitude. In one aspect we greatly desire, through our servitude, the unveilings of the profound mysteries of Allāh's care and mercy. To that effect, He Allāh has declared that only He holds those secrets. That His mercy is granted to whomsoever *He* wills, and *none* can decide for Him.

Given that, one may find themselves losing hope, especially when continual servitude seems not to alleviate one's destitution. This may lead one to abandon their servitude altogether to depend on predestination, and to that effect He has also declared that certainty in receiving His mercy is marked by sincerity in righteous deeds.

This is the balancing encouragement with the mystery of Allāh's mercy, preventing complacency in action and fostering sincere devotion. It is human nature to long for assurance, hoping to know we are chosen recipients of Allāh's grace, that our continual devotion will indeed earn us His favour. However, Allāh reveals only what He wills, granting some and withholding from others, as His mercy is dispensed according to His wisdom. With this comes a warning that if we were to rely only on the knowledge of pre-eternal grace, we may end up neglecting personal responsibility in our servitude. For this reason, an assurance is given to encourage continuous striving and virtuous action. Here, Allāh's mercy is not limited to predestination but is assured as recompense to the efforts and devotion of His servants. This ensures that while His mercy is indeed a gift, it also has a relationship with human responsibility and action, urging us to persist in goodness.

This balance, in itself, is a mercy. It encourages gratitude and commitment, keeping the believer focused on their spiritual journey, while at the same time promising a return for one's strife and struggle.

---

78   Sūrah āla 'Imrān 3:74

79   Sūrah al-A'rāf 7:56

۱۷۰

إِلَى الْمَشِيئَةِ يَسْتَنِدُ كُلُّ شَيْءٍ وَلَا تَسْتَنِدُ هِيَ إِلَى شَيْءٍ

Everything relies on the Will (of Allāh), but the Will does not rely on anything.

The existence and unfolding of all events in reality are governed not by causes and effects, as perceived by the human mind, but by a higher power, meaning that every occurrence, no matter how trivial or grand, is imbued with intelligent design, existential purpose, and righteous intention. Such is the worldview of the believer. It carries a deep sense of humility, as it beckons us to recognize our place in existence, where every thread is woven by the Hands of the Almighty. And by it we understand that Divine Will is not contingent upon any factors, circumstances, or the will of His creation. It is independent from all that is created, free from the constraints of time and space.

In our reality, we perceive how human agency often leads to a myriad of consequences, but seldom do we perceive Divine Will at play, that does not require validation or support from the created order. We encounter the effects of evil caused by the agents of evil, and we may think that this could not possibly be Divine Will. For how can Allāh, Most Merciful, Most Benevolent, allow such evil to manifest? Such thought has led many to conclude the non-existence of God, using this flawed logic as the basis of their convictions, or lack thereof. But the realization that Allāh's Will ultimately manifests all that is manifested in reality, and nothing can influence that Will, be it good or evil, can liberate the human being from all the doubts and anxieties of dependence upon causality.

·──────·

۱۷۱

رُبَّمَا دَلَّهُمُ الْأَدَبُ عَلَى تَرْكِ الطَّلَبِ اعْتِمَادًا عَلَى قِسْمَتِهِ وَاشْتِغَالًا بِذِكْرِهِ عَنْ مَسْأَلَتِهِ

Etiquette may guide them to abandon seeking, rely on His portioning, and be occupied with His remembrance instead of asking for their needs.

Adab, as we discussed before,[80] is the inner discipline of the seeker. It entails commitment and perseverance, humility and cordiality in the seeker's approach to guidance. This approach may ultimately lead them to transcend the rank of being a mere seeker to become content with the proportions of Allāh's provision, freeing them from preoccupation with their worldly necessities and become preoccupied solely in His remembrance. Indeed, true nobility transcends perpetual asking to becoming content and grateful with what is given.

·──────·

---

80 Hikam 126

(١٧٢)

إِنَّمَا يُذَكَّرُ مَنْ يَجُوزُ عَلَيْهِ الإِغْفَالُ،

وَإِنَّمَا يُنَبَّهُ مَنْ يُمْكِنُ مِنْهُ الإِهْمَالُ

Indeed, only those capable of heedlessness are reminded, and indeed only those susceptible to neglect are warned.

The heedless are reminded. The neglectful are warned.

Heedlessness is a state of forgetfulnesses, a state of mindlessness, a state embodied when the distractions succeed in their distraction and overwhelm the heart. It necessitates a reminder from other than the distraction to realign the heart and return it to the pathway.

Neglect, on the other hand, is deliberate. It is a lack of responsibility where responsibility is demanded, and is unbefitting a state to be in. Neglect has no excuse, and such an individual must be admonished lest their neglect lead to profound loss and injustice. Yet Mercy supersedes wrath, to give the neglectful fair chance at rectification before the arrival of retribution.

Both the reminder and the warning are acts of Divine Compassion. Both are sent to save and prevent disgrace and eternal damnation. While both may seem an attack upon the self, they are, if given a chance, welcomed by the heart that is humble and sincere. The human being is prone to lapse in conscious awareness, and this is a weakness we must acknowledge for the reminders and warnings to serve their purpose.

---

(١٧٣)

وُرُودُ الفَاقَاتِ أَعْيَادُ المُرِيدِينَ

The arrival of destitution (times of need) are the festivals for the seekers.

(١٧٤)

رُبَّمَا وَجَدْتَ مِنَ الْمَزِيدِ فِي الْفَاقَاتِ مَا لَا تَجِدُهُ فِي الصَّوْمِ وَالصَّلَاةِ

You may find benefit in direness what you do not find in fasting and prayer.

(١٧٥)

الْفَاقَاتُ بُسُطُ الْمَوَاهِبِ

Dire needs are the domain for Divine Gifts.

（١٧٦）

إِنْ أَرَدْتَ وُرُودَ الْمَوَاهِبِ عَلَيْكَ صَحِّحِ الْفَقْرَ وَالْفَاقَةَ لَدَيْكَ

﴿ إِنَّمَا الصَّدَقَتُ لِلْفُقَرَآءِ وَالْمَسَٰكِينِ ... ﴾

If you desire the arrival of gifts upon you, rectify poverty and neediness within yourself. 'Indeed, charities are (rightfully) only for the poor and destitute' [81]

Difficulty on the path is not an obstacle preventing advancement, rather every difficulty is a doorway through which, when the seeker passes successfully, reaches ever closer to the destination. When Allāh places a need within one's heart, it serves as a summons, a reminder of the soul's ultimate dependency on Him. Needs become opportunities for inner purification and the renewal of spiritual commitment. Much like a festival that brings joy and community, these moments of need draw seekers into the presence of the Divine, where they can find solace and strength. It is not the alleviation of need that fulfills the seeker, but the experience of communion with Allāh that each moment of yearning engenders. Indeed, certain forms of spiritual elevation are discovered uniquely through the experience of need.

While fasting and prayer are profound acts of devotion, the vulnerability inherent in genuine need can open doors of realization that structured acts of worship may not. Dire need invites the seeker to approach and embark the path with receptivity and humility, understanding that unmet desires or difficult times, though not worshipful acts, are powerful opportunities for seeking immediate communion with Allāh. Need exposes the soul, laying bare its weaknesses and illusions of independence, which, in turn, sharpens one's awareness and spiritual presence. When nothing in the world can satisfy the longing, the heart turns inward and upward, reaching toward the only true source of sufficiency.

Needs are the carpets of Allāh's gifts. This is both comforting and profound in meaning, in that within the seeming barrenness of need lies a hidden abundance. Each difficulty or shortfall becomes a foundation upon which Allāh's generosity is extended. For the seeker, this encourages a reevaluation of hardship as an essential space for Allāh's grace to manifest. It is not that the needs lead to gifts, but that they become a sacred arena for self-disclosure. In such a state of desperation, the seeker is forced to subdue his ego, thereby heightening his receptivity and allowing the gifts of insight, patience, and resilience to unfold in ways that would otherwise remain hidden. This teaches that every lack is a precursor to abundance, an invitation to look behind and see how far one has come, and to look ahead with sincere aspiration, to understand beyond the apparent hardship and witness Allāh's wisdom at work. This is what being in a state of destitution entails.

81 Sūrah at-Tawbah 9:60

Finally, this is not about material lack but about acknowledging one's essential dependency on Allāh. Given that alms and charity are rightfully for the poor and destitute, His gifts are naturally inclined toward those who recognize their spiritual neediness. This 'poverty' refers to an inner state where one sees beyond their personal resources and attributes all sufficiency to Allāh. The alms are the gifts of wisdom, spiritual insight, and inner peace, bestowed upon those who have humbled their hearts and embraced their vulnerability. The seeker who perfects this inward state of dependence will find themselves among the primary recipients of boundless gifting, for they have, through their destitution, emptied their 'selves' from themselves, and in doing so, have created the capacity to receive Light upon Light.

(١٧٧)

تَحَقَّقْ بِأَوْصَافِكَ يُمِدُّكَ بِأَوْصَافِهِ،

تَحَقَّقْ بِذُلِّكَ يُمِدُّكَ بِعِزِّتِهِ،

تَحَقَّقْ بِعَجْزِكَ يُمِدُّكَ بِقُدْرَتِهِ،

تَحَقَّقْ بِضَعْفِكَ يُمِدُّكَ بِحَوْلِهِ وَقُوَّتِهِ

Realizing your qualities reinforces you with His Attributes,
Realizing your humility reinforces you with His Pride,
Realizing your incapacity reinforces you with His Ability,
Realizing your weakness reinforces you with His Protection and Power.

Realization is a prime requisite of the path. No spiritual experience can be regarded as a true experience without realization. This realization is not sensory, in as much as the experience is also not sensory. It is a deep awareness within the heart, an untainted understanding of reality in which attribution, pride, ability, and power are attested to Allāh through the attestation of humility, incapacity, and weakness in the servant.

The former are 'realized' through the awareness of the latter that comprise the human condition, which in turn opens them to receive the qualities of honour, capability, and strength. Such that by fully acknowledging our created limitations, we invite Allāh's infinite, uncreated qualities to fill and uplift us. Understanding our human qualities, and truly inhabiting them with humility, leads to receiving support from Allāh's own attributes. Here, 'realizing' oneself in one's qualities refers to an honest awareness and acceptance of who we are in our human condition, rather than striving to transcend or deny our limitations. This realization is a kind of spiritual humility, where we no longer resist our nature as creatures. When we come to terms with our lack of inherent power, we open ourselves to Allāh's power, a limitless source that can guide and sustain us precisely because we have ceased to seek it within ourselves. Surrender, in this regard, does not mean to simply resign to our limitations but instead to find strength to rectify them through guidance. This surrender is not passive but a dynamic act of faith and intelligence, rationalizing and transcending the rationality of our nature as finite beings, to realize that we are sustained by the Infinite.

١٧٨

رُبَّمَا رُزِقَ الْكَرَامَةَ مَنْ لَمْ تَكْمُلْ لَهُ الإسْتِقَامَةُ

Miracles may be granted (even) upon those for whom righteousness is not complete.

Miracles are not the sole gifts of the pious and righteous. One may be granted miracles even though they have not attained complete uprightness, which is to say that miracles are not proof of one's spiritual station or signs of Allāh's complete favour. The seeker does not embark the path to encounter spiritual experiences, but to gain inner integrity and steadfastness.

This is the quality of continuous commitment to the straight path of devotion and ethical existence. It requires a steady heart, humility, and a persistent alignment with Allāh's commandments. The miracles arrive as extraordinary occurrences as gifts to remind the seeker of the Divine Promise, to grant respite to the heart, and draw them away from the distractions of the world of the mundane. This can be granted to any individual with a sincere heart, saint or otherwise, and though remarkable in and of themselves, they are not the core measure of one's spiritual closeness to Allāh.

The path itself, and steadfastness upon it, is of greater significance than the experiences encountered, because it reflects a more profound commitment to the qualities that draw one near to Allāh. For one might ask, which is the greater reward? The miracles, which are but traces of Allāh's power and majesty? Or His Divine Presence wherein His power and majesty are fully realized?

So do not aspire for extraordinary signs as proof of your spiritual progress but value the quiet, unseen virtues of sincerity and patience. These, in themselves, are miraculous, for very few can attain those qualities, while most remain comfortable in the mundane. This is the true testament of spiritual maturity, requiring continuous effort and strife. It demands a cultivation of unwavering faith and inner consistency, for it is through such virtues, and not through miraculous occurrences, that one attains true proximity to the Divine. This teaching preserves the purity of one's intention with the constant reminder that the path to Allāh is about refining the heart, not chasing wonders.

(١٧٩)

مِنْ عَلَامَاتِ إِقَامَةِ الْحَقِّ لَكَ فِي الشَّيْءِ إِقَامَتُهُ إِيَّاكَ فِيهِ مَعَ حُصُولِ النَّتَائِجِ

From among the signs of Al-Haqq's establishment for you in something, is His establishment in it, only for you, with achieving the results.

From among the signs that Allāh has established you in something is that He maintains you in it and grants you its fruits. Often one finds themselves in an endeavour, confused, whether they are upon the truth, whether their acts are in accordance with Divine Will. One may find certainty in a sign that unfolds it two ways, that they find consistency and the will to persevere in their deeds, and that their deeds bear righteous outcomes. The believer thus understands that when Allāh wants them in a particular role, state, or situation, He not only fashions the role solely for them, but establishes them there in addition to facilitating their success and bringing forth tangible outcomes from their efforts. Thereby the believer also understands that genuine outcomes stem from Divine Will, not merely from their own personal ambitions or desires.

When Allāh 'establishes' a person in something, He provides both the opportunity and the means for it to flourish. This includes stability and endurance, qualities that are often accompanied by a flow of beneficial results. Thus, a person who is genuinely guided by Allāh in their pursuits will witness a natural unfolding of events, and fruits that validate their efforts, which in themselves will appear miraculous. These outcomes are a kind of affirmation and consolidation for the heart, not because the person has exerted control over their success, but because they are aligned with Allāh's wisdom and purpose.

Underlying all this is also the need for humility and trust in Allāh's wisdom. Not every endeavor, even if pursued earnestly, with the right means and the proper channels, will yield results. Sometimes, Allāh's wisdom dictates otherwise. Sometimes, the yields are delayed or withheld altogether. If one is not granted success in a particular pursuit, it may be a sign that it is not meant for them at this time or perhaps not aligned with their ultimate spiritual good. Or perhaps, these outcomes are but means to greater outcomes ahead, and the ultimate yield is yet to be realized. Thus, the believer must cultivate a reflective approach, where one discerns their placement in life not merely by effort or desire, expecting immediate results, but by observing the fruits of their actions as signs of their establishment. It may be that the fruits were not meant for the doer of the deed, and their recipient was someone else. It may be that your role was to serve as a means for the prosperity of others. That, in itself, is a fruit of one's endeavours. So cultivate a balanced approach to both striving and surrender. Recognize success as a blessing rather than a product of your own doing, and embrace a deeper trust in Divine placement.

(١٨٠)

مَنْ عَبَّرَ مِنْ بِسَاطِ إِحْسَانِهِ أَصْمَتَتْهُ الإِسَاءَةُ،

وَمَنْ عَبَّرَ مِنْ بِسَاطِ إِحْسَانِ اللهِ إِلَيْهِ لَمْ يَصْمُتْ إِذَا أَسَاءَ

One who traverses the dais of his own goodness, silence prevails him over
wrongdoing, while one who traverses the dais of Allāh's goodness to him, does
not remain silent when he faces wrongdoing.

One who acts out of their own kindness is sometimes silenced when
their selflessness towards others is met with unkind reciprocation or no
reciprocation whatsoever. It hurts to be shunned and disgraced, but it only
hurts because the act of kindness originated from the self and was driven
by the self. When kindness arises from a sense of personal expectation, it
is vulnerable to discouragement and offense when met with ingratitude
or harm. However, when one acts out of Allāh's kindness to them, out
of selflessness solely for His sake, such a person is not silenced by the
harm of others. When one's kindness stems from an awareness of Allāh's
boundless grace, it is resilient, unshaken, and unaffected by the unkind
actions of others.

This is the distinction between the one whose kindness is rooted
in their own perception of goodness, and one who finds solitude in
Allāh's kindness. Human generosity, based on personal virtue alone,
often has conditions and expectations. When one's subjective perception
of goodness is met with equally subjective mistreatment or lack of
appreciation, the individual may feel disheartened, even silenced, as
they encounter the limitations of their own capacity for patience and
forgiveness. Their will falters, revealing that it was perhaps entangled with
subtle desires for acknowledgment or praise. But when a person acts out
of an awareness that all kindness ultimately originates from Allāh, they
see themselves merely as conduits of His grace, not as the source. This
realization shields them from disappointment or frustration when others
respond poorly, because their generosity is anchored in Allāh's approval,
not in the responses of others. Such a person continues to give and act
with goodness, irrespective of how others respond, seeing their actions as
a humble reflection of Allāh's infinite mercy.

So elevate your intentions, such that your acts are not manifest for
personal validation but as instruments of Allāh's kindness, sustaining
a generosity that is both enduring and selfless. Do not place yourself
between kindness and the anticipation of reciprocation. Kindness is an
attribute of the Divine. It was never yours to give. You were but entrusted
to carry it forward. Save yourself the disappointment and heartache of
others by readying yourself for the approval and pleasure of your Lord.
People will betray your selflessness. Your Lord will never betray you.

(١٨١)

تَسْبِقُ أَنْوَارُ الْحُكَمَاءِ أَقْوَالَهُمْ ، فَحَيْثُ صَارَ التَّنْوِيرُ... وَصَلَ التَّعْبِيرُ

The lights of the wise precede their words, so wherever illumination occurs... there discernment follows.

(١٨٢)

كُلُّ كَلَامٍ يَبْرُزُ وَعَلَيْهِ كِسْوَةُ الْقَلْبِ الَّذِي مِنْهُ بَرَزَ

Each word emerges, and upon it is the garment of the heart from which it emerges.

(١٨٣)

مَنْ أُذِنَ لَهُ فِي التَّعْبِيرِ فُهِمَتْ فِي مَسَامِعِ الْخَلْقِ عِبَارَتُهُ، وَجُلِّيَتْ إِلَيْهِمْ إِشَارَتُهُ

Whoever is granted the ability to express, his expressions are understood by the ears of people, and revered by them are his allusions.

The luminance of the people of wisdom precedes their words. Their very presence speaks volumes. And wherever there is illumination of their wisdom, its expression follows. Every word emerges clothed in the garment of the heart from which it came, and only those who are permitted to express will have their words understood by the ears of creation, and their subtle indications made clear to the recipients.

Expressiveness is of two kinds. There is the expression of the self, the type of expressiveness oft advocated by the shallow worldview of the godless. Then there is the expression of the heart, a type of expressiveness that the godless never realize, the foolish can never encompass, and the wise are ever cautious of. For the tongue that utters the expression is only a translator for the heart from whence the expression originates. The word emerges with the same garment it was clothed with in the heart. A heart that is corrupt will express a word that is corrupt. A heart that is righteous will do likewise. Speech is never independent of the heart's condition; rather, words carry the essence of the heart from which they spring.

This emphasizes the primacy of inner enlightenment over outward expression in true wisdom. This *nūr* نور is an intimate awareness of Divine truths, cultivated through sincerity, devotion, and self-purification, for authentic wisdom does not arise from mere words or intellectual formulations but from a deep, inner light that shapes and inspires the wise before they even speak. True insight is first an internal transformation, before it naturally flows into expression, and only when the heart is fully illuminated by Divine guidance. This is the inner illumination bestowed by Allāh, a form of spiritual clarity that transcends knowledge acquired through study alone.

The wise do not seek to impress others with their words; rather, their insights arise naturally from the radiance of their inner state. For them, expression is effortless and authentic, communicating not only knowledge but a palpable presence that resonates with others. The true power of wisdom does not lie in the expressive ability, in the proficiency of language, logic, rhetoric, or the cleverness and eloquence of one's speech. Rather, it lies in its source, in a heart lit by spiritual knowledge.

Here is a profound reminder for one to focus more on inner transformation than outward displays of knowledge. In spiritual discourse, the substance of one's heart matters more than the form of one's words. The wise do not need to force or embellish their expressions. Their words carry weight and truth because they stem from a deep, illuminated place within. When the heart is truly aligned with higher wisdom, the words to express that wisdom will flow naturally, carrying an authenticity that no amount of rhetoric could replicate. Moreover, true impact in communication comes when Allāh grants permission for one's words to reach others, imbuing them with clarity and resonance.

Thus when Allāh grants a person permission to speak, their words are not only heard by the ears, but are understood deeply by the hearts. This permission, however, is not a matter of outward authority but of facilitation, where Allāh makes the individual's words clear, impactful, and illuminating to the listener. Such permission is given to those who have refined their hearts, aligning their intentions with a higher purpose. Those who shift their perspective from external expression to inner sincerity, recognizing that the true weight of one's words lies in the heart from which they emerge and that it is Allāh's permission that grants them reach. And just as clothing covers and characterizes one's appearance, so does the heart shape and colour one's expressions. If the heart is pure and aligned with the Divine Presence, the words will carry sincerity, warmth, and wisdom. Conversely, if the heart is tainted by pride, anger, or insincerity, even the most eloquent words will wear those selfsame cloaks, diminishing their effect and resonance.

---

(١٨٤)

رُبَّمَا بَرَزَتِ الْحَقَائِقُ مَكْسُوفَةَ الْأَنْوَارِ، إِذَا لَمْ يُؤْذَنْ لَكَ فِيهَا بِالْإِظْهَارِ

Truths may emerge with veiled lights, if you are not permitted to manifest them.

The expression of truth is not contingent on one's ability to express, but on whether or not Allāh has permitted the truth to be revealed. When the truth emerges on the tongues of those expressing them, and it is not granted permission, it is veiled regardless of how righteous or pious the individual is. The wise understand that even profound truths, if shared without sanction, will emerge with obscurity and lack clarity.

---

(١٨٥)

عِبَارَاتُهُمْ إِمَّا لِفَيَضَانِ وَجْدٍ، أَوْ لِقَصْدِ هِدَايَةِ مُرِيدٍ،

فَالْأَوَّلُ حَالُ السَّالِكِينَ، وَالثَّانِي حَالُ أَرْبَابِ الْمَكِنَةِ وَالْمُحَقِّقِينَ

*Their expressions are either due to overflowing emotions, or to guide the
disciple. The former is the state of travelers on the path (beginners), and the
latter is the state of masters of enlightenment and those of certainty.*

(١٨٦)

الْعِبَارَاتُ قُوتُ الْعَائِلَةِ الْمُسْتَمِعِينَ وَلَيْسَ لَكَ إِلَّا مَا أَنْتَ لَهُ آكِلٌ

*The expressions are sustenance for the listeners, and not will you have save for
what you can consume.*

Expression of the truth occurs in two instances, and wherever else it
may appear, it is void of wisdom though it may bear semblance of truth
and wisdom. In the first instance, it occurs due to the overwhelming
emotion and ecstasy that the truth induces within the being, becoming
too weighty to keep contained. Those who encounter such instances are
the *sālikūn* سالكون, the ones on the path yet journeying towards realization
of the absolute truth. In the other instance, it occurs when guidance is
intended by Divine Will, and those who encounter such instances are
the masters of enlightenment, *arbāb al-makinah* أرباب المكنة, and the
muhaqqiqūn محققون, those of absolute certainty.

The distinction is between those whose words arise from an overflow
of spiritual experience and those whose words are carefully crafted with
the intention of guiding others, and each type of expression reflects the
spiritual state of the speaker.

Of the first type, the words come spontaneously, out of a heart filled
with the Divine Presence. This is often the case with the *sālikūn* who are
still traveling the path. Their experiences are fresh and immediate, and
their words reflect an unrestrained enthusiasm. In this state, their speech
may be unpolished or impulsive but is filled with sincerity and passion.
Such expressions are honest and raw, carrying the energy of one who is
still in the throes of discovery. However, while they may be inspirational,
they may also lack the focus and intentionality needed for sustained
guidance, as these seekers are often absorbed in their own journey.

Of the second type, those who speak with the intention of imparting
guidance, they are parted into two. The *arbāb* are the masters of
enlightenment, established, honed, and trained upon the path, while
the *muhaqqiqūn* are those who have certainty and conviction. Both are
considered to have reached spiritual maturity. Their words are not merely
expressions of their own state but are carefully chosen to benefit others,

reflecting a balance between knowledge and compassion. Such is the state of a spiritual master, as described;

$$﴿ ...ءَاتَيْنَٰهُ رَحْمَةً مِّنْ عِندِنَا وَعَلَّمْنَٰهُ مِن لَّدُنَّا عِلْمًا ﴾$$

... We granted him from Us kindness and inspired him from Us knowledge [82]

Their knowledge is inseparable from kindness, and they are inseparable from either. They are not caught in the fluctuations of their own experiences; instead, they have achieved stability and clarity that enables them to provide guidance with wisdom and precision. Their speech is deliberate and mindful, infused with gentleness and subtlety, crafted to uplift and direct the seeker without overwhelming them.

In either type, whether from overwhelming emotion, or through careful deliberations, the expressions are nourishment for the hungry listeners. However, one can only take from them or impart them to the fill of their capacity and readiness. The one expressing can only truly express what they have themselves embodied, leastways it may serve the listener, but serve no benefit to the speaker. Likewise, the listener must be readied to receive, for though the words are true and rich with wisdom, the listener's own limitations in understanding, paired with a lack of humility, will limit how much they can receive.

This reveals a profound distinction between the outward act of imparting wisdom and the inner act of embodying it. While words of wisdom may provide sustenance to the soul and spirit, genuine spiritual nourishment is derived only from what we ourselves deeply internalize and live by. Such is a call to recognize that true spiritual growth is not about what we articulate to others, but about what we actively integrate and embody within ourselves. True spiritual benefit comes from personal application rather than mere expression. Regardless of how much one shares with others, the only true gain for oneself comes from what is internalized and acted upon. One must aspire to go beyond the surface of intellectual knowledge or eloquent speech, and instead seek personal growth and transformation by 'consuming' and embodying the truths they encounter.

♦ ⬥ ❊ ⬥ ♦

(١٨٧)

$$رُبَّمَا عَبَّرَ عَنِ الْمَقَامِ مَنِ اسْتَشْرَفَ عَلَيْهِ وَرُبَّمَا عَبَّرَ عَنْهُ مَنْ وَصَلَ إِلَيْهِ$$
$$وَذَلِكَ مُلْتَبِسٌ إِلَّا عَلَى صَاحِبِ بَصِيرَةٍ$$

One may express the station they aspire to, and another may express it through realizing it. This remains ambiguous except to those with insight.

---

[82]   Sūrah al-Kahf 18:65

146

(١٨٨)

لَا يَنْبَغِي لِلسَّالِكِ أَنْ يُعَبِّرَ عَنْ وَارِدَاتِهِ؛

فَإِنَّ ذَلِكَ مِمَّا يُقِلُّ عَمَلَهَا فِي قَلْبِهِ وَيَمْنَعُهُ وُجُودَ الصِّدْقِ مَعَ رَبِّهِ

It is not appropriate for the seeker to express their spiritual experiences, as doing so diminishes their effects in his heart and prevents the presence of genuinity with their Lord.

The *sālikūn* express where they are on their journey and where they aspire to be, while the *arbāb* and the *muhaqqiqūn* express where they have been and to where they have arrived. However, neither can fully express their experiences without insight.

Insight, *basīrah* بصيرة, and sight, *basar* بصر, are both distinct in what they avail. The distinction is between the apparent outward and the hidden inward, between the form and the meaning. Though the two are linked, they do not carry the same virtue. Such is the difference between aspirational and experiential understanding on the spiritual path. The aspiration can be envisioned, the goal sighted on the horizon, but its reality can only be realized once one attains and experiences it. So while many may articulate spiritual stations from a place of longing or theoretical understanding, only those who have fully realized a station can speak from direct experience. This entails discernment, *'ibrah* عبرة, in recognizing authentic expression, as true insight lies in distinguishing aspiration from attainment.

Those who are at the stages of aspiration are drawn by the beauty and depth of certain spiritual realities, and they speak of them with sincerity but without the direct knowledge that comes from having fully attained them. These seekers are inspired by descriptions of spiritual states and express these ideals as they strive toward them. While such expression is heartfelt, it lacks the weight and authenticity of one who has 'arrived.'

Those who have arrived are those who have directly experienced these stations and can therefore speak with a clarity and authority born of true encounter. Their words are infused with the depth and nuance of actualized knowledge, revealing a level of understanding that cannot be feigned or intellectualized, meaning the conclusions they draw of reality cannot be reached through theoretical reasoning or scientific rationalizations.

In that regard, it is not fitting for the seeker to express their inspirations, for this diminishes their effect in the heart and prevents true sincerity with their Lord. Such inspirations or insights are personal gifts from Allāh, meant to deepen the seeker's heart and relationship with Him and help motivate them towards their aspired stations. By sharing these states prematurely or for the sake of self-display, a seeker risks reducing their depth and sincerity, and further risks falling in rank.

(١٨٩)

لَا تَمُدَّنَّ يَدَكَ إِلَى الْأَخْذِ مِنَ الْخَلْقِ إِلَّا أَنْ تَرَى أَنَّ الْمُعْطِيَ فِيهِمْ مَوْلَاكَ،

فَإِذَا كُنْتَ كَذَلِكَ ... فَخُذْ مَا وَافَقَ الْعِلْمَ

Do not extend your hand to take from creation unless you see that the giver through them is your Lord.
So should you be in this state, take what knowledge allows.

(١٩٠)

رُبَّمَا اسْتَحْيَا الْعَارِفُ أَنْ يَرْفَعَ حَاجَتَهُ إِلَى مَوْلَاهُ اكْتِفَائِهِ بِمَشِيئَتِهِ ...

فَكَيْفَ لَا يَسْتَحِي أَنْ يَرْفَعَهَا إِلَى خَلِيقَتِهِ؟

The knower may feel shy to raise his need to his Lord, satisfied with His will.
So how can he not feel shy to raise it to His creation?

Do not take any more than what has been provisioned by Allāh. Do not take other than what has been sanctioned by Allāh. Do not depend on what comes from others unless you have ascertained them as instruments of His provision. It is to understand that all sustenance ultimately comes from Allāh, and accepting assistance or resources from others is not a contradiction of reliance on Him. Instead, it is a recognition that He provides through various means, including the hands of creation. The distinction, however, is often too subtle and ambiguous to discern. It is not always evident for the seeker how much his allocation is, or whether what he is taking is truly belonging. Here the seeker is reminded to adhere to the prescribed guidelines and to apply knowledge in keeping safe.

As such, knowledge may reveal to the seeker a sense of shame to raise his need to his Lord, finding himself satisfied with what Allāh has already allocated and given him. This will in turn reveal in him a sense of shame in taking from creation. For such a person, if it feels audacious to appeal directly to the Provider and Sustainer, it should feel even more inappropriate to lower their needs to creation. Knowledge thus protects the seeker from breaching the parameters of consumption, and protects creation from being breached and becoming over consumed.

When one understands how much their need truly is, and that the need has already been alleviated if but they care to see and find the means already in place for them, then the delicate balance of the created realm and between created entities, is maintained. The world does not fall into corruption and ruination. And it is evident from what we see in reality that mankind has not allowed knowledge to penetrate their hearts. The world would otherwise not be as it is now.

148

(١٩١)

إِذَا الْتَبَسَ عَلَيْكَ أَمْرَانِ، فَانْظُرْ إِلَى أَثْقَلِهِمَا عَلَى النَّفْسِ فَاتَّبِعْهُ،

فَإِنَّهُ لَا يَثْقُلُ عَلَيْهَا إِلَّا مَا كَانَ حَقًّا

Should two matters appear to you, look at the heavier one upon the soul and follow it, for nothing burdens it except what is true.

(١٩٢)

مِنْ عَلَامَاتِ اتِّبَاعِ الْهَوَى الْمُسَارَعَةُ إِلَى نَوَافِلِ الْخَيْرَاتِ،

وَالتَّكَاسُلُ عَنِ الْقِيَامِ بِالْوَاجِبَاتِ

From among the signs of following desires is the hastening towards optional good deeds, while being lazy in performing obligatory duties.

The pathway always presents one with choices. Every unfolding moment necessitates decisive action, and often the seeker's options are apparent. Between good and evil, or between right and wrong, the correct choice is simple enough, but what if it were a choice between two goods, or worse, two evils?

The counsel given here is to look at which is heavier upon the self and follow it, for nothing is more burdensome to the self except that it is true. This is a profound spiritual insight into navigating moments of uncertainty. When faced with difficult choices, the path that feels most challenging is often the one aligned with truth, as the soul naturally resists what demands greater effort, sacrifice, or discipline, while it is inclined toward comfort and ease.

The self is naturally resistant to what is morally or spiritually weighty. This resistance is not necessarily indicative of aversion due to harm, but rather to the self's inclination toward convenience and aversion to accountability. For example, fulfilling obligations, speaking truthfully, or choosing humility over pride may feel burdensome, though these actions align with Divine command and ethical integrity. Using the weight of an action on the self as a tool for discernment solves the indecision, particularly in moments of ambiguity where clarity is lacking.

A clear example is when the believer finds themselves inclined to voluntary and supererogatory acts of worship because they are convenient and less demanding. He is eager and willing to fulfill them as they are quick and easy. Yet, when they are called upon to fulfill obligations, the self begins to find excuses. People look for the best way to avoid the act, even if it means scouring the law books to find a lenient ruling. And if they run out of ways to escape the act, they perform it most hastily, at the very last moment of its obligation, just to have it recorded as done.

149

This is a warning against self-deception in religious practice, against the tendency to seek out the shortest most quickest path to paradise. Indeed, some individuals may find joy in optional acts of worship because they bring a sense of spiritual accomplishment, yet they may neglect the foundational duties that truly define sincere devotion. This is an indication of the soul's tendency to indulge in religious displays that feed the ego rather than uphold the humility required by core responsibilities.

The believer must always prioritize the steeper path, for it bears the greatest yield. Prioritize the difficult but necessary obligations over actions that merely appear pious, in recognizing that the path of truth often involves hardship and that sincere devotion is reflected in fulfilling duties before pursuing extra acts.

---

(۱۹۳)

قَيَّدَ الطَّاعَاتِ بِأَعْيَانِ الأَوْقَاتِ كَي لَا يَمْنَعَكَ عَنْهَا وُجُودُ التَّسْوِيفِ،
وَوَسَّعَ عَلَيْكَ الْوَقْتَ كَي يُبْقِيَ لَكَ حِصَّةُ الاخْتِيَارِ

He stipulated specific times for acts of obedience, so that the presence of procrastination would not prevent you from them (their reward). And He expanded upon you the time (to perform them) so that you would have a share of choice (leeway in performing them).

Obligatory acts of obedience are bound to specific times so that procrastination does not deprive the believer from their rewards. At such times, the believer is compelled to fulfill the obligation and cannot delay them any further. The gaps of duration between these acts have also widened so that the privilege of choice is retained by the believer. He may choose to perform the act at its time, at a slight delay, or at the moment of its final call. This ensures that duties are fulfilled regularly and not delayed indefinitely. Yet, there is flexibility in performing them, granting the believer a degree of personal choice, as circumstances and necessities are ever shifting. Through this balanced approach, guidance and revelation disciplines the believer while also respecting Divinely granted human freedom.

---

(۱۹٤)

عَلِمَ قِلَّةَ نُهُوضِ العِبَادِ إِلَى مُعَامَلَتِهِ ، فَأَوْجَبَ عَلَيْهِمْ وُجُودَ طَاعَتِهِ ، فَسَاقَهُمْ إِلَيْهِ بِسَلَاسِلِ
الإِيجَابِ، قَالَ النَّبِيُّ صَلَّى اللهُ عَلَيْهِ وَسَلَّمَ
عَجِبَ اللهُ مِنْ قَوْمٍ يَدْخُلُونَ الْجَنَّةَ فِى السَّلَاسِلِ

He knew the reluctance of His servants to engage with Him, so He made it obligatory upon them to obey Him. He then led them to Him with the chains of obligation.

The Holy Prophet ﷺ said, 'Your Lord is amazed at a people who are dragged to Paradise in chains.' [83]

(۱۹٥)

أَوْجَبَ عَلَيْكَ وُجُودَ طَاعَتِهِ، وَمَا أَوْجَبَ عَلَيْكَ إِلَّا دُخُولَ جَنَّتِهِ

He obligated upon you to obey Him, and not does He obligate upon you except entry into His Paradise.

It is not due the strengths of the human being that worship is obligatory, rather those who exhibit spiritual strength do not worship to only fulfill their obligations. They are made obligatory due to human weakness, through which they are forced to go to Him. It is due to mercy and compassion for humanity's limitations, that Allāh has established mandatory acts of worship that gently compel people toward spiritual fulfillment. These obligations are the guiding force, directing souls toward Him even when their immediate inclinations might pull them elsewhere. The weakness being spoken of is the tendency to succumb to distractions, procrastination, and apathy in matters of worship. Knowing this, Allāh instituted obligations like prayer, fasting, and charity, providing a structure that holds believers accountable and keeping them on the path to spiritual growth. It curtails the risk of neglect, ensuring that even those whose hearts may not immediately yearn for Him are not deprived of the path to closeness. And just as chains may restrict physical movement, obligatory acts restrict the self from straying and gently bind it to the upright path. For some, these duties initially feel burdensome, yet through consistent practice, the heart opens to their inner beauty, and the chains transform into bonds of love and devotion.

This is the amazement of all amazements, that despite being promised paradise, despite the overwhelming love and compassion from Allāh, that would naturally compel an individual to serve Him, there remains a vast majority who are forced to receive a chance to enter His presence by being obligated to serve. Yet, even despite that, most never earn the right.

What He has obligated upon the human being is not for other than the human being's benefit. He Allāh does not obligate other than what leads to His paradise. His ordinance is not in place for His amusement. His commands are not mere tests or arbitrary restrictions; rather, they cultivate qualities that bring the soul closer to its true purpose and to the Creator Himself. Every obligatory act prescribed leads to paradise, and every act prohibited prevents from leading anywhere but paradise.

۱۹٦

مَنِ اسْتَغْرَبَ أَنْ يُنْقِذَهُ اللهُ مِنْ شَهْوَتِهِ

وَأَنْ يُخْرِجَهُ مِنْ وُجُودِ غَفْلَتِهِ فَقَدِ اسْتَعْجَزَ الْقُدْرَةَ الإِلَهِيَّةَ

﴿ ... وَكَانَ ٱللَّهُ عَلَىٰ كُلِّ شَىْءٍ مُّقْتَدِرًا ﴾

Whoever finds it strange that Allāh saves him from his desires and removes him from a state of heedlessness has underestimated the Divine Power. '...And Allāh has complete power over all things.' [84]

Whosoever thinks it strange and thus finds it improbable that Allāh, Most Merciful and All-Powerful, would save him from his desires and awaken him from his heedlessness has indeed underestimated Divine power. For in the end, it is not the individual that changes, but that Allāh grants him the grace to change. It is not the individual who gains victory, but that Allāh gives him the ability to be victorious. *He* Allāh is *All-Powerful.* No soul is beyond the reach of His mercy, no matter how deeply it may be entrenched in desires or heedlessness.

This is indeed a common spiritual struggle; the feeling of being trapped by one's own inclinations, attachments, or addictions. Many resign themselves to their weaknesses, feeling that these inner battles are too difficult to overcome. But such resignation is only induced by our perceived limitations and a lack of trust in Allāh's limitless capacity. The essence of faith is to recognize that transformation is possible, even when it seems beyond our reach. To doubt this is to underestimate the expansive and boundless mercy of Allāh, who is always near and capable of intervening in even the darkest moments of the soul.

The journey to spiritual awakening is not a burden one must bear alone. While human effort is essential, it is ultimately Allāh's grace that liberates the soul from the shackles of desire and the fog of heedlessness. It is upon us to ask with humility and awe, recognizing that even if our own will falters, the Divine Will *never* betrays, and one should never disgrace themselves for loss of hope.

۱۹۷

رُبَّمَا وَرَدَتِ الظُّلَمُ عَلَيْكَ، لِيُعَرِّفَكَ قَدْرَ مَا مَنَّ بِهِ عَلَيْكَ

It may be injustice befell you so that you realize the extent of the favour that He has bestowed upon you.

---

84   Sūrah al-Kahf 18:45

(۱۹۸)

مَنْ لَمْ يَعْرِفْ قَدْرَ النِّعَمِ بِوِجْدَانِهَا عَرَفَهَا بِوُجُودِ فِقْدَانِهَا

Whoever does not recognize the value of blessings by their presence will recognize it by their absence.

(۱۹۹)

لَا تُدْهِشْكَ وَارِدَاتُ النِّعَمِ عَنِ القِيَامِ بِحُقُوقِ شُكْرِكَ،

فَإِنَّ ذَلِكَ مِمَّا يَحُطُّ مِنْ وُجُودِ قَدْرِكَ

Let not the arrival of blessings astonish you from fulfilling your obligations of gratitude, for that is what diminishes your worth.

Though Allāh is Just, sometimes He may allow injustice to befall His servants solely that they realize the true extent of His favours upon them. So that they find themselves in a state of profound reflection on gratitude, the recognition of blessings, and the subtle relationship between light and darkness in spiritual growth. So that they understand the ways in which blessings and their apparent absence can truly cultivate a more profound understanding in the seeker, encouraging humility and conscious thankfulness.

And thus darkness may descend upon you, if only to make you appreciate the value of what He has bestowed upon you. Moments of difficulty or obscurity are there only as reminders of His favour. When one is caught in hardship or confusion, therein rises an opportunity for self-reflection, a time to appreciate the blessings that one may have taken for granted. This darkness is not intended as punishment but as a way to cultivate gratitude.

Yet, whoever does not recognize the worth of blessings by their presence will surely come to know them by their absence, for it is a human tendency to only appreciate a thing when it is taken away, when the blessing is temporarily withdrawn, allowing the soul a chance to confront its dependency on that grace, instilling a deeper recognition of its value. This loss, or the perceived withdrawal, humbles the soul and encourages a refined gratitude that is more complete and resilient. Thus, gratitude in the presence of blessings is enriched by the wisdom gained through their absence.

So let not the arrival of blessings distract you from fulfilling the obligations of gratitude, that due to their absence, you become so overwhelmed by their coming that you lose awareness of them as being gifts from Allāh. Doing so diminishes your spiritual worth, lowering your rank in His eyes. True gratitude is active and mindful, not merely a fleeting acknowledgment of a blessing's arrival. Instead of becoming complacent or dazzled by the gifts, the seeker is urged to respond by honouring the responsibility of gratitude, which involves using blessings purposefully and remembering their Source. A distracted heart fails to grasp the significance of Allāh's generosity, whereas true gratitude elevates one's spiritual state, aligning the soul with the His Will and maintaining humility in the face of endless blessings.

﴾٢٠٠﴿

تَمَكُّنُ حَلَاوَةِ الهَوَى مِنَ القَلْبِ هُوَ الدَّاءُ العُضَالُ

The sweetness of desire that dominates the heart is a disease incurable.

Desire is sweet, and its delight is sweeter, but greater still is its fulfillment, as from it comes ecstasy and euphoria. Once the human being has had but a taste of that sweetness, all his thought is bent on seeking it. When desire becomes a deeply ingrained attachment, it takes on a seduction that distorts one's perception and impairs the soul's ability to recognize truth and pursue higher spiritual goals. The soul's obsessions then become the heart's obsessions, and it, the heart, forgets why it is here. Such desires may initially appear harmless or even pleasurable, but as they slowly seep into the heart, they exert a strong, often unnoticed control over one's inner life. This is the mark of an addict.

The phrase 'sweetness of desire' حلاوة الهوى is key here. It is the disguise of pleasure that the desire adorns itself with. Desires are not always obvious sins or overt temptations; they can be subtle inclinations or attachments to worldly comforts, ambitions, or relationships. The sweetness of these desires makes them difficult to renounce, as they mask their harmful effects by satisfying immediate wants and creating a false sense of contentment. Once this 'sweetness' takes hold, it blinds the heart, making it harder for the seeker to see beyond it or to yearn for anything higher. This is why it is described as an *'incurable disease,'* not because it is absolutely beyond healing, but because it requires an exceptional effort to overcome.

Prevention is better than cure. To heed the warning and be cautious of the trap is the most sensible approach. The disease, once it takes hold, is near incurable, but one can still heal from it. Acknowledgment is the first step, by admitting addiction. Repentance is the medicine prescribed, and must be taken with consistency and commitment. The cure ultimately lies in redirecting the heart toward piety, finding sweetness in remembrance, worship, and the pursuit of inner clarity rather than in fleeting desires. This process of inner struggle, known as *mujāhada* مجاهدة, is both challenging and necessary, as it gradually replaces the alluring sweetness of worldly attachments with the true and lasting sweetness of the HereAfter. Through this, the heart can be freed from the chains of desire and returned to its natural state of seeking the Divine Presence.

(٢٠١)

لَا يُخْرِجُ الشَّهْوَةَ مِنَ القَلْبِ إِلَّا خَوفٌ مُزْعِجٌ أَو شَوقٌ مُقلِقٌ

Nothing dispels lust from the heart save for vexing fear and disquieting eagerness.

Fear or reward. Carrot or stick. The only two motivators that trigger the human being's psychological mechanisms for change.

The force of worldly desires, deeply rooted within the heart, can only be dislodged by equally powerful motivators. Either an intense fear that shakes one's being or a passionate longing that redirects the heart's focus. Both of these forces, though unsettling, are dramatically life-changing. They are responsible, where reason fails, for compelling the heart into a stasis of change and redirection toward a higher purpose.

The 'fear' in this regard refers to the fear of spiritual or moral failure, the realization of life's fleeting nature, and an acute awareness of accountability before Allāh. When the heart is vexed by such fear, it awakens to the consequences of capitulating to unchecked desires and the soul's ultimate responsibility. This fear is not paralyzing but rather invigorating. It brings about a sense of urgency and clarity. In this sense, fear becomes a means of liberation, encouraging the individual to transcend superficial desires and aspire for something greater and more enduring.

On the other hand, the disquieting eagerness, the unsettling longing is the rewarding motivator that arises from a deep, almost painful yearning for closeness to Allāh, His presence being the ultimate reward. This longing can be more powerful than fear, as it fills the heart with a sense of incompleteness and restlessness, propelling it to strive toward tranquility and contentment. Such longing often leads to a reorientation of one's desires, where the sweetness of worldly attachments is replaced by the sweetness of Divine love. Through such a powerful yearning, the heart begins to perceive that true fulfillment lies not in transient pleasures but in the eternal connection with Allāh. It trembles in awareness of the His presence and longs passionately for Him.

(٢٠٢)

كَمَا لَا يُحِبُّ العَمَلَ الْمُشْتَرَكَ ... لَا يُحِبُّ القَلْبَ الْمُشْتَرَكَ، العَمَلُ الْمُشْتَرَكُ لَا يَقْبَلُهُ، وَالْقَلْبُ الْمُشْتَرَكُ لَا يُقْبِلُ عَلَيْهِ

Just as He does not like a deed associated (with others beside Him) so too does He not like a heart allied (to others). The deed associated (with others) is not accepted by Him, and the heart allied (to others) is not approachable to Him.

Shared devotion does not embody the true meaning of love. How can a heart that is divided claim to love and claim love in reciprocation? Much like an act of love done for one cannot then be dedicated to another, the heart that professes love for one cannot then profess the same love for another. Indeed, Allāh does not love a heart that is divided, just as He does not love an act dedicated to other than Him. For if the heart is divided, it cannot truly turn to Him when its gaze is already set upon other than Him. Thus does He declare;

$$﴿ ... إِنَّمَا يَتَقَبَّلُ ٱللَّهُ مِنَ ٱلْمُتَّقِينَ ﴾$$

... Indeed, Allāh only accepts from the righteous [85]

When the heart is divided, its energies and affections are scattered, drawn to various other interests, and distracted from the singular focus that true devotion requires. It is a heart preoccupied with competing loves and concerns, one whose attention vacillates between devotion to Allāh and the lure of desires, ambitions, or fears. This divided focus weakens the heart and hinders its prime purpose of realizing true contentment. Such diluted offerings are not worthy of acceptance, for true worship requires sincerity and purity of intention. A heart that is truly devoted will find that Divine Love fills its every longing, leaving no space for competing desires, and will be able to experience the sweetness of unbroken devotion.

(٢٠٣)

$$أَنْوَارٌ أُذِنَ لَهَا فِي الْوُصُولِ، وَأَنْوَارٌ أُذِنَ لَهَا فِي الدُّخُولِ$$

There are lights permitted to arrive, and there are lights permitted to enter.

(٢٠٤)

$$رُبَّمَا وَرَدَتْ عَلَيْكَ الْأَنْوَارُ فَوَجَدَتِ الْقَلْبَ مَحْشُوًّا بِصُوَرِ الْآثَارِ ...$$
$$فَارْتَحَلَتْ مِنْ حَيْثُ جَاءَتْ$$

Perhaps the lights came to you, and they found the heart filled with forms of creation, so they departed from whence they came.

(٢٠٥)

$$فَرِّغْ قَلْبَكَ مِنَ الْأَغْيَارِ يَمْلَأْهُ بِالْمَعَارِفِ وَالْأَسْرَارِ$$

Empty your heart of otherness, so He may fill it with knowledge and secrets.

---

85   Sūrah al-Māʾidah 5:27

Some knowledge is permitted to reach the heart, but not permitted to penetrate it. That permission only comes when the light of knowledge finds no blemish to bar its entry. A vessel that is already full cannot take more, and when the heart is full of forms and imageries of the created realm, which blemish it, the lights of knowledge and inspiration cannot find entry, and they return to where they originated from. For such lights serve no benefit if the heart is distracted by otherness.

Such are the subtle dynamics of spiritual illumination and the state of receptivity within the heart. The lights that reach the heart, but do not penetrate, are a fleeting presence, a momentary awareness or insight that touches the heart's surface but does not transform it. Upon finding the heart preoccupied with worldly images and attachments, these lights may retreat, leaving the heart as it was. But when they are permitted entry, they transform into a deeper level of illumination that truly settles within, filling the heart with understanding and nearness to Allāh. This difference is reflected in the heart's state. While certain lights can grace its threshold, only a heart prepared through purity and focus can truly embrace these lights and let them grow into spiritual knowledge. Just as a container can only hold what it has space for, a heart filled with distractions, desires, or attachments naturally lacks the capacity to fully absorb Divine Light. These *āthār* آثار, or impressions of worldly things, act as veils, barring deeper insights and blessings from taking root. When the seeker learns to purify their inner world, to empty themselves of themselves and the distractions of others, they create a space that can now be filled. Such emptiness is not mere detachment, but an intentional freeing of the heart from dependencies and attachments, making it a vessel for Divine Wisdom. When the heart is cleansed of *aghyār* الأغيار, the 'otherness' or foreign distractions, it becomes fertile ground for the *ma'ārif* المعارف, Divine Knowledge, and the *asrār* الأسرار, Divine Secrets.

﴾٢٠٦﴿

لَا تَسْتَبْطِئْ النَّوَالَ، وَلَكِنِ اسْتَبْطِئْ مِنْ نَفْسِكَ وُجُودَ الإِقْبَالِ

Do not find slow the gifts, but find slow from yourself your approach.

Do not become impatient for gifts that have already been promised and assured for you. Forget not that you took this path to ready yourself for those gifts, but the gifts themselves were never the true objective. For what bears greater value? The gift? Or meeting the Giver? Rather be impatient with yourself for lacking true turning toward Him, for directing your efforts in exchange for His gifts rather than His presence, and for thus losing sight of what truly matters. Worse still that one should lose sight of both the Giver and the gifts, to focus instead on its delay, while being unwary of the poor cordiality they present.

(۲۰۷)

حُقُوقٌ فِي الأَوْقَاتِ يُمْكِنُ قَضَاؤُهَا، وَحُقُوقُ الأَوْقَاتِ لَا يُمْكِنُ قَضَاؤُهَا،

إِذْ مَا مِنْ وَقْتٍ يَرِدُ إِلَّا وَلِلَّهِ عَلَيْكَ فِيهِ حَقٌّ جَدِيدٌ، وَأَمْرٌ أَكِيدٌ،

فَكَيْفَ تَقْضِي فِيهِ حَقَّ غَيْرِهِ وَأَنْتَ لَمْ تَقْضِ حَقَّ اللهِ فِيهِ ؟

There are rights within time that can be fulfilled, and there are rights of time that cannot be fulfilled.
For every moment that passes, there is a new right that Allāh has upon you, and this is an emphatic matter.
So, how can you fulfill in it (the moment) the right of others when you have not fulfilled in it the right of Allāh?

Every unfolding moment contains a Divine Command that must be fulfilled, and to each servant is entrusted a command within their capacity to fulfill. Each command is thus a right of the One issuing it, and some are fulfilled, while others, if missed, cannot be reclaimed.

These rights are unlike those ordinary obligations that can be deferred. The demands of each moment in time are fleeting and cannot be retroactively honoured, as each one is imbued with a particular invitation from Allāh. The highest awareness and vigilance is required from the believer, lest they miss the grandest of all opportunities to serve.

The urgency of fulfilling these unique rights lies in the fact that every moment in a believer's life is endowed with a specific "حق" or right that Allāh has over them. Each moment calls upon the believer to engage in worship, reflection, or action that fulfills a higher purpose. This creates an awareness that the heart's attention cannot afford to drift, as the rights of the present cannot be deferred without a spiritual cost. The believer must avoid filling their present with past obligations or futuristic distractions, and be ever aware and vigilant of the moment to be in readiness for the unique call. This is the sacredness of each unfolding moment as a fresh opportunity to serve Allāh, rendering time itself a trust that must be honoured as it unfolds. The true seeker is present in the present, for he understands that what is required of him right now is not random or accidental— it is Decreed.

· ·—+—·◄●►◄●►◄—●—+· ·

(۲۰۸)

مَا فَاتَ مِنْ عُمُرِكَ لَا عِوَضَ لَهُ ، وَمَا حَصَلَ لَكَ مِنْهُ لَا قِيْمَةَ لَهُ

What has passed from your life cannot be substituted, and what you have gained from it cannot be quantified.

What is meant for you will reach you. What missed you was never yours, and if even it was, it cannot be replaced. This is the nature of Time, and its irreplaceable value. What is gone of one's life can never be recovered, and what one gains of virtue and righteousness in those days past is indeed of immeasurable worth.

Such are also the words of the Holy Prophet ﷺ when he said;

* وَاعْلَمْ أَنَّ مَا أَخْطَأَكَ لَمْ يَكُنْ لِيُصِيبَكَ، وَمَا أَصَابَكَ لَمْ يَكُنْ لِيُخْطِئَكَ *

And know, that what missed you was never meant for you, and what befell you was not meant to miss you [86]

Examine both the transience of time and the infinite value in every moment lived with purpose and reflection. By acknowledging that missed time cannot be compensated, the believer is urged to value each moment deeply and to live with a sense of responsibility and awareness of their purpose in this world. Those moments filled with other than what cultivates one's HereAfter are wasted, until in old age their dreams are replaced by regrets of opportunities missed. Whereas those moments filled with purpose, with spiritual and experiential insights, are priceless. The growth, wisdom, and understanding one gains from life is beyond material valuation; it cannot be quantified or replaced. True wealth lies in the depth of one's experiences, especially those that shape one's character from what they are to who they become. We are encouraged to reflect on the *quality* of life lived, not its quantity, where the journey itself, filled with moments of self-awareness and righteous conduct, becomes the most significant and invaluable attainment of one's life.

(٢٠٩)

مَا أَحْبَبْتَ شَيْئًا إِلَّا كُنْتَ لَهُ عَبْدًا، وَهُوَ لَا يَرْضَى أَنْ تَكُونَ لِغَيْرِهِ عَبْدًا

You do not love a thing but that you become its slave, and He is not pleased that you be a slave to other than Him.

One does not truly love a thing except that they become its servant, and indeed Allāh does not desire for you to be a servant to anything other than Him. Love binds the soul, and whatever one gives their heart to ultimately possesses them. In this way, love can become an unseen shackle, transforming what was once a desire or attachment into a form of servitude. This servitude is subtle yet powerful, as it reorients one's focus and energy toward the object of affection. Would that object, for the believer, be a created thing, or the Creator Himself? And remember, the heart cannot divide its devotion between the two.

---

86 Imām an-Nawawī's Forty, Hadīth 19

(٢١٠)

لَا تَنْفَعُهُ طَاعَتُكَ وَلَا تَضُرُّهُ مَعْصِيَتُكَ، وَإِنَّمَا أَمَرَكَ بِهَذِهِ وَنَهَاكَ عَنْ هَذِهِ لِمَا يَعُودُ إِلَيْكَ

Your obedience does not benefit Him, nor does your disobedience harm Him. He has only commanded you this (obedience) and forbidden you from that (disobedience) for what ultimately returns to you.

(٢١١)

لَا يَزِيدُ فِي ـهِ إِقْبَالُ مَنْ أَقْبَلَ عَلَيْهِ، وَلَا يَنْقُصُ مِنْ ـهِ إِدْبَارُ مَنْ أَدْبَرَ عَنْهُ

Not does His Nobility increase by the approach of those who turn towards Him, and not does His Nobility diminish by the retreat of those who turn away from Him.

This is a fundamental aspect of the relationship between the human being and his Lord. Commands and prohibitions are not for the sake of commanding and prohibiting, as they are not to His benefit or harm, but for the benefit of those who adhere to them. They serve to refine, elevate, and purify the individual, allowing the soul to grow closer to its source and experience wisdom and love. Obedience strictly leads to paradise, and prohibition strictly protects from other than paradise. Thus Allāh commanded His servants to do one and forbade them from the other for what ultimately returns to His servants.

Most approach obligations with a mindset rooted in transactional exchanges; give and take, benefit and harm. Here rises the challenge on that limited perspective by reminding us that Allāh's commands transcend human notions of need or gain. He is beyond all reliance, free from dependence on His creation, for His reality is Absolute, while creation is contingent upon Him. Those who turn toward Him with obedience do not in any way increase His already infinite and limitless nobility, nor is His nobility affected by those who turn away. The former, by their surrender, have everything to gain and nothing to lose, while the latter, from their defiance, have everything to lose and nothing to gain.

When we see the Divine Decree in this light, it becomes a profound expression of mercy rather than mere restrictions. The Law is guidance, not a burden, a path crafted to foster inner peace and protect us from self-inflicted harm. In turning away from disobedience, we protect ourselves from the inner disturbances and regrets it often brings, while through obedience, we build resilience, discipline, and a closer bond with our Creator. One must therefore approach the Law, not with fear of consequences or a sense of duty alone, but with a deep understanding of the love and wisdom that underpins every command, recognizing that all good ultimately 'returns to us' in the form of reward.

(٢١٢)

وُصُولُكَ إِلَيْهِ وُصُولُكَ إِلَى الْمَعْرِفَةِ بِهِ، وَإِلَّا فَجَلَّ رَبُّنَا أَنْ يَتَّصِلَ بِهِ، أَو يَتَّصِلَ هُوَ بِشَيْءٍ

*Your arrival to Him is your arrival to the knowledge of Him; elseways,
Majestic is our Lord that He be attached to any thing.*

(٢١٣)

قُرْبُكَ مِنْهُ... هُوَ أَنْ تَكُونَ مُشَاهِدًا لِقُرْبِهِ، وَإِلَّا فَمِنْ أَيْنَ أَنْتَ وَوُجُودَ قُرْبِهِ

*Your closeness to Him... is that you be in a state of witnessing His closeness,
otherwise, where are you and (where is) His closeness?*

One's journey and their arrival to the Divine Presence is not a physical motion. We are not beings in motion through space and matter, though our temporal existence is embodied by matter which occupies space. Our journey is through time, in how each moment is unfolded and the choices that we make in those moments. The human being is inseparable from the expenditure of time. It is the only true precious commodity granted to him, and he is, in his present existence, but a number of days. Each moment spent is exchanged either for that which is intrinsic or that which is extrinsic. He either acquires what sustains his spiritual aspect or that which sustains his material being. And in the spiritual aspect, there are only two entities that sustain him. Faith and Knowledge, both intertwined and inseparable.

The search for the eternal and absolute is not a physical motion nor a physical acquisition. Reaching the Divine Presence does not entail a materialization of oneself in some higher dimension. It entails a knowledge of the highest degree, an understanding that cannot be encompassed in the lower earthly plane. There are no words that can express or articulate that understanding, for such knowledge does not originate from causality. Almighty Allāh is too Majestic to be causally attached to anything lower than His Majestic Throne. Hence Divine Proximity is not a literal, material, or physical meeting or connection with Allāh, who is, Himself, transcendent and beyond any material or spatial connection. Rather, 'reaching' Him means attaining understanding and spiritual awareness of His reality, as Allāh exists beyond human conceptions of space, form, or limits. Our journey is thus a pursuit of gnosis or deep knowledge of Him. It is to reach an understanding of *who* He is, rather than a physical destination of *where* He is.

For the believer, nearness to Him is to witness His nearness to you, for how can one otherwise comprehend His nearness? And this is not about reducing some physical distance but rather becoming aware of Allāh's presence that is ever-close. This nearness is an awakening within the heart to perceive His intimate presence.

161

In that regard, our inability to grasp the nature of Divinity directly or fully should not lead us to despair, as it is in becoming aware of His nearness to us that we experience true closeness. This nearness, as we said, is less about approaching a 'where' or a 'when' and more about awakening the heart to the truth of His proximity, which exists without bounds and at all times. It is a nearness experienced in knowledge, not in tangible terms. It is when the heart attains a living, experiential knowledge of Allāh's ever-present reality, transforming every moment into an opportunity to recognize His closeness. This is a knowing that instills a sense of humble awe for the Absolute Majesty of the Lord of the Worlds.

(٢١٤)

الْحَقَائِقُ تَرِدُ فِي حَالِ التَّجَلِّي مُجْمَلَةً ، وَبَعْدَ الْوَعْيِ يَكُونُ الْبَيَانُ

﴿ فَإِذَا قَرَأْنَهُ فَاتَّبِعْ قُرْءَانَهُ ۞ ثُمَّ إِنَّ عَلَيْنَا بَيَانَهُ ﴾

The realities are manifested in a comprehensive state of revelation, and after understanding (of the Revelation), comes the elucidation.
'So when We have recited it [through Gabriel], then follow its recitation [O Muhammad]. Then upon Us is its clarification [to you].'"[87]

The truth of reality is not arrived at through facts and figures, or through particulate and semantic analysis. Truth is universal and is arrived at through the comprehension of universals, axioms, and fundamental principles which once affirmed cannot be altered. These universal truths arrive in the form of unveilings to the heart, and clarity in them follows with awareness of these truths being from the Divine. They first come to the seeker in a form that might be overwhelming or ambiguous, akin to a flash of light that briefly illuminates but does not immediately reveal every detail. These initial unveilings of truth are called *tajalliyāt* تجليات and are often indirect and obscure, offering a glimpse that stirs the heart yet remains just beyond complete comprehension. Only as the seeker matures in awareness and understanding do these truths gradually unfold in clarity, enabling them to grasp their depth and meaning.

Such is the nature of the grandest of all revelation, being the Divine Speech of Allāh. When it is *re*-cited to the human being through the chosen Messenger ﷺ, the foremost objective of the recipients is to further the revelation in recitation. While the apparent meanings are availed upon receiving it, the deeper meanings are a privilege granted by Allāh to be revealed at His discretion in the innermost dimensions of the heart. By this one understands that it is He Allāh who initiates the revelation of truth and then, from His own wisdom and at a time of His own choosing, He provides clarity and understanding.

---

[87] Sūrah al-Qiyāmah 75:18-19

The scholars say that the best exegete of Revelation is Time itself. The seeker's role is to remain receptive and patient, to follow the guidance as received. Whether one is able to immediately rationalize it or not, he must trust that Allāh will clarify its meanings. Complete understanding unfolds according to His wisdom rather than human urgency, irrespective of one's intellectual acumen or academic proficiency. In this gradual revelation, the search for spiritual insight, for those universal truths and axioms of reality, becomes a journey of patience, humility, and openness. It is unbefitting for the believer to assume to know, when the knowing is not an initiation of the self, rather is grant of the Divine. One should not rush to interpret or define Revelation based on initial impressions or their own mental projections. They risk compromising the unveiling of these insights and further deluding themselves into believing they have attained clarity when in reality they remain obscure.

(٢١٥)

مَتَى وَرَدَتِ الْوَارِدَاتُ الْإِلَهِيَّةُ عَلَيْكَ هَدَمَتِ الْعَوَائِدَ عَلَيْكَ

﴿ ... إِنَّ ٱلْمُلُوكَ إِذَا دَخَلُوا قَرْيَةً أَفْسَدُوهَا ... ﴾

When there come Divine Inspirations upon you, they tear down the habitual customs in you. 'Indeed, when kings enter a city, they neutralize it...'[88]

(٢١٦)

الْوَارِدَاتُ تَأْتِي مِنْ حَضْرَةِ قَهَّارٍ، لِأَجْلِ ذَلِكَ لَا يُصَادِمُهُ شَيْءٌ إِلَّا دَمَغَهُ

﴿ بَلْ نَقْذِفُ بِٱلْحَقِّ عَلَى ٱلْبَطِلِ فَيَدْمَغُهُ فَإِذَا هُوَ زَاهِقٌ ... ﴾

The inspiration comes from the presence of the Dominant (Allāh), and for this reason, nothing confronts it except that it (the inspiration) triumphs it (defeats what attempts to confront it).
'Rather, We cast the truth upon falsehood, that it (the truth) triumphs it (falsehood). And behold, it (falsehood) perishes.'[89]

(٢١٧)

كَيْفَ يَحْتَجِبُ الْحَقُّ بِشَيْءٍ، وَالَّذِي يَحْتَجِبُ بِهِ هُوَ فِيهِ ظَاهِرٌ وَمَوْجُودٌ حَاضِرٌ

How can the truth be concealed by some thing, when that which conceals it is itself evident and present?

---

88 Sūrah al-Naml 27:34

89 Sūrah al-Anbiyāh 21:18

Due to the nature of their origin, Spiritual Inspirations do not conform to the customs of causality, rather, when they arrive, they disrupt and demolish all habituations. Such is the power of Divine Intervention, likened to powerful kings, who, when they enter a city in conquest, they tear down everything so as to rebuild to their liking. These inspirations are like the arrival of a sovereign force that comes with sweeping changes to the believer's inner state. When they enter the being, they have the power to dismantle the established habits and attachments that have rooted themselves in the heart over time.

They arrive in moments of spiritual awareness, when one's sensitivity to Allāh's presence is heightened, and the heart is directly touched by His light. Such moments can be jarring because they demand a reordering of one's priorities, perspectives, and life choices. Just as the arrival of a conquering king disrupts the existing order in a city, the presence of these inspirations uproots what was once familiar, urging the seeker to abandon those mundane customs that hinder their progress toward the Divine Presence. Old habits, comforts, and even some of the personal identities built around worldly matters are 'laid to ruin' so that new space is created for authentic spiritual growth and alignment with a higher purpose.

In the face of these inspirations, as originating from the 'Presence of the Most Powerful' من حضرة قهار, being Allāh's attribute as the Ultimate and Irresistible Power of Truth, الحق, all else becomes availed as false and folly, helpless and crumbling. Falsehood has no origin, no foundation, no existential reality. It is, as defined, a feeble fabrication.

When these inspirations arise, they obliterate anything of illusion that stands in their path, just as Truth, when it is cast, shatters and dispels all falsehood. They dissolve the veils of ego, attachment, and delusion, and purify the heart by illuminating it with the presence of Al-Haqq, rendering any form of resistance or self-deception void.

Such moments of insight or spiritual awakening penetrate the core of one's being, establishing truth within and extinguishing anything contrary to it. They invite the individual to surrender, knowing that any attempt to resist Divine Illumination is like attempting to shield one's eyes with gossamer from the glare of the sun.

For how can the luminance of the Divine ever be veiled by anything, given that He is the very essence and existence of all things? He is not only present but manifest within all that exists.

The idea of something 'veiling' Him, and likewise veiling the Truth, is an illusion. Any supposed barrier is itself permeated by His presence, and so too is that which emanates from Him as the Truth, to enter the being as its inspiration. The heart's inability to see this reality stems not from a lack of Allāh's presence, but from the limitations imposed by the self. In essence, Al-Haqq is never truly concealed, rather it is the awareness of the individual that fluctuates, sometimes perceiving, sometimes veiled. Any such 'veil' is but an illusion, dissipated by the Light of Absolute Truth.

(٢١٨)

لَا تَيْئَسْ مِنْ قَبُولِ عَمَلٍ لَمْ تَجِدْ فِيهِ وُجُودَ الْحُضُورِ،

فَرُبَّمَا قُبِلَ مِنَ الْعَمَلِ مَا لَمْ تُدْرِكْ ثَمَرَتَهُ عَاجِلًا

Do not despair of the acceptance of a deed in which you do not perceive the Presence (of the Divine), for it may be that what is accepted from the deed is its fruit that you have not presently realized.

(٢١٩)

لَا تُزَكِّيَنَّ وَارِدًا لَا تَعْلَمُ ثَمَرَتَهُ، فَلَيْسَ الْمُرَادُ مِنَ السَّحَابِ الإِمْطَارَ،

وَإِنَّمَا الْمُرَادُ مِنْهُ وُجُودُ الثِّمَارِ

Do not augment what is coming without knowing its outcome (result). For it is not the rain that is sought from the clouds. Rather, only fruitful outcomes are sought from it (the rain).

Here is a common spiritual concern—the anxiety over the efficacy and acceptance of one's deeds when the heart feels distant or absent from them. We are cautioned against despairing over an action where one has not felt a tangible presence of heart or mind. Often, seekers may worry that a prayer or act of devotion performed without full attentiveness is worthless. Yet, we are reminded that a deed may still be accepted, even if its immediate fruits or impacts are not apparent. Allāh, in His mercy, may accept acts of worship done with sincerity, even if they fall short of ideal concentration or are not performed to perfection. This is an encouraging thought, to have patience and perseverance in worship, recognizing that the ultimate value of a deed lies beyond what one perceives of it in the immediate moment. It does not befit one to judge a deed without knowing its outcome, for it is not the rain that is sought from the cloud, but rather the fruits that will blossom from the rain. The deed is only a vessel for the sincerity of one's intention. What truly matters is not the fruition of the deed, but the fruition of one's sincere intention.

So do not place undue judgment on any spiritual inspiration or insight without understanding its deeper impact or fruit. The mere presence of rain-bearing clouds does not fulfill their purpose. True benefit arises only when they bring forth fruit-bearing rain. Similarly, the mere arrival of insight or spiritual inspiration is not necessarily transformative or beneficial. For it to be an authentic insight, for it to bring lasting change or enlightenment, it must be preceded by growth and deeper understanding in one's spiritual journey. This guards against self-deception, as by themselves, they are but fleeting insights, and do not inherently contribute positively to one's development. It is the distinct importance of substance over appearance in both worship and spiritual experience that it is the true fruit, the deep, internal transformation that signifies an accepted deed or a meaningful inspiration. This subtle discernment between transient feelings and genuine, enduring benefits protects one from false satisfaction and guides them to a more profound and genuine relationship with their Lord.

٢٢٠

لَا تَطْلُبَنَّ بَقَاءَ الوَارِدَاتِ بَعْدَ أَنْ بَسَطَتْ أَنْوَارَهَا وَأَوْدَعَتْ أَسْرَارَهَا،

فَلَكَ فِي اللهِ غِنًى عَنْ كُلِّ شَيْءٍ، وَلَيْسَ يُغْنِيكَ عَنْهُ شَيْءٌ

Do not seek the perpetuation of inspirations after they have spread their lights and entrusted their secrets. For you have sufficiency in Allāh from everything, yet nothing can make you independent of Him.

It is a warning to the believer against seeking permanence in those fleeting, illuminating moments of spiritual insight or inspiration, as such moments, though they come with a radiance and unique clarity that unveil aspects of higher secrets and knowledge, they are not meant to linger. Their purpose is to open the heart and reveal certain truths, not to become a permanent state. They depart once their purpose has been fulfilled, and by clinging to these moments, one risks becoming attached to the experience itself, rather than to what was intended by it.

True richness lies not in the possession of transient states, no matter how enlightening, but in the abiding presence of Allāh within one's heart. He alone is the ultimate source of wealth, satisfaction, and contentment. No experience or state, however blissful or profound, can substitute for the essence of His closeness. Seeking permanence in these momentary experiences can inadvertently lead to dependency on them rather than cultivating true reliance on Allāh as the One who sent the inspiration. And He sends it not to delight and bring joy, for even though they do, they are purposed to act as openings to Him.

This is what attaining a state of inner independence entails, where one is enriched solely by their relationship with Allāh by using the inspirations received as stepping stones in their ascent. In such a state, they are no longer swayed by the coming and going of spiritual states, but rather find stability and fulfillment in the Divine Presence itself, transcending the need for any intermediary experience. In the end, one's goal must be to turn the mediated and assisted experiences into an immediate and intuited state of being. This transformation is not a negation of the spiritual experiences, but an invitation to go beyond them and realize that Allāh alone suffices as the Eternal, Unchanging Reality.

166

(٢٢١)

تَطَلُّعُكَ إِلَى بَقَاءِ غَيْرِهِ دَلِيلٌ عَلَى عَدَمِ وِجْدَانِكَ لَهُ،

وَاسْتِيحَاشُكَ بِفِقْدَانِ مَا سِوَاهُ دَلِيلٌ عَلَى عَدَمِ وُصْلَتِكَ بِهِ

Your endeavour for the permanence of otherness is evidence of your lack of conscience with Him, and your melancholy (state) by the loss of what is other than Him is evidence of your lack of arrival to Him.

Where does one place their ultimate sense of comfort and security? Yearning for the permanence of anything besides Allāh indicates a lack of true realization of the His Presence. Its realization is not passive and does not come when one's attention is elsewhere. When one fully turns their attention to Him, they come to see that He alone is constant, while all else is subject to change and loss.

This endeavour towards the longevity of anything worldly or even spiritual shows that one's heart has not yet fully found the satisfaction and contentment in the Divine Presence alone, and has hence not fully realized the true value of that presence in their heart.

The sense of alienation then arises when one loses the very thing they sought permanence in, and if such a loss, of any worldly or spiritual gain, brings about a sense of separation or isolation, it is an indication that the heart has not yet forged a deep, unbreakable connection with the Absolute. For if it were so then the heart would not feel alienated knowing that its has placed its trust in that which never diminishes. For the heart that is firmly rooted in Divine Presence, the departure of worldly matters or transient spiritual experiences does not disturb its stillness, as it knows that Allāh's presence is ever with it. The heart's spiritual maturity lies in deepening its trust in Allāh, such that nothing else, in its appearance or disappearance, disrupts its peace. It must transcend its reliance on the fleeting, and seek an unwavering attachment to the Divine. In this way, the heart becomes unshaken by gains or losses, immersed in the perpetual presence of Allāh, the Eternal, the only reality that is Absolute.

(٢٢٢)

النَّعِيمَ وَإِنْ تَنَوَّعَتْ مَظَاهِرُهُ إِنَّمَا هُوَ بِشُهُودِهِ وَاقْتِرَابِهِ،

وَالْعَذَابَ وَإِنْ تَنَوَّعَتْ مَظَاهِرُهُ إِنَّمَا هُوَ بِوُجُودِ حِجَابِهِ،

فَسَبَبُ الْعَذَابِ وُجُودُ الْحِجَابِ...

وَإِتْمَامُ النَّعِيمِ بِالنَّظَرِ إِلَى وَجْهِهِ الْكَرِيمِ...

The essence of bliss, be it complex, lies only in witnessing Him and drawing near to Him. The essence of punishment, be it complex, lies in the existence of His veil. Thus, the cause of punishment is the presence of the veil, while the completeness of bliss is in beholding His Noble Countenance.

(٢٢٣)

مَا تَجِدُهُ الْقُلُوبُ مِنَ الْهُمُومِ وَالْأَحْزَانِ فَلِأَجْلِ مَا مُنِعَتْ مِنْ وُجُودِ الْعِيَانِ

What the hearts experience of sadness and sorrow is due to what prevents them from the witnessing.

We establish first that the cause of the veil is not in its inherent presence, but by one's own doing, or lack of doing. We establish secondly that the veil is lowered through righteous conduct, and absence of such conduct results in retribution, for the void of righteousness is ultimately filled with wickedness, which in turn is reciprocated by punishment. In this sense both joy and suffering are entirely dependent on one's proximity to or distance from the Divine. They are not defined by their external forms or the variety of their expressions, but rather by the presence or absence of one's closeness to Allāh. True bliss, in all its diverse appearances, is a result of beholding and drawing near to Allāh. Conversely, true suffering, regardless of its outward manifestations, stems from the existence of a deliberate veil or barrier between the servant and his Lord.

This veil, then, is the prime cause of torment. It signifies spiritual separation, obscuring the light of the Divine Presence from the heart. The painful consequence of this separation is not simply the result of moral failings but arises from a state in which the heart loses its deeper purpose and deprives itself of the one source of true contentment. Likewise, the fulfillment of bliss is encapsulated in the witnessing of Allāh's Nobility and experiencing His beauty, closeness, and presence in a way that profoundly fulfills the heart's purpose. This alludes to the ultimate reward in the Hereafter, which for the believer is not only entry into paradise but also, and most significantly, one's unveiled experience of Allāh's majestic presence. Hence, true paradise is found in closeness to Him, while true despair lies in estrangement from Him.[90]

One's focus should be on removing those inner veils of selfish desires and heedlessness that distance the heart, to pursue a life of devotion and purification so that one might glimpse, even in this world, something of the nearness that is the true joy of the heart. In the end, it is to remember that all worldly pleasures and pains are mere reflections. It is the intimacy with Allāh that defines real bliss, just as absence from Him defines real suffering. Regardless of how complex, sophisticated, or diverse, in its varied forms the bliss or pleasure may be, it can be found only in close proximity with Allāh. The closer His presence, the truer the pleasure.

---

90 See Hikam 123.

As for distress, regardless of how complicated, sophisticated or diverse, in all its varied forms, it is found only in being distanced from Him. Thus the true cause of punishment is due to those things that widen the rift between the seeker and his Creator. Sin, disobedience, pride and arrogance, greed and desire, all contribute to dimming the Light with which to witness Allāh's Nobility in existence.

Ultimately, all the sorrows and anxieties that the heart experiences are, in their essence, due to a deprivation of true witnessing. The heart is burdened with the sorrow of trial and tribulation because it forgets, or neglects to acknowledge, that the trials came from Allāh. Separated from the clarity and the light that comes from such encounters, it is left in a state of inner unrest and disquiet, unable to see the wisdom in the suffering. What arises of sorrow and anxiety from worldly causes is but an outward shell of what has been sent by Allāh, and it is the lack of one's witnessing His Wisdom in the suffering that causes the pain. Thus does Allāh provide assurance that...

﴿ إِنَّ ٱلَّذِينَ قَالُوا۟ رَبُّنَا ٱللَّهُ ثُمَّ ٱسْتَقَٰمُوا۟ فَلَا خَوْفٌ عَلَيْهِمْ وَلَا هُمْ يَحْزَنُونَ ﴾

Indeed those who proclaim "Our Lord is Allāh!" thence they stay true [to their course], naught will there be fear upon them, not will they be sorrowful.[91]

The heart is inherently inclined towards its Creator, its ultimate source and true fulfillment. When it is prevented from attaining closeness with Allāh, the emptiness left by the absence His Light and Guidance naturally fills it with worldly concerns, fears, and griefs. These emotional burdens, then, are not simply challenges to endure, but can serve as indicators of a deeper need— the heart's yearning for Allāh's Light and Love which dispel the shadows of grief and fear.

So rise above mere surface solutions for inner peace, and turn instead to practices that facilitate closeness to your Lord. Engage in His remembrance, in sincere worship, and spiritual purification, for He has also said...

﴿ ...أَلَا بِذِكْرِ ٱللَّهِ تَطْمَئِنُّ ٱلْقُلُوبُ ﴾

... Unquestionably, by the remembrance of Allāh are the hearts assured.[92]

This is the only medicine for the heart by which one can heal the illness of heedlessness and attachments that obscure spiritual sight. By remembering who you are, what is your true purpose in this world, from whence have you come, and to where you are ultimately destined. In doing so, your heart will become realigned with its higher purpose and will gain a tranquility unlike anything in existence, one that is not easily disturbed by the causality and turbulence of worldly concerns.

---

91 Sūrah al-Ahqāf 46:13

92 Sūrah ar-Ra'd 13:28

(٢٢٤)

مِنْ تَمَامِ النِّعْمَةِ عَلَيْكَ أَنْ يَرْزُقَكَ مَا يَكْفِيكَ وَيَمْنَعَكَ مَا يُطْغِيكَ

From the completeness of the blessing upon you is that you are provisioned with what suffices you and withheld from what causes your transgression.

From the perfection of Allāh's complete favour upon His servants is Him providing not only what suffices for their needs but also in withholding what leads lead them to transgression.[93] Sustenance and prosperity is not only about abundance but also about balance, receiving precisely what fulfills one's necessities in order to prevent a breach in one's psychological and spiritual well-being.

(٢٢٥)

لِيَقِلَّ مَا تَفْرَحُ بِهِ يَقِلُّ مَا تَحْزَنُ عَلَيْهِ

Let what brings you joy be little, and what saddens you will also be little.

Joy is contained within sorrow, and sorrow contained within joy. While one may sit beside you as a friend, the other eagerly awaits your company. When one tires, the other resumes its place. Hence, the greater the worldly delight, the greater the sorrow that comes with it. So, if you were to seek some worldly joy, seek it in its most minimal yield. Its sorrow will also be just as minimal.

By reducing one's attachments to worldly things, the believer naturally reduces both the excessive joys and sorrows in them. This does not entail a complete elimination of joy or love, but to center them on more enduring foundations, so that the heart finds joy primarily in that which is lasting and meaningful, and be less dependent on fleeting external circumstances. This disciplines the believer to temper his desires and lessen his preoccupations in a way that helps him achieve greater stability and peace of heart.

(٢٢٦)

إِذْ أَرَدْتَ أَنْ لَا تُعْزَلَ فَلَا تَتَوَلَّ وِلَايَةً لَا تَدُومُ لَكَ

If you want not to be forced to step down, then seek not authority from what has no permanence for you.

---

93   Sūrah al-Mā'idah 5:3

Be wary of becoming overly attached to positions of authority or influence that are inherently temporary. By anchoring oneself to transient forms of power or recognition, one only sets the stage for eventual disappointment when these roles or titles are inevitably lost. The counsel here is to seek something more enduring and stable, avoiding attachments that bring with them the pain of inevitable separation.

Positions of worldly power, be they roles of leadership, wealth, or societal status, are, by their very nature, fleeting. When one identifies with such positions, they create a false sense of permanence in something that is inherently unstable. Eventually, whether by circumstance, time, or personal limitation, one must step down or be replaced. The resulting sense of loss can be deep and painful, as it strikes at the ego and the sense of identity tied to that role.

Instead, cultivate a form of leadership or status that does not fade, that is rooted in virtue, humility, and compassion. These inner qualities are not dependent on external validation and do not waver with worldly changes. By investing in such enduring qualities, one finds a sense of stability and fulfillment that is not susceptible to the impermanence of external titles and positions. This inward focus helps to build resilience and contentment, ensuring that one's sense of self remains intact even as external roles come and go.

(٢٢٧)

إِنْ رَغَّبَتْكَ البِدَايَاتُ زَهَّدَتْكَ النِّهَايَاتُ... إِنْ دَعَاكَ إِلَيْهَا ظَاهِرٌ نَهَاكَ عَنْهَا بَاطِنٌ

If beginnings attract you, let the endings detach you. If the outward calls you to them, let the inward dissuade you from them.

Arm yourself with the distinction between initial attraction and eventual disillusionment. When we find ourselves enticed by the beginnings, whether it is the thrill of a new endeavor, the allure of success, or the excitement of material gains, then, often, the endings will come as a reminder of their emptiness, stripping away our illusions. What initially seemed fulfilling or enticing tends to lose its appeal as we begin to understand its limitations.

When something calls to us on the surface, a deeper, spiritual awareness may caution us. There is often an inner knowing, a subtle insight from within that recognizes the fleeting nature of such pursuits. If such occurrences appease you in their initiation, then discern them to their end such that the realities of their finalities repulse you from indulging in them. And should their outward allures invite you to indulge in them, let your insight reach such depths that their inward ugliness discourages you from approaching them.

171

(٢٢٨)

إِنَّمَا جَعَلَهَا مَحَلًّا لِلْأَغْيَارِ وَمَعْدِنًا لِوُجُودِ الْأَكْدَارِ تَزْهِيدًا لَكَ فِيهَا

He only made it (this world) a place for otherness and a source for troubles, so you would abstain from it.

This is the fundamental truth about the transient nature of the world.[94] It is a place of distractions and a source of impurities, with inevitable challenges, sorrows, and disappointments. Material achievements, fleeting relationships, and personal aspirations, while temporarily fulfilling, only lead to hardship. Yet, these elements serve a purpose. Once the heart discerns the nature of the world as a place of imperfections and fluctuations, it is naturally encouraged to seek fulfillment beyond its confines. The trials of this life are not meant to embitter or disillusion, but to reorient the heart toward a purer form of love and fulfillment that is transcendental.

---

(٢٢٩)

عَلِمَ أَنَّكَ لَا تَقْبَلُ النُّصْحَ الْمُجَرَّدَ، فَذَوَّقَكَ مِنْ ذَوَاقِهَا مَا يُسَهِّلُ عَلَيْكَ فِرَاقَهَا

He knew that you do not accept pure advice, so He allowed you to taste from its bitter flavours that made parting with it (the worldly) easier for you.

Human psychology is naturally inclined towards truth and sincerity. Through our intellectual abilities, we are able to distinguish and keep away from superficial counsel, provided, of course, we employ guided intelligence. We have been given the ability to recognize false counsel and distinguish it from sincere counsel, and this is what is meant by 'tasting of its bitter flavours.' For there is also another aspect of human nature, the tendency to resist pure counsel, especially when it suggests detachment from the fulfillment of a rationalized desire. This is a desire, though not righteous in its outcome, is sound in logic. The indulgence seems to make sense, while making abstinence from it seem illogical. And it is primarily for this reason that we are allowed to experience its bitter consequences, so as to gain ease in accepting sound counsel. When counsel alone is insufficient, experiencing the 'taste' of desire's true nature serves as an experiential lesson that mere advice might not convey.

Words alone rarely suffice in persuading one from desires or attachments. Whether due to love, ambition, or comfort, attachments can have an intense hold on one's heart, masking their inherent limitations. Even when advised against certain pursuits, one might not fully grasp their emptiness or potential harms.

94 See Hikam 14, 24, and 85

So, rather than simply *tell* the servant, Allāh, His Wisdom, may let him realize this truth directly by tasting the hardships or disappointments that often accompany their attachments. This subtle shift in guidance ultimately helps the believer make peace with detachment, seeing it not as a loss but as a path to spiritual freedom.

Allāh's wisdom in allowing us to experience both the joys and sorrows of attachment is a mercy. For one might not truly believe until they have had a taste of reality. A lesson taught by real experience, albeit hard learned, has enduring effects. By experiencing the outcomes of our resistance to the truth firsthand, we may find ourselves better prepared to turn our hearts toward a more lasting source of contentment.

(٢٣٠)

العِلْمُ النَّافِعُ الَّذِي يَنْبَسِطُ فِي الصَّدْرِ شُعَاعُهُ، وَيَنْكَشِفُ بِهِ عَنِ القَلْبِ قِنَاعُهُ

Beneficial knowledge is that whose rays expand in the chest, and by it is unveiled from the heart its mask.

(٢٣١)

خَيْرُ العِلْمِ مَا كَانَتِ الخَشْيَةُ مَعَهُ

The best knowledge is that which is accompanied with God-Consciousness.

(٢٣٢)

العِلْمُ إِنْ قَارَنَتْهُ الخَشْيَةُ... فَلَكَ، وَإِلَّا... فَعَلَيْكَ

Knowledge, if it is accompanied with God-Consciousness, is to you (your benefit). Elseways, it is against you.

Knowledge is neither good nor bad; neither right nor wrong. It simply is… Knowledge.

From it one may derive benefit and also harm. The issue lies not in the knowing, but in what one knows or seeks to know. One's knowledge is only beneficial if it is illuminating and if its rays expand the heart and dispel its veils, and such knowledge is not merely intellectual or rational but rather the kind that penetrates deeply, reshaping one's inner world. It is the kind of knowledge that foremost dispels the illusions of one's subjective whims, exposing the self to the self. Through it, one uncovers and purifies the soul's numerous masks and veils, guiding toward spiritual clarity and sincerity. This knowledge is not cold information. It does not comprise facts, figures, and theories. It is a radiant realization, an inner guide that steers the being closer to Absolute Truth and Certainty.

This knowledge then transforms into a higher form of understanding when it meets Revelation and is accompanied by a sense of awe or *khushū'* خشوع, a reverent and conscious humility before the Divine Presence. It embodies the hierarchy of نور على نور, the Light of Revelation over the light of reason. As it expands the heart, it unveils the mysteries and secrets of reality. Any approach to knowledge that lacks this humility is incomplete and even perilous, for without awe, knowledge can lead to pride and self-deception. Only knowledge that is coupled with humility benefits the seeker; otherwise, it only weighs against one's soul by increasing arrogance and heedlessness, serving no benefit. Such a person bears...

$$ ﴿ ...كَمَثَلِ ٱلْحِمَارِ يَحْمِلُ أَسْفَارًا... ﴾ $$

... the likeness of a donkey laden with books...[95]

The true measure of knowledge and the value of seeking it lies not in the abundance of information or one's intellectual accomplishments, but in one's ability to cultivate humility and reverence. Knowledge imbued with awe nurtures the soul, steering it toward the Divine. If this awe accompanies one's learning, it is a blessing; if absent, it becomes a burden, serving merely as an intellectual vanity. Knowledge that *does not* lead to an understanding of a higher Truth is vain and useless, while knowledge that does, but is not accompanied by conscious humility poisons the heart. As a principle, true knowledge is not in the cumulation of information, narrations, and opinions. True knowledge is a Light that Allāh places in the heart of the believer.[96]

(٢٣٣)

مَتَى آلَمَكَ عَدَمُ إِقْبَالِ النَّاسِ عَلَيْكَ، أَوْ تَوَجُّهُهُمْ بِالذَّمِّ إِلَيْكَ...

فَارْجِعْ إِلَى عِلْمِ اللهِ فِيكَ،

فَإِنْ كَانَ لَا يُقْنِعُكَ عِلْمُهُ ...

فَمُصِيبَتُكَ بِعَدَمِ قَنَاعَتِكَ بِعِلْمِهِ أَشَدُّ مِنْ مُصِيبَتِكَ بِوُجُودِ الأَذَى مِنْهُمْ

When you are pained by people's lack of acceptance, or their condemnation towards you, return to the knowledge of Allāh concerning you.
If you are not satisfied with His knowledge of you, then your misfortune in lack of conviction in His knowledge is greater than the affliction of any harm from them (people/others).

---

95 Sūrah al-Jumū'ah 62:5

96 Attributed to Imām Mālik 🙵, although numerous other scholars have also been cited to have stated the same, or similar.

(٢٣٤)

إِنَّمَا أَجْرَى الْأَذَى عَلَى أَيْدِيهِمْ كَيْ لَا تَكُونَ سَاكِنًا إِلَيْهِمْ ، أَرَادَ أَنْ يُزْعِجَكَ عَنْ كُلِّ شَيْءٍ حَتَّى لَا يَشْغَلَكَ عَنْهُ شَيْءٌ

He only allowed harm by their hands that you do not find peace with them. He wanted that you be agitated from everything, until nothing preoccupies you from Him.

Your lack of trust or faith in His good opinion of you is far greater a misfortune than the apparent poor opinion of others upon you. Because what they think and say of you lives and dies with them. But your faith carries on with you into His Eternal Presence. With what integrity will you then hold yourself before His Majesty and Power knowing that He held such poor an opinion of you.

The believer must understand that ultimately one's worth is not measured by the opinions of others. For they too will stand before Allāh's judgment. Rather, when faced with criticism and appreciation, one must turn their gaze inward and evaluate themselves from a higher lens. If one finds Allāh's opinion of them to be low, then the real struggle is not with the world. The real struggle lies in one's own lack of satisfaction with Allāh's knowledge of them. For He, Almighty, Most Merciful and Most Benevolent, never holds a poor opinion for His righteous servants.

If He allows harm to befall you by the hands of others, it is only so you can find refuge in Him. So that your state of agitation in everything else, coupled with a yearning for tranquility and contentment, leads you to seek out only that which will take away your agitation and grant you peace, found only in the protection of your Lord Almighty. It is deliberate on His part to place you in a state of agitation, so that you do not become too comfortable where you are, so that you are ever vigilant and aware of your state, and so that you place all your trust and reliance upon Him, Almighty, always seeking only His pleasure, His love, and His protection from all else.

(٢٣٥)

إِذَا عَلِمْتَ أَنَّ الشَّيْطَانَ لَا يَغْفُلُ عَنْكَ، فَلَا تَغْفُلْ أَنْتَ عَمَّنْ نَاصِيَتُكَ بِيَدِهِ

When you know that Shaytaan is not heedless of you, then do not become heedless from the One in whose Hands lies your destiny [97]

97 The term ناصِيَة literally means 'forelock' or the frontal hairs of the head, used here metaphorically since it also carries the meanings of 'concern', 'affairs', or 'situation'.

(٢٣٦)

إِنَّمَا جَعَلَهُ لَكَ عَدُوًّا لِيَحُوشَكَ بِهِ إِلَيْهِ، وَحَرَّكَ عَلَيْكَ النَّفْسَ لِيَدُومَ إِقْبَالُكَ عَلَيْهِ

He made him (shaytān) an enemy to you that you be, by him (shaytān)
conscious of Him (Allāh), and He inflamed your soul (lower self) to persevere
in your inclination towards him.

One of the most striking proofs of demonic existence, which our
times afford us, is found in the fact that the minds of people have been
so deluded regarding spiritual realities, that most do not believe in the
existence of the devil, and this is perhaps the trickster's greatest trick.
After all, the deceiver's power is his ability to convince others that he does
not exist, and if he does, it is not as a deceiver but as a sincere advisor.[98]

There is a subtle wisdom in the presence of adversity and inner
struggle, specifically in the context of the devil (*shaytān* شيطان) and the ego
(*nafs* نفس), and the incredible affiliation between the two in that though
they differ in their ethereal and material compositions, they both possess
the same essential qualities. This similarity is what enables the devil to do
what he does, and likewise also motivates his actions. His passion rests in
the ease with which he is able to manipulate and influence, and so long as
that passion is alive, he does not rest from his quest. And since the devil
never ceases his efforts to lead us astray, we, too, must remain vigilant of
his machinations.

The devil's role as a deceiver and eternal adversary of the human being
is deliberate. Once the enemy is known, the heart immediately seeks
out an ally, and an absolute enemy prompts the search for an absolute
ally. The devil's existence and the relentless promptings of the ego, once
known, urge the believer to strive for refuge in Allāh. The struggles we
face with temptation and inner discord are less of a burden, and more a
mechanism meant to awaken us from the devil's illusions and fabrications.
Evil is the contrast by which Good is illuminated, and in this way, every
hardship, including the whispers of the devil or the rebellion of the ego,
all contribute to strengthening our resolve to remember Allāh and seek
His protection and guidance.

(٢٣٧)

مَنْ أَثْبَتَ لِنَفْسِهِ تَوَاضُعًا فَهُوَ الْمُتَكَبِّرُ حَقًّا،

إِذْ لَيْسَ التَّوَاضُعُ إِلَّا عَنْ رِفْعَةٍ،

فَمَتَى أَثْبَتَّ لِنَفْسِكَ تَوَاضُعًا فَأَنْتَ الْمُتَكَبِّرُ حَقًّا

---

98   Sūrah al-Aʻrāf 7:21

One who asserts humility for himself is in reality arrogant, for humility is not but from a high rank. So, when you assert humility for yourself, you are in reality the arrogant one.

(۲۳۸)

لَيْسَ الْمُتَوَاضِعُ الَّذِي إِذَا تَوَاضَعَ رَأَى نَفْسَهُ فَوْقَ مَا صَنَعَ،

وَلَكِنَّ الْمُتَوَاضِعَ الَّذِي إِذَا تَوَاضَعَ رَأَى نَفْسَهُ دُونَ مَا صَنَعَ

Not does the humble one, who, when he is humble, sees himself above what he has accomplished, but rather the humble one is he who, when he is humble, sees himself lower what he has accomplished.

(۲۳۹)

التَّوَاضُعُ الْحَقِيقِيُّ هُوَ مَا كَانَ نَاشِئًا عَنْ شُهُودِ عَظَمَتِهِ وَتَجَلِّي صِفَتِهِ

True humility is what arises from witnessing His greatness and the manifestation of His attributes.

Humility is the devil's greatest weakness, and the believer's greatest strength against the devil. *Shaytān* is marked with pride and arrogance, the very antithesis of humility. His downfall was driven by these because he refused to humble himself before his Creator. Humility does not need an extrinsic assertion. It being from a praiseworthy rank, can assert itself through sincerity. Hence the very act of claiming oneself to be humble becomes a demonstration of arrogance.

In these reflections, we are offered profound insight into the nature of true humility and the subtle dangers of self-assigned modesty. One who consciously attributes humility to themselves, in reality, be cloaked in pride. True humility can only arise as a virtue, not from a sense of self-importance, but as a response to recognizing the majesty of Allāh. Humility, though an innate quality, demands great effort against the self to truly manifest, which by its nature is prideful. By regarding oneself as naturally humble, one risks falling into an apparent form of arrogance, for this self-assigned humility becomes a means of self-glorification, obscuring the purity of genuine lowliness before the Divine Master.

The believer must understand that true humility is not achieved by someone who, after displaying humility, perceives themselves as having done something noble and virtuous, or considers themselves humble and modest having done a righteous deed. Rather, the genuinely humble individual considers even their humblest acts to fall short of what is truly due. They do not see themselves as virtuous for displaying modesty but are instead always aware of their inadequacy before the greatness of Allāh, who deserves infinitely more reverence than any mortal can offer.

（٢٤٠）

لَا يُخْرِجُكَ عَنِ الوَصْفِ إِلَّا شُهُودُ الوَصْفِ

You cannot part from the Divine Attributes save by witnessing the Attributes.

Allāh is indescribable, for there is nothing like unto Him.[99] Knowing Him can only be possible by seeing and realizing His manifestation in reality, as all of reality bears witness to His Being. It is impossible to 'see' Him, in all His Majesty, save by acknowledging His manifested attributes. And it is impossible to part from seeing His attributes, in order to see Him, until one moves from merely 'seeing' His attributes, to truly 'witnessing' them.

Recognition and acknowledgment of Allāh's attributes are fundamental to maintaining one's faith. Witnessing the manifestation of His attributes are the experiential reflections and realizations that the believer encounters on their journey of life, which reinforce their understanding and appreciation of who their Lord is.

His attributes are not merely abstract concepts but are experienced and internalized through personal encounters and moments of enlightenment. When a believer truly witnesses and comprehends these attributes, they become deeply ingrained in the heart with a profound sense of reverence for His Majesty as the Lord of the worlds. This internal witnessing acts as a safeguard, ensuring that the believer remains aligned with the Allāh's Will and resistant to distractions or deviations that might otherwise lead them away from their spiritual path. The affirmation here is that genuine understanding and witnessing of Allāh's attributes fortify the believer's faith and commitment.

（٢٤١）

المُؤْمِنُ يَشْغَلُهُ الثَّنَاءُ عَلَى اللهِ عَنْ أَنْ يَكُونَ لِنَفْسِهِ شَاكِرًا،

وَتَشْغَلُهُ حُقُوقُ اللهِ عَنْ أَنْ يَكُونَ لِحُظُوظِهِ ذَاكِرًا

The believer is preoccupied with praising Allāh, removed from being appreciative of himself, and he is preoccupied with the rights of Allāh, removed from being concerned with his own share.

The believer is preoccupied with praising Allāh, leaving no time to praise himself, and is ever absorbed in fulfilling Allāh's rights, leaving no room to think about his own share. This is a subtle aspect of the believer's relationship with Allāh, being the selflessness that true worship and

---

99 Sūrah al-Shūrā 42:11

devotion demand. The act of glorifying Allāh with praise and sanctifying Him is an angelic quality and of the rank of Allāh's most beloved, as when the Angels attested:

$$ ﴿ ...وَنَحْنُ نُسَبِّحُ بِحَمْدِكَ وَنُقَدِّسُ لَكَ... ﴾ $$

... and we glorify You with praise and sanctify You... [100]

Truly, His grandeur surpasses any thought of self-congratulation or personal credit. The believer's gratitude is directed solely toward Him, as he realizes that every success or blessing is ultimately from Allāh and belonging to Him alone, leaving no place for self-praise.

(٢٤٢)

$$ لَيْسَ الْمُحِبُّ الَّذِي يَرْجُو مِنْ مَحْبُوبِهِ عِوَضًا وَيَطْلُبُ مِنْهُ عَرَضًا، $$
$$ فَإِنَّ الْمُحِبَّ مَنْ يَبْذُلُ، لَيْسَ الْمُحِبُّ مَنْ يُبْذَلُ لَهُ $$

Not is the lover one who hopes from his beloved compensation (for his love) or seeks purpose from them. Indeed, the true lover is the one who sacrifices. Not is the true lover one for whom sacrifices are made.

The true lover is one who strives for his beloved, not the one who expects his beloved to strive for him. The true lover does not hope for compensation from his Beloved nor does he seek a personal aim, for the lover is the one who gives, not the one to whom is given. This is the essence of selfless love. Genuine love is about self-sacrifice and devotion, while conditional love is driven by personal gain with the expectancy of recompense and reciprocation of one's love. Love, by its very nature is selfish, and only he who loves but does not expect is considered selfless. In the context of Divine Love, this teaching reveals that the truest love for Allāh is one that is free of expectations and desires, reflecting a pure and unconditional commitment.

The idea that love should be transactional is unbefitting of what love truly is. Most approach their relationships with expectations of receiving something in return, be it recognition, affection, or material benefits. However, upon the spiritual path, such a love is incomplete. The true lover does not measure their love by what they receive but rather by what they willingly and unconditionally offer. This is especially true in one's relationship with Allāh. A true lover serves, obeys, and worships not for rewards, but purely out of a deep, abiding love and reverence. This selflessness transcends any earthly notion of reciprocity or personal gain, aiming instead for union with the Divine.

---

100 Sūrah al-Baqarah 2:30

(٢٤٣)

لَوْلَا مَيَادِينُ النُّفُوسِ مَا تَحَقَّقَ سَيْرُ السَّائِرِينَ،

لَا مَسَافَةَ بَيْنَكَ وَبَيْنَهُ حَتَّى تَطْوِيَهَا رِحْلَتُكَ،

وَلَا قَطِيعَةَ بَيْنَكَ وَبَيْنَهُ حَتَّى تَمْحُوَهَا وُصْلَتُكَ

Were it not for the arenas of selves, naught would be realized of the journey of those who are journeying. There is no distance between you and Him unless your journey enfolds it, and there is no rift between you and Him unless your reach erases it.

The fruit of the journey is only truly realized by the strife of the journey itself. If it were a journey without effort, it could not truly be a journey. For in reality, there is no distance between you, the seeker, and Him, the One sought. And there is no rift between you, the desirous, and Him, the One desired. If there is no distance to be traversed, and no rift to be closed, how can one claim to be on a journey to the Divine Presence. In truth, then, the journey is the strife and struggle through the arena of selfishness for the victory of selflessness. With each battle won against the self, the distance is shortened and the rift is lessened. The very essence of the journey is in overcoming the self, hence were it not for the challenges of the self, the journey would not be realized. In reality, Allāh is already near, closer than any form of connection or concept of nearness. There is no true distance between you and Him that a physical journey might cover, nor any separation that a material link might erase. There is no literal distance to traverse, no spatial or temporal separation to overcome. Rather the journey is within the self, in overcoming the inner obstacles and illusions that veil this closeness.

The ego and its inclinations serve a purpose by creating resistance, much like how physical obstacles build strength when overcome. The struggle with the self provides a field in which the believer's commitment to Allāh is tested, refined, and strengthened. Rather than lamenting the difficulties within, the believer is urged to see them as a necessary aspect of the journey, knowing that Allāh's presence is already with him, and he but needs to realize it by cleansing the heart of the clouds of the ego's judgments. This understanding reframes the seeker's journey as one of unveiling and purifying, rather than moving toward a far-off destination. The only distance is the illusion created by the self's attachments and misconceptions. There is no intrinsic separation between the seeker and the Divine, except in the mind and heart. The process entails peeling away the layers that the self has created, and thus reaching a realization that it was never about attaining something new but about recognizing what has always been.

(٢٤٤)

جَعَلَكَ فِي الْعَالَمِ الْمُتَوَسِّطِ بَيْنَ مُلْكِهِ وَمَلَكُوتِهِ لِيُعْلِمَكَ جَلَالَةَ قَدْرِكَ بَيْنَ مَخْلُوقَاتِهِ ،
وَأَنَّكَ جَوْهَرَةٌ تَنْطَوِي عَلَيْهَا أَصْدَافُ مُكَوَّنَاتِهِ

*He placed you in the intermediate realm between His material domain and
His spiritual dominion to teach you the magnificence of your status among His
creatures, and that you are a gem contained within the shells of His creations.*

(٢٤٥)

وَسِعَكَ الكَوْنُ مِنْ حَيْثُ جُثْمَانِيَّتُكَ، وَلَمْ يَسَعْكَ مِنْ حَيْثُ رُوحَانِيَّتُكَ

*The universe encompasses you in your physical aspect, but it does not encompass
you in your spiritual essence.*

(٢٤٦)

الْكَائِنُ فِي الكَوْنِ وَلَمْ يُفْتَحْ لَهُ مَيَادِينُ الغُيُوبِ، مَسْجُونٌ بِمُحِيطَاتِهِ وَمَحْصُورٌ فِي هَيْكَلِ ذَاتِهِ

*The being existent in the universe, unopened to him the realms of the unseen,
is imprisoned by his surroundings, confined within the frame of his selfsame.*

(٢٤٧)

أَنْتَ مَعَ الأَكْوَانِ مَا لَمْ تَشْهَدِ الْمُكَوِّنَ ، فَإِذَا شَهِدْتَهُ كَانَتِ الأَكْوَانُ مَعَكَ

*You are with the realms as long as you have not witnessed the Creator. When
you witness Him, the realms are with you.*

The human *being's* cosmological placement is in the intermediary
between the material and the spiritual, a unique placement that is not
shared by any other creature in existence. The body serves as the outward
shell, while the Spirit as the inward. Through this unique placement,
the being has access to both the material domain of the *Mulk* المُلك, and
the spiritual dominions of the *Malakūt* المَلَكوت. The being is thus able to
discern the unseen meanings from the seen forms, and it is through this
that he gains knowledge, enlightenment, and spiritual ascension.
Thus does Allāh say,

﴿سَنُرِيهِمْ ءَايَتِنَا فِي ٱلْآفَاقِ وَفِيٓ أَنفُسِهِمْ حَتَّىٰ يَتَبَيَّنَ لَهُمْ أَنَّهُ ٱلْحَقُّ...﴾

*We will show them Our Signs on the horizons and in their selves, until it
becomes clear to them that it (the Revelation) is the Truth* [101]

The Soul is likened to the horizon, being the meeting place between the Heavens and the Earth, wherein the witnessing of the manifest Signs of Allāh takes place, and through their discernment, the Truth is realized. This meeting place is the realm of signs and symbols, the domain of language, of words and their significations, and access to this domain is what truly distinguishes the human being from the rest of creation, being the only entity that can, through discernment, realize the Majesty of the Lord Almighty, and this is what makes him a gem, or a pearl, contained within a shell among the rest of creation.

Existent in this state, the cosmos lay readily opened to the being, if the ability to discern is actively executed. This entails both intellectual and spiritual effort, and entails a shift from the semantics and particularities of the created world to the universals and axioms that define it, as these universals and axioms do not originate from creation. They originate from the Creator, and their discernment leads to an affirmation of His Eternal Majesty.

If the being exists, despite this unique placement, but does not discern reality in its seen and unseen aspects, he is imprisoned by his selfsame shell, subservient to forms and symbols, never expanding his understanding. For the cosmos is expansively vast compared to the being's physical, corporeal form, and has encompassed the being entirely. It is not, however, vast compared to the being's spiritual essence and cannot truly encompass or contain the being within it, as Imām 'Alī is noted to have said;

أتزعم نفسك جرم صغير ... وفيك انطوى العالم الأكبر

You think yourself a particulate grain (an insignificant thing)... Yet within you reside vast realms; [102]

Hence, so long as the being remains dormant in his discernment and, as a result, heedless of his Creator, he also remains a prisoner to creation, in that the being and his abilities are in *their* possession. For he has failed in his ability to discern, and has only discerned, if at all, other shells like himself. Only when the human being, through his discernment, witnesses the Creator, is he truly freed from creation, and creation then comes under his possession. As one might say, you are not truly free, until you are freed from the subjugation of a created thing to submit to the Creator Himself. True freedom lies in seeing what is greater and beyond oneself. Seeing oneself as the greatest becomes the limitation of one's potential and ultimately one's own prison.

When the human being's awareness shifts from the created world to the Creator, his perception is transformed in all interactions. Worldly matters no longer dominate the mind, as their chains no longer bind the soul. Creation then becomes a companion, no longer a distraction, aiding the human being in his journey rather than hindering it.

102   From the *Dīwān* of Imām Alī, a collection of his poems and sayings.

（٢٤٨）

لَا يَلْزَمُ مِنْ ثُبُوتِ الْخُصُوصِيَّةِ عَدَمُ وَصْفِ الْبَشَرِيَّةِ،

إِنَّمَا مَثَلُ الْخُصُوصِيَّةِ كَإِشْرَاقِ شَمْسِ النَّهَارِ ظَهَرَتْ فِي الْأُفُقِ وَلَيْسَتْ مِنْهُ،

تَارَةً تُشْرِقُ شُمُوسُ أَوْصَافِهِ عَلَى لَيْلِ وُجُودِكَ،

وَتَارَةً يَقْبِضُ ذَلِكَ عَنْكَ فَيَرُدُّكَ إِلَى حُدُودِكَ،

فَالنَّهَارُ لَيْسَ مِنْكَ وَإِلَيْكَ وَلَكِنَّهُ وَارِدٌ عَلَيْكَ،

The establishment of uniqueness does not necessitate the absence of the characteristics of humanness. An example of uniqueness is like the rising of the day's sun; it manifests on the horizon but is not of it. Sometimes, the suns (rays of light) of His attributes illuminate the night of your existence, and other times, He withdraws them from you, returning you to your human limits. Thus, the light of day is not from you and does not belong to you, rather it (only) comes to you.

Finding oneself at an established rank with Allāh, being granted His favour, or reaching the unique waystations on the spiritual path, does not separate one from their human attributions. Human nature is still, and will remain a part of the individual, rather the only difference that may exist before the rank and after is that human nature might become subservient to the individual, rather than the individual being subservient to it. This is only possible when the individual himself is entirely subservient to Allāh, and that is, ultimately, the highest rank one might achieve, which is in turn only possible when that nature is illuminated, its strengths and weaknesses revealed and laid bare. It happens briefly, sometimes in fleeting moments, in the form of revelation or inspiration. Lights of the Divine Attributes arrive in these unique moments and once the illumination is complete, they recede, returning the individual to their prior state. And having glimpsed what was intended, it is hence upon the individual to realize their humanness and right their way.

This is likened to sunlight as it illuminates the world, glorious and majestic in its capacity, yet ultimately external to and independent of what its light touches. The sun's light reaches the earth but retains its origin because it does not belong to its intended destination. The analogy being that the experience of spiritual insight does not dissolve one's inherent humanity. It only illuminates briefly, bringing wisdom without negating one's essence. Just as sunlight shines upon the earth without becoming part of it, so does Divine Light reach the human soul without altering its essential nature. This external illumination enlightens without eliminating the night of human limitations. The self is still bound to its earthly form, its nature remaining unchanged.

In this regard, spiritual elevation does exigently shed or rectify human nature. The purpose of this Divine Favour, which may come as moments of clarity or in the form of spiritual insight, is to touch one's life without erasing their human frailties. Humanity, with its fluctuations and struggles, remains intact, even when grace briefly transforms one's experience. Such moments come with two axiomatic purposes, and both are as a mercy to the human being.

Foremost, it is to keep the individual grounded, knowing that any momentary transcendence is a gift, not a permanent state. This protects one from delusion and false acclamation. For some may end up believing that the elevated moment is a permanent sign of their arrival to the Divine Presence, in as much as one might think that the sun's warm glow means that one no longer needs to light their lamps. Yet come nightfall, only a fool will find themselves confounded, as it is known that the sun rises and sets, its light comes and then goes, and one must prepare to navigate the darkness of night. Likewise, the spiritual insight arrives and illuminates what is praiseworthy and what is blameworthy of oneself, then it departs. The wise then prepare to safeguard the praiseworthy from corruption by refraining from self-acclaim, and likewise, with the clarity that the moment brings, they cleanse the blameworthy of corruption and save themselves from delusion.

Thereafter, these moments make them aware of who they truly are and what purpose they must serve. The human being was not established on earth to 'have a spiritual experience' in a mundane sense of the expression. If this was the intent, he would have been established in the spiritual domains. Why send him to earth for an experience not found on earth? The experience, though it comes, is but a means to an end, not the end itself. Its purpose is to illuminate *your* purpose by reminding you of the ultimate spiritual destination. Which is to say that such illumination does not arrive to raise one, as a matter of course, to an angelic state, rather it arrives to reveal one's humanness, and the magnificent attribute with which the human being was created and to further illuminate what must be done to rise, attain, and retain that higher rank.

And just as the sun illuminates the earth and withdraws, so too do the 'suns' of Allāh's attributes. They inspire and offer insight by shining upon the 'night' of His servants' existence. They are sent momentarily and are then withheld, returning the servants to their limits. These moments of spiritual insight come and go just like moments of expansion and constriction. When one feels the light of Allāh's presence, one's 'night' is illuminated. The light reveals of their nature what darkness conceals. It disillusions the illusions of the causal world and offers clarity. It is under no obligation to intervene and rectify or alter that nature, nor does it expunge the distractions of causation. Its task is simply to reveal, and upon completing its task the light recedes, and the obligation to change one's nature and turn away from the distractions, falls upon the individual.

(٢٤٩)

دَلَّ بِوُجُودِ آثَارِهِ عَلَى وُجُودِ أَسْمَائِهِ،

وَبِوُجُودِ أَسْمَائِهِ عَلَى ثُبُوتِ أَوْصَافِهِ،

وَبِثُبُوتِ أَوْصَافِهِ عَلَى وُجُودِ ذَاتِهِ،

إِذْ مُحَالٌ أَنْ يَقُومَ الوَصْفُ بِنَفْسِهِ،

فَأَهْلُ الْجَذْبِ يَكْشِفُ لَهُمْ عَنْ كَمَالِ ذَاتِهِ، ثُمَّ يَرُدُّهُمْ إِلَى شُهُودِ صِفَاتِهِ،

ثُمَّ يَرُدُّهُمْ إِلَى التَّعَلُّقِ بِأَسْمَائِهِ، ثُمَّ يَرُدُّهُمْ إِلَى شُهُودِ آثَارِهِ،

وَالسَّالِكُونَ عَلَى عَكْسِ هَذَا،

فَنِهَايَةُ السَّالِكِينَ بِدَايَةُ الْمَجْذُوبِينَ، وَبِدَايَةُ السَّالِكِينَ نِهَايَةُ الْمَجْذُوبِينَ،

لَكِنْ لَا بِمَعْنًى وَاحِدٍ، فَرُبَّمَا التَقَيَا فِي الطَّرِيقِ،

هَذَا فِي تَرَقِّيهِ... وَهَذَا فِي تَدَلِّيهِ...

The proof of the existence of His traces is in the existence of His Names,
And the existence of His Names affirms His Attributes,
And by the affirmation of His Attributes is His essence,
For it is impossible for the attribute to stand on its own.
As for those who are drawn towards Him, they witness the perfection of His
essence, then they are returned to witness His attributes, then to relate to His
names, and then they are returned to witness His traces.
Conversely, the seekers are the opposite (of the ones drawn to Him);
The end of the seekers (path) is the beginning of the attracted, and the beginning
of the seekers (path) is the end of the path of the attracted.
But they do not carry the same meaning, only that they may meet on the path:
This one in their ascent... and the other in their descent...

The journey to knowledge and enlightenment of the Divine Presence
has two points of initiation. There are some who begin from a distance,
and these are the seekers. Others begin in proximity, and these are among
those drawn to Him by a powerful force or by His deliberate placement
of them in His proximity.

The former are the *sālikūn* سالكون,[103] who begin from the outward
realities to arrive at the inward illuminations, progressing from discerning
the signs among creation to reach an understanding of the Creator.

---

103   The *sālik* is one whose existence وجود is in a state of searching وجد or
finding. He is hence a finder or seeker until he finds يوجد the One described as
Absolutely Existent واجب الوجود

The Seekers are those who actively pursue spiritual enlightenment and knowledge. They move from the outward traces to discerning the inward realities of creation. This leads them to knowing the Creator through His Names, by which He may be invoked, by which He unveils to them an understanding of His Beautiful Attributes. These then take the seekers to understanding who *He* is. The name necessarily represents the attribute and the attribute necessarily represents the essence, as the name cannot exist without an attribute, and the attribute cannot exist without an essence. This, when unhindered, is a natural progression from Rational Intelligence to Spiritual Intelligence. Through this path of knowing, one ultimately arrives at the very essence sought. The seekers, in this regard, are favoured in a way that their counterparts are not, in that they begin in a state of not knowing to reach a state of knowing and, through much strife and effort, receive a reward most worthy and deserving.

The latter, who are the *majdhūbūn* مجذوبون,[104] begin with glimpses of Divine Completeness and are then directed back to the tangible signs among creation. The wisdom of being distanced after experiencing this state is evident, as such an experience is axiomatically overwhelming upon any part of creation. Witnessing the Divine Presence without a filter can permanently alter one's state, inducing an ecstatic love that can drive one to lunacy and insanity. For this reason, after the experience, they are guided, by Allāh's Mercy, to return to a state of rational normalcy and retain their sanity by witnessing His attributes, then His names, and then His outward expressions. Such individuals are drawn towards Allāh through an experience or a 'spiritual awakening.' In this awakening, they begin their journey by witnessing His Presence. They are then turned back to His Attributes, and then to His Names, until they witness His traces in the world. Such people are favoured in a way that their counterparts are not, in that they begin in a state of witnessing and their descent allows them to understand reality from a lens of that witnessing. They see, if they should see with truth and sincerity, the world as it was intended and created, as opposed to what it merely is or should be.

The difference between the two, though both are on their respective journeys, is that the seekers reach a certain milestone where they begin to understand what it was that initially attracted their counterparts, while the attracted, in turn, reach a point where they begin to understand what it is that the seekers initially sought. Thus in essence, they may meet on the path, where one is in their ascent, from the traces to the Essence, while the other is in their descent, from the Essence to the traces. And so, despite their different starting points and destinations, there can be a convergence or meeting point where both groups gain a deeper understanding of their Creator.

---

104 From جذب which means to attract, enchant, magnetize, or lure. One of the meanings of a *majdhūb* مجذوب is one who is powerfully captivated or fascinated, which, incidentally, also carries the meaning of lunacy and ecstasy.

(۲۵۰)

لَا يُعْلَمُ قَدْرُ أَنْوَارِ الْقُلُوبِ وَالأَسْرَارِ إِلَّا فِي غَيْبِ الْمَلَكُوتِ،

كَمَا لَا تَظْهَرُ أَنْوَارُ السَّمَاءِ إِلَّا فِي شَهَادَةِ الْمُلْكِ

Nothing can be known of the full extent of the lights of hearts and secrets save only in the unseen of the dominions, just as the lights of the sky only appear in the witnessing of the domain.

The spiritual unveilings do not take place save in spiritual dimensions, just as discernment of the outward manifestation can only take place in the physical realm. One cannot discern the nature of the world, the cosmos, and all that there is in creation, by spending all their thoughts in the spiritual domain, much in the same way that one cannot understand what is occurring in the physical world while they are asleep and in a dream state. Likewise, that which is unveiled of the innermost, of the hearts and secrets, cannot be discerned during the wakeful turbulence of the physical world. Such unveilings can only be realized in spiritual states, when the gateways of the senses are shut.

Just as the heavens become visible in the earthly sky, illuminating the material realm, the light of the heart finds its true expression in the spiritual realm. The seen and unseen are intertwined, with each offering insights into the other. What we observe in the outer world invites us to a contemplation of the hidden realities, as the inner spiritual illumination points to the greater truths within the unseen world.

---

(۲۵۱)

وِجْدَانُ ثَمَرَاتِ الطَّاعَاتِ عَاجِلًا بَشَائِرُ الْعَامِلِينَ بِوُجُودِ الْجَزَاءِ عَلَيْهَا آجِلًا

The conscience finds the fruits of obedience immediately, while the rewards for those who strive for them are promised in the future.

Experiencing the fruits of worship in life may serve as a sign for the devout, giving them hope of greater rewards in the afterlife, but the immediate benefits of sincere devotion are consciously experienced as a foretaste of the blessings and as glad tidings of the recompense awaiting those who act out of love and submission to Allāh. These may be in the form of spiritual serenity, clarity, and fulfillment that sincere acts of devotion bring. For those who seek closeness to Allāh, the peace and inner joy felt in worship suffice as a confirmation of His favour. However, it is important for the believer to remember that these experiences are not the ultimate reward; only indications that greater blessings await.

---

(٢٥٢)

كَيْفَ تَطْلُبُ الْعِوَضَ عَلَى عَمَلٍ هُوَ مُتَصَدِّقٌ بِهِ عَلَيْكَ؟

أَمْ كَيْفَ تَطْلُبُ الْجَزَاءَ عَلَى صِدْقٍ هُوَ مُهْدِيهِ إِلَيْكَ؟

How can you seek recompense for a deed He has bestowed upon you?
Or how can you seek reward for sincerity that He gifted you?

Every good action performed, though it may be performed by one's own volition, driven by one's own intentions, is in truth, a gift from Allāh. For it is He who grants each individual the strength, the ability, the means and opportunity, as well as the inspiration to form the intention and the passion to perform the deed. He even sends the recipients of the deeds your way, manifesting every condition and variable necessary for the deed to take place. So, how can anyone, who understands this, seek compensation for an act that He Himself has granted?

In the end, our deeds are not *our* achievements, though they are performed by us. Rather they are, in a higher reality, manifestations of Allāh's Grace. We are only recipients of the opportunity to do good, conduits and vessels for the manifestation of Allāh's Will and Decree.

This is also true for sincerity, a quality central to true worship, rather the very condition that determines the acceptance of a deed. It too, as an innate quality of the human being, is a gift, for it is in the Wisdom of Allāh to create the human being with such a quality.

Recall then, what it was that severed the bond between the Prophet Mūsa ﷺ and Al-Khadir ﷺ,[105]

﴿ فَٱنطَلَقَا حَتَّىٰٓ إِذَآ أَتَيَآ أَهْلَ قَرْيَةٍ ٱسْتَطْعَمَآ أَهْلَهَا فَأَبَوْا أَن يُضَيِّفُوهُمَا

فَوَجَدَا فِيهَا جِدَارًا يُرِيدُ أَن يَنقَضَّ فَأَقَامَهُۥ قَالَ لَوْ شِئْتَ لَتَّخَذْتَ عَلَيْهِ أَجْرًا ۝

قَالَ هَٰذَا فِرَاقُ بَيْنِي وَبَيْنِكَ... ﴾

Thus they proceeded until they came upon a people of a town. They sought food from the people, but were denied hospitality. And then they found there a wall on the verge of collapse, and he (al-Khadir) erected it. He (Mūsa) said, "Had you wished, you would have sought payment for it."
He (Al-Khadir) said, "This is the parting between you and I..."[106]

---

105 Conventionally pronounced as 'Al-Khidr', although this is an incorrect transliteration. The title itself is written as الْخَضِرُ with a *Fat'hah* (َ) on the *Kha* خ and *Kasra* (ِ) on the *Dhad* ض, and therefore should be properly pronounced as 'Al-Khadiru' in the nominative case, not 'Khidr'.

106 Sūrah al-Kahf 18:66-67

They sought food and provision from the people but were denied any form of hospitality, and yet, despite that, Al-Khadir did the town a service by repairing a broken wall. In the outward one might judge justly, as Mūsa did, that fair compensation for a good deed is deserving. But Al-Khadir was also right in his conviction, for he did not perform the deed in anticipation of reward or recompense. His actions were guided and inspired by Allāh's Decree, as was his sincerity in the act.

So, reconsider your spiritual motivations. Pursue worship out of love and gratitude rather than for gain. Do not use rewards as a unit of measure for your closeness to Allāh, such that you become self-centered in your devotion. Reflecting on this principle deeply should humble the seeker and help him realize what role he truly serves when performing righteous actions, for it does not befit one to take credit not due to them. Asking for rewards based on one's sincerity is akin to demanding payment for a gift freely given, and such a thing is ignoble and unbecoming of a sincere servant, as one cannot be grateful for a gift and in the same instance expect a reward for using the same gift.

The ability to worship, to act sincerely, or to perform righteous deeds is granted by Allāh, as it is He who empowers the soul with the means and inclination to approach Him through goodness. Recognize that even piety, sincerity, and actions are gifts, not innate talents or skills. The ability to do good and to do it with sincerity is a privilege, which, when truly understood in its essence would not so easily be squandered. Especially not in an age where digital documentation of one's actions is so prevalent that it has become the norm to seek immediate reward, recompense, and recognition for one's actions, and such a thing is indeed a psychological and sociological phenomenon unprecedented in human history.

(٢٥٣)

قَوْمٌ تَسْبِقُ أَنْوَارُهُمْ أَذْكَارَهُمْ،

وَقَوْمٌ تَسْبِقُ أَذْكَارُهُمْ أَنْوَارَهُمْ،

وَقَوْمٌ تَتَسَاوَى أَذْكَارُهُمْ وَ أَنْوَارُهُمْ،

وَ قَوْمٌ لَا أَذْكَارَ وَلَا أَنْوَارَ،

نَعُوذُ بِاللَّهِ مِنْ ذَلِكَ

There are those whose supplications precede their illuminations, and there are those whose illuminations precede their supplications, and there are those whose supplications and illuminations are balanced, and there are those who have neither supplications nor illuminations.
We seek refuge in Allāh from these.

There are essentially four states that correspond to the interaction between the human being and Allāh.

The first speaks of a people whose *'light precedes their supplications.'* These are individuals whose hearts have been illuminated by guidance even before engaging in outward acts of devotion. For them, the inner light is the very source and initiator of their worship, supplication, and remembrance. Their connection to the guidance is so strong that their worship flows naturally, as an organic response to an already-present spiritual enlightenment. Those in this state know Allāh, but do not know His ordinance. When they act, they do so out of love and affection, but are not free from error and flaw, for it is the law that protects one from error, and often, without realizing, they risk falling into error.

The second are those whose *'supplications precedes their light.'* For these individuals, the practice of worship, supplication, and remembrance is a means of seeking enlightenment. They may begin their journey with diligence and conscious effort in remembering Allāh, often feeling distant from Him, yet with the hope that such practice will eventually bring about enlightenment and understanding. They represent a stage where discipline and consistent devotion leads the soul toward a growing awareness of Allāh's presence, but the inner light is something that must be attained progressively through dedicated effort. Those in this state know Allāh's ordinance, but do not know Allāh Himself. When they act, they do so purely in accordance to the law, but do not understand the wisdom, essence, or spirit of His ordinance.

The third are those who represent a balanced state where supplication and luminance are synchronized, meaning they experience both simultaneously and in harmony. When they act, they do so freely and without much deliberation, and their actions are always accompanied with a righteous will and sincere intent. Though they are not exempt from error or flaw, their actions and their knowledge of the law have become so intuitive that they no longer require an external prompt to perform them. Those in this state know Allāh and also know His Ordinance. They know what they must do and how it is to be done, and they do it without hesitation while fully aware of their actions. This is the state that one must strive for, as it reflects the highest level of spiritual maturity, where the soul has moved beyond the need for causal reminders, being naturally aligned with Allāh's Ordinance.

Finally, we are warned of a state devoid of both supplication and luminance. These individuals neither remember Allāh nor experience His illumination, and are in a state of a profound spiritual disconnect due to heedlessness. It is a condition in which the soul is trapped in forgetfulness and has deprived itself of the very purpose of its existence. These are a people who neither know Allāh nor do they know His Ordinance. When they act, if they do, it is without guidance, and they manifest naught but error of which they are neither remorseful nor willing to rectify.

Indeed, we seek refuge in Allāh from such a state!

(٢٥٤)

ذَاكِرٌ ذَكَرَ لِيَسْتَنِيرَ بِهِ قَلْبُهُ فَكَانَ ذَاكِرًا،

وَذَاكِرٌ اسْتَنَارَ قَلْبُهُ فَكَانَ ذَاكِرًا،

وَالَّذِي اسْتَوَتْ أَذْكَارُهُ وَأَنْوَارُهُ فَبِذِكْرِهِ يُهْتَدَى وَبِنُورِهِ يُقْتَدَى،

One who remembers in order to illuminate his heart becomes a rememberer, and one whose heart is illuminated by remembrance (also) becomes a rememberer.
As for the one whose remembrance and illumination are equal, through his remembrance he is guided, and through his illumination he is emulated.

(٢٥٥)

مَا كَانَ ظَاهِرُ ذِكْرٍ إِلَّا عَنْ بَاطِنِ شُهُودٍ وَفِكْرَةٍ

Not is there an outward manifestation of remembrance save from an inward witnessing and contemplation.

Dhikr is not that which manifests on the lips or the string of beads, but rather that which comes from the heart in both realization and contemplation to then manifest on the tongue and fingers. While the relationship between *dhikr* ذكر and *nūr* نور varies, each has a distinct role in one's spiritual growth, and each is a gifted privilege from Allāh.

The one who engages in *dhikr* with the intention of illuminating the heart is aware that the light of the Divine Presence is not yet deeply felt within and therefore maintains their *dhikr* as a way of nurturing that light. In this stage, the *dhikr* is a meditative tool to cleanse the heart of distractions, preparing it to receive that *nūr*. This approach demands a deliberate and mindful effort, where one actively seeks spiritual light, understanding that it may be acquired over time through sincere and persistent devotion.

As for the one whose heart has already been illuminated, and from this inner illumination, *dhikr* naturally flows, the Divine Light is not a distant goal but a present reality. Their *dhikr* springs from a heart already softened by Allāh's Grace and filled with light, making the *dhikr* intuitive and reflective of an established relationship with Him. In this state, the *dhikr* is less about striving and more about expression, a natural outpouring of gratitude and presence stemming from an already-enlightened heart.

The third type embodies a harmony between *dhikr* and *nūr*, where both are present and in balance. This person's remembrance is guided by *nūr*, and that light, in turn, is sustained and amplified through remembrance. Such an individual represents an ideal synthesis, where *dhikr* and *nūr* are not separate phases but simultaneous experiences.

191

This state is described as both guiding and exemplary, such that one finds guidance through constant remembrance, and his actions are emulated and imitated by others due to their illumination. Such an individual not only finds personal guidance in remembrance but also becomes a beacon for others through the consistency of their inner light and outward devotion. They understand that true *dhikr* arises from a deep, internal awareness and presence. It is genuine and meaningful, rooted in an inner state of reflection and spiritual perception.

(٢٥٦)

أَشْهَدَكَ مِنْ قَبْلِ أَنْ يَسْتَشْهَدَكَ،

فَنَطَقَتْ بِأُلُوهِيَّتِهِ الظَّوَاهِرُ، وَتَحَقَّقَتْ بِأَحَدِيَّتِهِ الْقُلُوبُ وَالسَّرَائِرُ

He made you witness before He asked your testimony.
Thus is spoken of His Divinity in the outward, and is realized of His Oneness
in the hearts and the innermost.

Allāh's existence and unity are self-evident in reality, revealed through both the outward signs and the inner realizations of the heart, such that before the human being can reach testimony he has long already witnessed Divinity. Before the human being could give his affirmation, he was made to witness;

﴿ وَإِذْ أَخَذَ رَبُّكَ مِنۢ بَنِىٓ ءَادَمَ مِن ظُهُورِهِمْ ذُرِّيَّتَهُمْ وَأَشْهَدَهُمْ عَلَىٰٓ أَنفُسِهِمْ أَلَسْتُ بِرَبِّكُمْ قَالُوا بَلَىٰ شَهِدْنَآ ... ﴾

And when your Lord gathered from Banū Ādam, from their loins, their
descendants, and made them witness of themselves... "Am I not your Lord?"
they affirmed, "Indeed, we testify!" [107]

This was the covenant established before the corporeality of man on earth, when both the witnessing and the testimony occurred without rational filters, hence without the taint of doubt. It is a testimony greater than the testimony of all else, for indeed all of creation stands as a testament to Allāh's existence and qualities. Each thing, from the minutest particle to the most vast of celestial entities, testifies to Divine order and purpose. But the testimony of the human being is not akin to the rest of the creation. Though it is of the utmost intelligence, conscious and aware, the testimony itself does not rely on the human being's rational and intellective abilities, but emanates directly from the heart, which when asked in alienation from the material world, speaks truthfully and openly of Allāh's greatness, power, and creativity.

---

107   Sūrah Al-Aʿrāf 7:172

Thus does the Almighty affirm;

﴿ وَلَئِن سَأَلْتَهُم مَّنْ خَلَقَ ٱلسَّمَٰوَٰتِ وَٱلْأَرْضَ لَيَقُولُنَّ ٱللَّهُ... ﴾

And were you to ask them, who created the Heavens and the earth, they would surely say 'Allāh'...[108]

﴿ وَلَئِن سَأَلْتَهُم مَّنْ خَلَقَهُمْ لَيَقُولُنَّ ٱللَّهُ... ﴾

And were you to ask them, who created them, the would surely say 'Allāh'...[109]

Thus, Allāh has already 'made' creation to be in a perpetual state of witnessing His reality, so that humanity merely recognizes a truth already embedded within the very fabric of its existence.

By the human being's placement in the intermediary between realms[110] both the heart and the soul are naturally inclined to seeking an understanding not only of Allāh's Eternal Existence but His Divine Unity, where there is no partner, rival, or equal. This realization touches the core of human experience, as the inner self, which is the higher self, instinctively recognizes and inclines toward Allāh's Presence.

The spiritual journey, therefore, is not a search for an unknown or unfamiliar truth but a return to an inner recognition embedded within the soul. It is to remember one's origins and return to that origin. Faith, then, becomes not so much an achievement as a rediscovery of something fundamentally real and ever-present. It frees one from the imposition to 'prove' God's existence or unity through intellectual means, and instead invites one to immerse themselves in both the external signs and internal realizations of God's presence. For once one witnesses that reality itself is testifying to Allāh's Majesty, all rationality and intellectual probing eventually also arrives at precisely the same testimony. Thus, if one was to ask, 'Who created the Heavens and the earth? Who created me?' the only conclusive answer is 'Allāh, the Most Merciful, Most Benevolent.'

The only difference, in this regard, is that the believer can effortlessly affirm his testimony, while the disbeliever struggles with manifesting it. This is why he is called a '*Kāfir* كافر,'[111] not because he does not want to become a Muslim, but because he is deliberately attempting to cover the truth by his unwillingness to affirm what he is witnessing.

---

108   Sūrah Luqmān 31:25

109   Sūrah az-Zukhruf 43:85

110   See Hikam 244-247

111   In its core meaning, the root word *kafara* كفر means to cover, conceal, or deny. *Kāfir* literally means 'one who covers or conceals.' In the old Arabic, a farmer might also be called *Kāfir* as 'one who covers the seed with soil,' and likewise the night might also be called *Kāfir* as the land is covered by its darkness. The theological application of *Kāfir* as a disbeliever or infidel is rooted in the meaning of 'one who covers the truth of God's existence with falsehood,' or one who denies that truth despite clear evidence.

٢٥٧

أَكْرَمَكَ بِكَرَامَاتٍ ثَلَاثٍ...

جَعَلَكَ ذَاكِرًا لَهُ وَلَوْلَا فَضْلُهُ لَمْ تَكُنْ أَهْلًا لِجَرَيَانِ ذِكْرِهِ عَلَيْكَ،

وَجَعَلَكَ مَذْكُورًا بِهِ، إِذْ حَقَّقَ نِسْبَتَهُ لَدَيْكَ،

وَجَعَلَكَ مَذْكُورًا عِنْدَهُ فَتَمَّمَ نِعْمَتَهُ عَلَيْكَ،

He honoured you with three kinds of honours:
He made you remember Him, and were it not for His grace, you would not
have been worthy of His remembrance.
He made you mentioned by Him, as He affirmed His relation to you.
He made you remembered in His presence, thus completing (perfecting) His
favour upon you.

The favours of Allāh upon His servants are boundless, limitless in their quantity and quality. But three stand out, unique, and for His most esteemed servants, upon whom the robe of honour descends, and each honour rises in greatness.

The first is that He has honoured the servant by establishing him as a '*dhākir* ذاكر' one who remembers his Lord. As we mentioned before, *dhikr* is a privilege,[112] and this privilege of remembering Him, though it may seem ordinary, is truly an honour. For had it not been for His grace, we would not have been worthy of His remembrance. Even the capacity to remember Allāh is a gift from Him, not an inherent right or accomplishment of the servant, which in turn reframes *dhikr* from a simple spiritual practice to an intimate connection with Allāh, where each utterance of His Magnificent Names and Attributes is an acknowledgment of His mercy and generosity.

By remembering Him, and showing gratitude for His favour and honour, Allāh says;

﴿ فَٱذْكُرُونِىٓ أَذْكُرْكُمْ وَٱشْكُرُواْ لِى وَلَا تَكْفُرُونِ ﴾

So remember Me, I will remember you, and be grateful to Me, and do not be
in ingratitude.[113]

This, then, is the second honour, of being 'remembered by Him,' as He opens the door to His servant, granting provision, bounty, and blessing. He makes Himself known through His names and attributes, affirming His relationship with His servant, in which the servant is 'mentioned by Him.'

---

112   See Hikam 254-255

113   Sūrah al-Baqarah 2:152

This leads the servant to an elevated position, one that is marked by belonging to Allāh's vast creation but having a unique rank as His beloved. This is the third and highest honour, in which the servant is 'remembered by Allāh and mentioned in His presence,' and in doing so, He completes His favour upon you, placing you among His beloved, such that all in the heavens and the earth are compelled to honour you, as has been said by the Prophet ﷺ;

> ﷽ إِنَّ اللهَ إِذَا أَحَبَّ عَبْدًا دَعَا جِبْرِيلَ فَقَالَ إِنِّي أُحِبُّ فُلَانًا فَأَحِبَّهُ،
>
> فَيُحِبُّهُ جِبْرِيلُ... ثُمَّ يُنَادِي فِي السَّمَاءِ فَيَقُولُ إِنَّ اللهَ يُحِبُّ فُلَانًا فَأَحِبُّوهُ،
>
> فَيُحِبُّهُ أَهْلُ السَّمَاءِ... ثُمَّ يُوضَعُ لَهُ الْقَبُولُ فِي الْأَرْضِ ﷽

Indeed, Allāh, when He loves a servant, He calls upon Jibrīl and says, 'Indeed, I love such and such. You, Jibrīl, also must love him.' So Jibrīl loves him. Thereafter, he (Jibrīl) calls to the Heavens and says to them, 'Indeed, Allāh loves such and such, so you also must love him.' So the inhabitants of the heavens love him. Thereafter, honour is bestowed upon him in the earth. [114]

Take a moment and reflect upon the words of our beloved Prophet Muhammad ﷺ. That Almighty Allah, Majestic as He is, Himself declares His love for His servant and commands Jibrīl ؏, highest in the Angelic Rank to do the same. Being a direct command, Jibrīl obeys without hesitation, and extends that command to all among the Heavens and the Earth, animate and inanimate. And being a command directly from the Lord of the World, not a single thing in existence would dare defy it. We ask... Could there possibly be, in all of existence, a higher honour than this?

Aspire then, if you should aspire for honour, to be among those remembered by Allāh, and thus remembered by His creation. For such is an everlasting honour; not an honour that vanishes with the vanishing of creation. [115]

﴾٢٥٨﴿

> رُبَّ عُمُرٍ اتَّسَعَتْ آمَادُهُ وَقَلَّتْ أَمْدَادُهُ،
>
> وَرُبَّ عُمُرٍ قَلِيلَةٌ آمَادُهُ كَثِيرَةٌ أَمْدَادُهُ،

Many a life has a lengthy endurance, but lessened fruition, and many a life has lessened endurance, but abundant in fruition.

---

114   Sahīh Muslim 2637a

115   See Hikam 86

(٢٥٩)

مَنْ بُورِكَ لَهُ فِي عُمُرِهِ... أَدْرَكَ فِي يَسِيرٍ مِنَ الزَّمَنِ مِنْ مِنَنِ اللهِ تَعَالَى مَا لَا يَدْخُلُ تَحْتَ
دَوَائِرِ الْعِبَارَةِ، وَلَا تَلْحَقُهُ الْإِشَارَةُ

Whoever is blessed in their age, may realize in the span of their life from the grace of Allāh what cannot be attained under the peripheries of expressions or captured by signs (and indications).

Some lives are long in their quantity, in the number of years, but less in their quality, in their fruitfulness and contentment. Yet, other lives are short in their number of years, but abundant in their fruitfulness. In that regard, it is less the length of one's life and more what one chooses to do with what has been given to them. None can know how long they have; but all can decide what to fill each moment with.

Know then, that it is not the size of the vessel, but what it is filled with that determines its worth. Is not a small cup filled with honey worth more than a large container filled with mud?

The true measure of life is not in its length nor in its embellishment, but in the spiritual richness and contentment that it contains. For one may live many long years yet be miserable and void of any experience, having little to no spiritual growth, or entirely bereft of Allāh's guidance. Such a life, while lengthy in earthly terms, lacks substance in the realm of the soul. Time alone does not equate to spiritual progress; without active remembrance of God, devotion, or inner purity, a long life may merely pass without bringing any happiness, regardless of wealth or health.

Yet, one may have a life, though short, but imbued with a profound spiritual connection, transformative moments through Allāh's guidance, moments that magnify one's worth. Such is the life of those who, though they may have fewer years, find each moment to be filled with remembrance, spiritual insight, and closeness to God. For them, time is not measured by its quantity, but by the intensity of their servitude and contentment in what is received. The brevity of their lives is compensated by the depth of their spiritual achievements.

In that regard, the essence of a meaningful life lies not in how many years we live but in how those years are spent. A brief life filled with sincerity and devotion surpasses a long life spent heedlessly. Contentment and gratitude are the pillars of life, for whether it is long or short, the true gift is in how one uses the time allocated to them by earning Allāh's blessing upon the journey. Such a blessing is beyond the scope of language and description, cannot be confined by time or fully conveyed through words. It transforms the believer's limited time into an avenue for boundless fruitions and achievements, such that one may accomplish what might otherwise take a lifetime, or even several, to attain.

(٢٦٠)

الْخِذْلَانُ كُلُّ الْخِذْلَانِ ...

أَنْ تَتَفَرَّغَ مِنَ الشَّوَاغِلِ ... ثُمَّ لَا تَتَوَجَّهَ إِلَيْهِ،

وَتَقِلَّ عَوَائِقُكَ ... ثُمَّ لَا تَرْحَلَ إِلَيْهِ،

The folly of all folly... Is to free yourself from the preoccupations, yet not direct yourself towards Him. And lessen your obstacles, yet not journey towards Him.

There is a powerful insight in these words, into the true nature of spiritual abandonment. It is folly indeed that one succeeds in parting from the distractions of otherness and preoccupations with other than Allāh, yet fail in directing his attention towards his Lord. Thereby, he also succeeds in removing all the barriers and impediments that prevent him from obeying his Lord and witnessing His Majesty, and yet fail to make the effort of drawing closer to Him.

This is indeed a profound a misfortune. Such heedlessness is a tragedy; to have the opportunity ready at hand and yet neglect it. Truly, trials and suffering are inevitable following the failure to pursue that higher purpose when one is granted the blessing of ease and freedom to do so. When distractions and burdens are lifted, the soul is left with a clear path to devotion, not seizing the opportunity is a deep form of neglect because it reflects a deliberate *choice to distance* oneself from Divinity, such that true misfortune lies not in the presence of trials but in ignoring the Higher Call when external impediments are minimal.

Herein lies the danger of spiritual apathy, as often, people might wish for fewer distractions to focus on spiritual growth, yet, when given the chance, they may still fail to act. Such inaction is a form of inner poverty because it demonstrates a lack of true motivation and sincerity toward one's ultimate purpose. It is false testimony to desire a change of state as a condition of servitude, for if servitude was indeed one's passion, it would be achieved regardless of their state.[116] In the end, each one's servitude is guaranteed, whether willingly or unwillingly. But the arrival of an opportunity to serve willingly, and with clear intention and sincerity is an unquantifiable blessing. There could not possibly be a higher folly as to squander such an opportunity, knowing that there are people who exist under such incredible constrictions, they can barely spare a moment to reflect upon the Signs of Allāh. The arrival of ease should therefore be a bounty to be prioritized and capitalized, not a mere option among other options. Foolish indeed is the one who, when granted ease from causation, fails to turn his gaze inward and instead only expands his capacity to accommodate more distractions.

---

116   See Hikam 19

(٢٦١)

الْفِكْرَةُ سَيْرُ الْقَلْبِ فِي مَيَادِينِ الْأَغْيَارِ

The Thought is the journey of the heart through the fields of otherness.

(٢٦٢)

الْفِكْرَةُ سِرَاجُ القَلْبِ... فَإِذَا ذَهَبَتْ فَلَا إِضَاءَةَ لَهُ

The Thought is the lamp of the heart... so when it departs, there is no illumination for it (the heart).

(٢٦٣)

الْفِكْرَةُ فِكْرَتَانِ... فِكْرَةُ تَصْدِيقٍ وَإِيمَانٍ، وَفِكْرَةُ شُهُودٍ وَعِيَانٍ،
فَالْأُولَى... لِأَرْبَابِ الْاعْتِبَارِ، وَالثَّانِيَةُ... لِأَرْبَابِ الشُّهُودِ وَالِاسْتِبْصَارِ،

The thought is twofold... The thought of conviction and belief, and the thought of witnessing and perception. The first is for the people of discernment, and the second is for the people of witnessing and insight.

Thought فكر is the progressive form of reflection تفكر. In the Qur'ān the former often carries a negative connotation, while the latter always carries a positive one. This is because thought originates from the being, and its outcome is entirely dependent on its origin. Additionally, thought is also influenced by four sources. The Divine, the Angelic, the Self, and the Demonic. The former two are rare and praiseworthy, which the latter two are common and, evidently, blameworthy.

Reflection, on the other hand, comes into the being, as he reflects on what already is rather than what he supposes to be. Its point of origin is not an assumption or speculative wonder, rather it comes from an origin that is Absolutely True and Certain.

In this regard, thought, when sourced from other than what is True and Certain, can be destructive, as illustrated;

﴿ إِنَّهُ فَكَّرَ وَقَدَّرَ ۞ فَقُتِلَ كَيْفَ قَدَّرَ ۞ ثُمَّ قُتِلَ كَيْفَ قَدَّرَ ۞ ثُمَّ نَظَرَ ۞ ثُمَّ عَبَسَ وَبَسَرَ ۞
ثُمَّ أَدْبَرَ وَاسْتَكْبَرَ ۞ فَقَالَ إِنْ هَٰذَا إِلَّا سِحْرٌ يُؤْثَرُ ۞ إِنْ هَٰذَا إِلَّا قَوْلُ الْبَشَرِ ﴾

Indeed, he thought and deliberated. So may he be destroyed for how he deliberated. Then may he be destroyed for how he deliberated. Then he considered. Then he frowned and scowled. Then he demurred and became arrogant. So he said, 'This is but witchcraft. This is but the words of man.' [117]

---

[117] Sūrah al-Muddathir 74:18-25

This is the destructive power of thought, for it always attempts to follow a logical and rational pattern. The fault of it does not lie in its logic or rationality. Both may make sense so long as their rules are observed. The fault lies inward, at the point of origination. The primary input, the assumption, or supposition that initiates the logic, if faulty, will lead to a destructive outcome. The admonition here is paramount, for it encapsulates the entirety of what this book contains. There is a wisdom that originates from the human mind, and a wisdom that descends from the Divine. The latter necessitates reflection, not scrutiny, while the former, incumbent on thought, must first be scrutinized. And thus thought can either be a guiding light if rightly executed, or, if absent, become a profound darkness. So pay heed to the following three statements.

Firstly, thought is what facilitates the heart's journey through the realm of otherness. It is through deep thought that the heart navigates safe passage in a world that is alien to it. Thought facilitates for the heart a gateway that leads beyond its immediate surroundings, through which it enters a metaphysical space, allowing it to seek Truth and recognize the Essence behind worldly appearances. Thought, therefore, is not a passive mode of the mind, but a movement from the forms, through their symbols, and towards their meanings. When rightly executed, following the prescribed methodologies and epistemic processes, thought may successfully strip away superficiality, and lead the heart closer to the Divine Presence by transcending worldly distractions.

Secondly, thought is a source of inner illumination, guiding the heart and helping it sift through the murkiness of causality. Just as light reveals what is hidden in darkness, contemplation reveals spiritual truths and nurtures insight. When this light is extinguished, often due to false assumptions and speculations, the heart becomes vulnerable to ignorance and confusion, losing the guidance it so direly needs.

Lastly, thought is of two kinds. One that leads to belief and faith, the other that leads to intelligent testimony. These are the two innate qualities of the heart, Faith and Knowledge. And so the heart's thoughts, when pure and praiseworthy, will generically seek to fulfill either, or both, of these qualities. This is the mark of distinction for the seeker, by which he may expel any thought that is not beneficial or praiseworthy. If the thought does not lead to an increase in faith or an increase in worthy knowledge, the thought is, by necessary attribution, destructive. And anything that originates such a thought is equally, by attribution, blameworthy. The believer must be vigilant of his rational and intellective faculties, for nothing in this world bears the capacity of great destruction wrought upon oneself than by one's own thoughts.

And this marks the end of the Book of Wisdoms

A BRIEF DISPOSITION ON WISDOM

The most intriguing aspect of this subject is that while many may speak on wisdom, share wisdom, indeed regard wisdom as a virtue, no one can say what wisdom actually is. Even the philosophers, whose very institute of '*philo sophia*' being a 'love of wisdom' struggle to understand its nature. It has no quantifiable form, no bounds or limits, and no blameworthy attribute, for who ever heard of 'bad wisdom' or 'evil wisdom'? Never has there been a line that blurs, never a gray area that contains doubt as to the distinction between wisdom and foolishness.

The closest we might come to understanding a thing is to give it a rational definition, and perhaps the most profound definition of wisdom, in our view, comes from Al-Farābī who, as a brilliant logician, defined it as 'the knowledge of causes,' not merely as an understanding of *what* things are or *how* they occur, but an inquiry into the deeper understandings of *why*. It is the kind of holistic understanding that is layered over the scientia, elevated above empirical knowledge, that unveils the delicate fabric of reality, revealing its subtle interconnections and inherent meanings. It is not confined to rational comprehension, rather it blossoms into action, manifesting thought and intention in reality, to become part of one's existence. It enables the virtuous to harmonize their insights with the Divine Word that manifests all of reality.

In that regard, it is the highest form of intellectual and spiritual attainment. The wise individual is not only a contemplative observer and articulator of aphorisms, but also a virtuous actor, whose insights into the universal order enable him to guide society toward justice and harmony. Wisdom for such a person integrates the *'ilm* علم (*theoria*) with its practical application *'amal* عمل (*praxis*), resulting in excellence and luminance *lam'a* لمع (*sapientia*),[118] becoming both an intellectual virtue and an ethical imperative.

Ibn Sīnā, in his magnum opus *Al-Shifā* (The Cure), extended Al-Farābī's definition by linking wisdom to the human soul's ascent toward its highest perfection. For Ibn Sīnā, attaining wisdom requires the mastery of logic, natural sciences, and metaphysics, which would act as the stepping stones of intellection leading one from semantics and fragmented particularities to the sublime universal realization of Divine Unity (*Tawhīd* توحيد). To know and understand that ultimate reality, he argued, is to intelligently align one's being with the heavenly order of existence, thereby achieving a form of spiritual immortality. Wisdom itself must transform the knower to situate them as an integral participant in the harmony of existence, lest one become an insignificant passing entity in life that eats, copulates, entertains, sleeps, and ultimately dies.

In the Islāmic tradition, the pursuit of wisdom is inseparable from the quest for truth (*haqq* حقّ). The Qur'ān repeatedly extols *hikmah* حكمة as a gift, bestowed upon the Prophets ﷺ and those chosen to guide humanity. This sacred grounding informed the scholars' understanding of wisdom as inherently tied to all ethical and metaphysical truths.

In his *Mishkāt al-Anwār* (The Niche of Lights), Imām Al-Ghazzālī argues that true wisdom arises only when reason and revelation are harmonized, this being the precedence of Light upon light نور على نور,[119] that is, the Light of Revelation over the light of reason. He critiques those who rely solely on speculative reason, asserting that their wisdom, if any, is incomplete without the illumination of Allāh's Guidance.

For the truth to be fully realized its search must first be understood as a two-part journey, where the first part involves the soul's efforts through the praiseworthy rational inquiry that brings it to the threshold of truth.

---

118 Note how all three words are constructed from the same three root letters ع ل م. This is unique in Arabic whereby the words formed from the same letters often have related meanings. In this regard, knowledge علم with action عمل results in excellence لمع.

119 Sūrah an-Nūr 24:35

The second part of the journey is granted leave by Allāh, where the meanings are unveiled to the soul. One's rational inquiry will only reach as far as the formal truth, no further, while the entire truth remains spiritually transcendental, or as we might say, always beyond the reach of logic and rationality.

Through this synthesis of rational inquiry and spiritual insight, wisdom is considered a holistic endeavor that unites the mind, heart, and soul. It is not enough to discern the truth intellectually; one must embody it through ethical action and spiritual discipline. In the end, one must trust it to be unveiled to them, not on the condition of their earnings, but as a gift from their Creator.

However, this only constitutes one type of wisdom, which we may term as 'human wisdom.' It is the kind of wisdom which is permitted by Allāh to be sourced through human experience and learning, which originates from the light of reason as mentioned prior. The other kind of wisdom, which is much higher and more profound, is Divine Wisdom, which exclusively originates from the Allāh through Revelation. While the human endeavour can unveil *what* and *how* reality is, only He can unveil *why* it is.

This wisdom *always* sits in judgment over human wisdom, as wisdom itself dictates recognizing this order, for failure to adhere to the axiom of the Light of Revelation over the light of reason essentially nullifies both, leaving the being in a state bereft of wisdom altogether, regardless of the extent and strength of one's rational faculties. Rationality might define the parameters of human thought, but wisdom will enable one to respect them.

While scholars have written extensively on the theoretical aspects of wisdom, they did not confine their reflections to abstract dimensions. They have continually emphasized its practical applications at the individual, societal, and political levels as a resolution to the conflicts resultant from the human condition.

Al-Farābī's vision of the virtuous city, *al-Madīnah al-Fādilah* المدينة الفاضلة, exemplifies this integration. In his political philosophy, he places wisdom as the cornerstone of governance, requiring leaders who understand the metaphysical order and can translate it into just policies. He calls the ideal ruler a 'philosopher-king,' whose wisdom as a master of both reason and revelation enables him to guide his subjects toward both worldly and spiritual flourishing. He posits that both reason and revelation translated as philosophy and religion, are derived from and dependent upon what comes from Allāh through His prophets, and that, if rightly understood and acted upon, there should be no contradictions in governance for the individual and the society.

Ibn Sīnā similarly stressed the ethical responsibilities of the knowledgeable and wise. In his treatises on ethics, he emphasized the role of wisdom in cultivating virtues such as justice, courage, and temperance. Though these are themselves defined by the Sharī'ah, their understanding and application must come from reason. A wise person is not only one who perceives the truth but also one who acts in accordance with it, as he is responsible for being a moral exemplar to others.

While conservative-minded individuals have heavily criticized the likes of Al-Farābī and Ibn Sīnā, they cannot deny that there is truth to these presented theories. Even Al-Ghazzālī, who cautioned against the over-reliance on philosophy as a source of wisdom, acknowledged its importance in one's life. In the Ihyā' Ulūm al-Dīn, he provides practical guidance on how to live wisely, from managing one's time to purifying the heart. Wisdom, in this view, is the art of living in constant awareness of God, making every action a reflection of Divine Harmony.

We understand, then, that wisdom, for the Muslim, is more a spiritual endeavour than a rational or intellectual enterprise. In the Islāmic worldview, wisdom is not a static possession embedded in poetry and emotionally stimulating aphorisms. Rather it is regarded as a dynamic process of growth, introspection, and alignment with the ultimate reality. It bridges the material and spiritual realms as they culminate in the heart, illuminating the path toward a life of purpose and fulfillment.

As such, whether through the rational rigor of Al-Farābī and Ibn Sīnā, the philosophical ponderings of Al-Kindī and Fakhr ad-Dīn ar-Rāzī, the jurisprudent firmness of Ibn Taymiyyah and Ibn al-Jawzī or the spiritual depth of Al-Ghazzālī and Ibn 'Atā'illāh, the collective wisdom of our scholars is foundational in understanding and rectifying the human condition, especially in an age increasingly fragmented by materialism and superficiality. The teachings of these individuals are the guiding lights through the complexities of the manifesting deceptions of modern societies and ideologies. We cannot hope to solve our problems through revolutions and political protests. Certainly not by waving flags and shouting slogans in the streets. In the age of the Dajjāl, the only true visionary is the righteous believer with spiritual insight. We cannot base our understanding of reality upon the 'scientific' discoveries of the godless. For how can those, void of morals and ethics, distanced from God and His Guidance, be beacons of light? To follow them would be equally bereft of any wisdom.

Indeed, we would be fools.

I deliberately chose to put this chapter at the very end of the book to keep all bias at bay, to present the words of one, whom some consider wise while others consider deviant, in the most objective and untainted manner possible. It is for you, dear reader, having traversed these pages, to conclude what wisdom truly means to you in light of what it means to the great exemplars mentioned in this book. Do not become so opinionated as others have, that you end up forsaking the precious gems and pearls of wisdom that these scholars have dedicated their lives to bring into our hearts. Consider that the book you hold in your hands was not a random spontaneous occurrence. If it has offered you even the slimmest glimpse of that truth, then its purpose is fulfilled. You were meant to read it in as much as I was meant to compile it, that if Almighty Allāh has chosen to put in your way even a rice grain's worth of knowledge and wisdom, He has indeed intended blessing for you. Take it, nurture it, and let it grow and bear fruit, for in wisdom lies the path to both knowledge and the Eternal Light of the Divine.

سبحانك
وبحمدك
نشهد أن لا إله إلا أنت
نستغفرك ونستخيرك ونتوب إليك

MORE BOOKS BY ABUBILAAL YAKUB

abubilaal@ironheartpublishing.com
abubilaal@ieschatology.org

THE AMULETS OF SIHR

Book One of an Eight-Part Fictional Series entitled
THE OATH OF KINGS.

Mukhtar's life is upturned when he uncovers a dark secret concealed by his father. Life is brutal and harsh, even harsher while the empire only looks after its own, and the rest of the people are left to fend for themselves. In an impulsive moment Mukhtar frees four slaves from their captors. Little does he know how this would shape his destiny. As the turmoil unfolds, his mother unveils her most guarded secret - an ancient and powerful amulet once belonging to his long-lost father. The Amulet sets Mukhtar on a path to unraveling a grim and dark part of his bloodline.

Now, at the crossroads of good and evil, he must face his life's greatest trials yet in order to save the empire from annihilation.

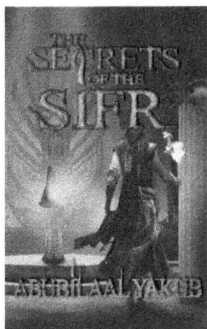

THE SECRETS OF THE SIFR

Book Two of THE OATH OF KINGS Series.

Mukhtar's tale continues as he sets out to right the wrongs of his father. As the King lies on his deathbed, the Empire hinges on the whims of his successors while evil forces both from within and without conspire to conquer the world of man.

Mukhtar's brother, Zaki, establishes himself with the Crowned Prince, while Mukhtar, displeased with his brother's bureaucratic approach, takes matters into his own hands to find a resolution to the crises.

Along the lines, those whom they thought were their enemies are discovered to be mere pawns of an ancient order known as the Hidden Ones attempt to restructure civilization to their liking, all the while following the whispers of the Hand of Azazil who is on the cusp of breaking free from his bonds.

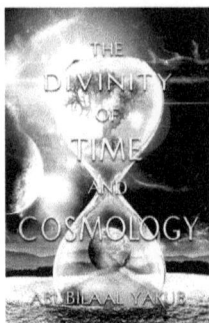

THE DIVINITY OF TIME AND COSMOLOGY

An abridgment of the much larger philosophical work entitled *Time, Light and Being.*

In a devious ploy of secularizing and institutionalizing education and academics, from childhood to adulthood, for generation after generation, the Modern Age has thus far succeeded in the secularization of the Golden Knowledge of Islāmic Sciences.

It is upon us, the Muslims, the Believers, to revive the Golden Age of Islāmic Knowledge and Sciences by revisiting the Knowledge of the Holy Qur'ān and Hadīth.

This book begins with the beginning, with the Elements of Creation, Time, Light and the Cosmos, with the hopes of enabling the Believer with the ability to see with his inner eye, and pierce through the Dajjalic veils of the Modern Godless Age.

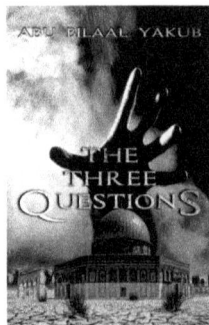

THE THREE QUESTIONS

This title on a unique unfolding during the Holy Prophet's time, which resulted in the Revelation of the anchor of Islāmic Eschatology in the Holy Qur'ān.

Close to the end of the Third Meccan Period, between 619 and 622 AD, in a desperate attempt to foil the unstoppable spread of Islām, the Ruling Tribe of the Qur'aysh sent a delegation to the Rabbis of Yathrib, returning with Three pivotal Questions to test the Holy Prophet of God. Three Questions that have sculpted the fate of mankind into the modern, secular age we live in today. This book explores these three questions to pierce the godless veils of deception, and better understand the strange unfolding of event in the world, hellbent on ushering the harbinger of evil, the Impostor Messiah, and the dawn of the End of Times.

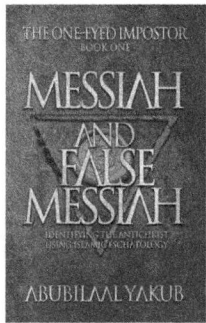

THE ONE-EYED IMPOSTOR
Book One
MESSIAH AND FALSE MESSIAH

An Eschatological work focusing on the subject of the center-most figure in the End Times Eskhatos. Humanity is no stranger to its finality. Only a fool is oblivious to the ultimate conclusion of man's existence in this world.

Our acknowledgement of this as the bedrock of a strange transformation, unprecedented in human history, is that this is a manifest fulfillment of Divine Prophecy.

This book seeks to examine the central figure, described as the One-Eyed Impostor, the Dajjal, the Antichrist, whose prime role is to set the stage for the final act mankind will play before the curtain is drawn on human history.

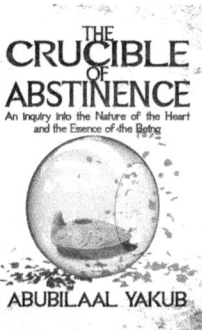

THE
CRUCIBLE
OF ABSTINENCE

An Inquiry into the Nature of the Heart and the Essence of the Being.

Who is this 'Being' that the Lord Almighty has created? What is its excellence? Where lay its origins? Where is he destined to be? Who is he destined to become? What is his Purpose of Being?

Modernity argues that the human being is a mere accident of spontaneous causes and effects. A random set of material events. Here to entertain and be entertained. But you must ask yourself, are you what they say you are? Will you pass a fleeting speck of dust. A bemoaner who never rose. Just a collection of flesh and bone. A consuming leech. A reactionary husk. Or will you be what your Creator wants you to be? One who is raised in rank, upon whose shoulders would descend the robe of honour, to become a being of purity in the Divine Presence.

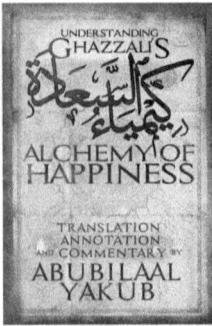

UNDERSTANDING GHAZZALI'S
ALCHEMY OF HAPPINESS

The happiness of this world is temporal and finite. It has no real value, measured only by external material factors, which fluctuate with the vicissitudes of time, rising and falling with the tide, emerging and dissipating without any real worth. They come to satisfy the carnality of the self, and depart just as swift, leaving you empty and hollow. True contentment is intrinsic. It cannot be measured by any object of this world, however valuable that object might be. It is of that garb whose cloth is not sown by the threads of carnality and worldly pleasure. This you must understand, if you wish to manifest for yourself a sound psychological state in a life that is meaningful and purposeful. And Ghazzālī's Alchemy is designed specifically to facilitate that understanding.

UNDERSTANDING ABHARI'S
TREATISE ON LOGIC

Sound psychological states are the product of sound reasoning and decision-making. The mind is inherently a logical entity operating in a logical world which functions and abides by rational principles that are both logically intelligible and comprehensible. Every cognitive and behavioural process, every law and axiom, is a manifestation of intelligibility.

The treatise presented in this book, as one of the oldest, most venerable compositions of the science of logic, also serves as a manual for cultivating the mind to be in harmony with nature and the natural algorithms of the world. Herein also lies proof that logic is not merely an abstract or theoretical construct, but a potent instrument for achieving clarity, wisdom, and mental equilibrium, whether one is a seasoned philosopher, or an initiate seeker of knowledge and understanding.

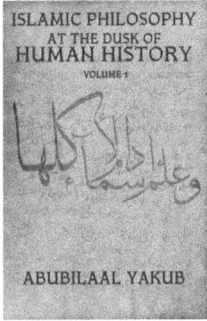

ISLĀMIC PHILOSOPHY AT THE DUSK OF HUMAN HISTORY vol.1

The first volume in a series that seeks to revive the true wisdom of Islāmic Thought in an age deprived of it. Philosophy, in the Muslim World, played an important role in cultivating deep and critical thinking to resolve queries into existential matters. In recent history, driven by certain influences, philosophy has been unjustly classified as *non grata*, deemed as something disapproved by Islāmic doctrine.

Yet the world is shaped by philosophies unfounded in religious thought, rendered unchallenged to reign free. This series seeks to revive the critical thinking once beheld by the Muslim Civilization that challenges the ideologies of modernity.

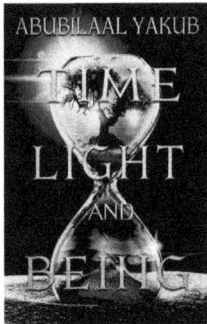

TIME, LIGHT, AND BEING

A philosophical work delving into the prime ontological elements that form the crux of existence for the human being.

Seldom does man think of his being, his purpose of existence, where he came from, where he is, who he is, and where he is destined.

Seldom does man think of his being, and what he is becoming.

Why did God create you?

Why are you here?